Congress and the Politics of Problem Solving

Congress and the Politics of Problem Solving shows how a simple premise – voters are willing to hold lawmakers accountable for their collective problem-solving abilities – can produce novel insights into legislative organization, behavior, and output. How do issues end up on the agenda? Why do lawmakers routinely invest in program oversight and broad policy development? What considerations drive legislative policy change? Knowing that their prospects for reelection are partly dependent on their collective problem-solving abilities, lawmakers support structures that enhance the legislature's capacity to address problems in society and encourage members to contribute to nonparticularistic policy-making activities. The resulting insights are innovative and substantial: incumbents of both parties have electoral incentives to be concerned about Congress's collective performance; the legislative issue agenda can often be predicted years in advance; nearly all important successful legislation originates in committee; many laws pass with bipartisan support; and electoral replacement, partisan or otherwise, is not the most robust predictor of policy change. The electoral imperative to address problems in society offers a compelling explanation for these findings and provides an important new perspective on the dynamics of lawmaking in legislatures.

E. Scott Adler is Associate Professor of Political Science at the University of Colorado, Boulder. Among his publications are the books *Why Congressional Reforms Fail: Reelection and the House Committee System* and *The Macropolitics of Congress*. He received a BA from the University of Michigan in 1988 and a PhD from Columbia University in 1996.

John D. Wilkerson is the Director of the Center for American Politics and Public Policy at the University of Washington. He received his PhD from the University of Rochester in 1991.

Congress and the Politics of Problem Solving

E. SCOTT ADLER
University of Colorado, Boulder

JOHN D. WILKERSON
University of Washington, Seattle

CAMBRIDGE
UNIVERSITY PRESS

CAMBRIDGE UNIVERSITY PRESS
Cambridge, New York, Melbourne, Madrid, Cape Town,
Singapore, São Paulo, Delhi, Mexico City

Cambridge University Press
32 Avenue of the Americas, New York, NY 10013-2473, USA

www.cambridge.org
Information on this title: www.cambridge.org/9781107670310

First published 2012

Printed in the United States of America

A catalog record for this publication is available from the British Library.

Library of Congress Cataloging in Publication data
Adler, E. Scott.
  Congress and the politics of problem solving / E. Scott Adler, John D. Wilkerson.
    p. cm.
  Includes bibliographical references and index.
  ISBN 978-1-107-02318-5 (hardback) – ISBN 978-1-107-67031-0 (paperback)
  1. United States. Congress.   2. Decision making – Political aspects – United States.
  3. Legislation – Political aspects – United States.   I. Wilkerson, John D.,
  1939– II. Title.
  JK1021.A45   2012
  328.73–dc23   2012006879

ISBN 978-1-107-02318-5 Hardback
ISBN 978-1-107-67031-0 Paperback

Contents

Tables and Figures

FIGURES

Preface

In this book, we offer a perspective on U.S. lawmaking that draws on long-term, large-scale patterns and developments in Congress. After gathering and analyzing information regarding thousands of proposed, enacted, and failed legislative proposals we came to a singular conclusion – contemporary legislative studies seem to be overlooking key aspects of what legislatures do. These studies tend to have a common theme – the institution no longer functions. The proffered causes are numerous – a politically polarized citizenry, ideologically rigid lawmakers, party strategy, increased electoral competition, campaign finance, economic inequality, etc. Certainly, we recognized the conflict and divisiveness that other studies emphasize. But our data also pointed to additional dynamics that were receiving much less attention. In particular, the issue area seemed to matter – a great deal.

Congress often surprises. The 111th Congress (2009–10) was frequently described as the most polarized of the last century – the epitome of a dysfunctional Congress. Yet, it ultimately turned out to be one of the most productive as well. How can this happen? Our answer highlights the question of how certain issues end up on the legislative agenda. Examining congressional agendas and policy change across many years, we find that policy making is often spurred by problem solving. Issues become the subject of new legislation for reasons that have less to do with party or lawmaker priorities, and more to do with events in society and established lawmaking routines that encourage policy updating. Lawmakers have electoral incentives to be responsive to such problems because most voters care as much (if not more) about *whether* problems are addressed as they do about *how* those problems are addressed.

A problem-solving perspective not only portends that Congress will be more productive than many contemporary perspectives suggest, but it also anticipates why. When we systematically examine the legislative agenda and policy change, we find that congressional politics revolves in large part around problem solving. Even when dysfunction seems to be at its peak, problem-solving motivations still give lawmakers reasons to search for common ground. The pages that follow explain the principles of our problem-solving perspective and how this approach reveals new insights about Congress's organization, operations, and output.

Over the many years it has taken us to complete this project (more years than we wish to recall), we have racked up quite a few debts of gratitude. Perhaps the best place to start is at the beginning: without sizable financial support from the National Science Foundation (NSF 00880066; 00880061; 9320922; 0111611), the Congressional Bills Project – which played a key role in formulating our thinking – would not exist. Additionally, grants from the University of Colorado Department of Political Science Legacy Fund, the University of Colorado Undergraduate Research Opportunities Program, and a Government of Spain External Investigator Award (to Wilkerson) provided further financial assistance throughout the project. The views expressed in this book are solely those of the authors, who also bear full responsibility for any errors, omissions, and gaffes it may contain.

As well, our home institutions provided productive environments, exceptional colleagues, talented students, and picturesque surroundings to keep us on track toward the book's completion. At the University of Washington, T. Jens Feeley deserves special recognition for getting the Congressional Bills Project up and running. Jens's dissertation research also provided inspiration for important ideas developed further in this book. In addition, Loren Collingwood, Ashley Jochim, Barry Pump, and Stephen Purpura provided exceptional research assistance along the way. We are also indebted to a long list of CAPPP Undergraduate Fellows for their essential collective contributions to the data used in this book, including Sean Freeder, who made an important research contribution that we reference in Chapter 9. Finally, Peter May was always willing to provide prompt (and encouraging) feedback on drafts.

The Bills Project crew at the University of Colorado included three lead research assistants: Dennis Still, Gregory Young, and Michael Berry. Under their guidance were several undergraduate and graduate students who provided invaluable assistance in the data collection: Amy Budner, Jeanette Bustamante, Rebecca Carr, Keith Edwards, Laurel Harbridge,

Jarrod Hayes, Inayah Hays, Jeff Howland, Thomas McFarland, Reyna Perez-Oquendo, Brittany Perry, Christa Watson, and Cheryl Williams. In many instances these students got more out of this project than just a paycheck. Independent research projects by Berry, Bustamante, Edwards, Harbridge, and Perry are included in our study in various ways. Additionally, a number of graduate students endured numerous hours of discussion both in and out of the classroom that helped to hone our thinking and analysis. Among them were Michael Berry, David Doherty, Sarah Hagedorn, Bill Jaeger, Josh Kennedy, Jeff Lyons, Josh Ryan, and Scott Minkoff. Finally, colleagues at the University of Colorado, both current and former, tolerated a seemingly endless barrage of questions and provided cheerful answers and critiques over the course of many years. These (unfortunate souls) include Ken Bickers, David Leblang, John McIver, Anand Sokhey, and Jennifer Wolak.

Thanks to the generosity of Yale University and Alan Gerber, Adler was able to spend a year at the Center for the Study of American Politics. This time and intellectual community allowed us to take stock of what the Bills Project was telling us. Among the outstanding scholars at Yale who gave so generously of their time and insights were Alan Gerber, Justin Fox, Don Green, Jacob Hacker, Greg Huber, Matt Levendusky, and David Mayhew.

We were also fortunate to present various iterations of our work at a number of excellent institutions including Columbia University; Fordham University; New York University; Sciences-Po (Paris); SUNY–Stony Brook; and the universities of Arhus, Bordeaux, Barcelona, Chicago (Harris School of Public Policy), Essex, Notre Dame, Pennsylvania, Pittsburgh, and Virginia, as well as several talks at our home universities. During these visits, at conferences, and individually, many scholars helped to improve the manuscript, including Scott Basinger, Christopher Berry, Sarah Binder, Laura Chaques, Jeff Cohen, Olivier Costa, Larry Evans, Avi Feller, Richard Fleisher, Gerald Gamm, Sandy Gordon, Christopher Green-Pederson, John Griffin, Emiliano Grossman, Thad Hall, Will Howell, Jeff Jenkins, Kris Kantak, George Krause, John Lapinski, Rene Lindstadt, Forrest Maltzman, Nolan McCarty, Becky Morton, Nate Monroe, Costas Panagopoulos, Kathryn Pearson, Wendy Schiller, Chuck Shipan, Boris Shor, David Skaggs, Tracy Sulkin, Rob Van Houweling, Jennifer Victor, Craig Volden, Greg Wawro, Alan Wiseman, Christina Wolbrecht, and Jonathan Woon.

As the manuscript came together, we had two opportunities to present the entire manuscript to captive audiences. The first workshop took place at the University of Texas, at the invitation of Bryan Jones and Sean Theriault, and included Scott Ainsworth (who also read the manuscript a second time), Jon Bond, Sam Workman, and several of their graduate students and UT colleagues. The second workshop was orchestrated by David Rohde for his Political Institutions and Public Choice (PIPC) Book Seminar at Duke University. In addition to Rohde, we were the beneficiaries of extensive comments by Frank Baumgartner, Jason Roberts, Sarah Treul, Frank Orlando, David Sparks, Aaron King, and Robi Ragan (who provided very helpful suggestions for the model in Chapter 5). The extensive suggestions and criticism we received in both instances came at precisely the right moment, and we are deeply grateful for these opportunities.

At Cambridge University Press, Lew Bateman believed in and supported our vision for this project. Lew ably guided the manuscript through the publication process, along with the assistance of Mark Fox, Shari Chappell, Christine Dunn, and Fred Goykhman.

Two scholars deserve special thanks. Michael Ensley and Gilad Wilkenfeld are listed as coauthors of two chapters (Chapter 3 and Chapter 9, respectively). Both also provided additional assistance and valuable feedback on other portions of the manuscript. Their efforts, skills, and patience played a very sizable role in bringing this project to completion.

An earlier version of Chapter 6 appeared as "Intended Consequences: Jurisdictional Reform and Issue Control in the U.S. House of Representatives," 2008 *Legislative Studies Quarterly* 33: 85–112. We thank *Legislative Studies Quarterly* for allowing us to use a modified version of the study for this book.

Finally, we are indebted to our families most of all. John thanks Barbara, Christopher, and Sean, who matter more than any book, and who undoubtedly wondered whether all of those hours John spent working on his laptop would ever lead to anything. Scott is indebted to Rose, Anna, and Pam for their cheerful support and loving encouragement. Yes, *now* it's done!

PART I

Congress and the Politics of Problem Solving

This is the most dysfunctional political environment that I have ever seen. But then you have to juxtapose that with [this Congress being] one of, at least, the three most productive Congresses since 1900.... Making sense of all that can make your head burst.

Norman Ornstein (Fahrenthold, Rucker, and Sonmez 2010)

This was, by far, the most productive Congress in American history.... Why? Because we heard the message the American people sent us last month: They don't want us to sit around and waste their time. They want us to work together and work for them.

Senate Majority Leader Harry Reid (Bolton 2010)

How is it that a legislature like Congress – so rife with dysfunction and partisanship – can nevertheless meet many of the demands of voters and pass much-needed legislation? In this book we consider why and how Congress is able to address problems in society despite the many reasons mustered for why it cannot. According to many recent accounts, congressional politics has become so polarized and dysfunctional that lawmakers are incapable of cooperating on even the most mundane issues. Reelection and partisanship are such all-consuming concerns that individual legislators no longer contribute to the work of the chamber. Congress has been variously described as the "Broken Branch" (Mann and Ornstein 2006), the scene of a "Second Civil War" (Brownstein 2007), and a venue for "Fight Club Politics" (Eilperin 2007).

Claims about congressional dysfunction are hardly new. A review of scholarly research reveals remarkably similar statements in previous decades. In the 1990s, scholars debated how to "fix" or "remake"

Congress (Robinson 1995; Thurber and Davidson 1995). In the 1980s, there was a "crying need" for reform (Penner and Abramson 1988). The 1970s saw a Congress that was "against itself" (Davidson and Oleszek 1977). In the 1960s it was "out of order" (Bolling 1965) and "in crisis" (Davidson, Kovenock, and O'Leary 1966). Even as far back as the 1940s, reforms meant to address a "Congress at the crossroads" (Galloway 1946) were ultimately judged to have "failed" to address Congress's ills (*Life Magazine* 1947). These are just a small taste of the many books, articles, and reports over the years that have portrayed Congress as an ineffective lawmaking body in need of serious restructuring.

All is not well with Congress. The institution rarely responds as quickly or as completely as many would prefer. Electoral dynamics sometimes create incentives for parties in Congress to highlight their differences rather than their common concerns. Yet, Congress also accomplishes more than is generally appreciated, and much more than many scholarly perspectives would lead us to expect. Contemporary legislative research often portrays the policy preferences of lawmakers as central to understanding policy making and change in Congress. We argue that preferences often take a back seat to another concern – problem solving. On many issues, legislators seek common ground because they share common electoral incentives. Evidence in support of this perspective is hiding in plain sight. As observers have concluded that Congress is broken or failing, the institution has been addressing significant societal problems – the struggle for civil rights, military conflicts in every part of the globe, access to affordable health insurance, environmental and energy crises, educational disparities, tax reform, economic recessions – and many other visible and less visible challenges.

Conflict in Congress is neither all consuming nor is it the defining characteristic of lawmaking. Research documenting partisan polarization focuses on the growing percentage of roll call votes that pit a majority of one party against a majority of the other (McCarty, Poole, and Rosenthal 2006; Roberts and Smith 2003; Theriault 2008). Yet, at the end of the day, partisan *agreement* has been the historical norm in congressional politics, even for important issues. Most bills in the modern era pass with bipartisan support (see Carson, Finocchiaro, and Rohde 2010; Lee 2005, 308). Similarly, although the number of laws passed by Congress has declined somewhat in recent decades (from an average of about 750 laws per term in the 1940s and 1950s, to approximately 450 laws per term in the 1990s and 2000s), the number of pages of legislation enacted has increased by more than 300 percent (from around 2,600 pages of statutory language per term, to well more than 6,000 pages). Congress also continues to engage in as much regular oversight of federal agencies and programs as it ever has (Aberbach 2002; Ainsworth, Harward and Moffett 2010). And as mentioned, the recent 111th Congress (2009–10), initially characterized as one of the most dysfunctional in years, turned out to be one of the most productive in generations (Fahrenthold, Rucker, and Sonmcz 2010; Hulse and Herszenhorn 2010).

Why, then, do criticisms of Congress overshadow its accomplishments? "Conflict," Pamela Shoemaker and Stephen Reese conclude, "is more inherently interesting than harmony" (1996, 117; see also Fiorina, Abrams, and Pope 2005). Given the options of portraying the congressional glass as half-full or half-empty – of focusing on conflict versus consensus – there seems to be a longstanding bias toward the latter (Durr, Gilmour, and Wolbrecht 1997; Hibbing and Larimer 2008; Ramirez 2009). Speaking to CNN, House Speaker John Boehner (R-OH) caustically remarked, "It would surprise people that 90 percent of the time, members of Congress on both sides of the aisle get along. But, you know, that's not news for those of you in the news business" (Boehner 2011). Rep. Henry Waxman (D-CA), reflecting on an important enactment that received little coverage, opined that the news media "are conditioned to assume that the most important political issues are the ones that create the greatest amount of public drama and culminate in gavel pounding showdowns on the House floor.... . This set me to pondering the old line about a tree falling in the forest: When a law of real consequence is enacted without anyone noticing, does it still count as an accomplishment?" (Waxman 2010, 136–7). A similar bias toward conflict also seems to pervade scholarly research on Congress, possibly for the same reasons. One goal of this book, in contrast, is to understand better the *agreement* that also seems to be such an important and understudied aspect of congressional lawmaking.

THE POLITICS OF PROBLEM SOLVING

We assert that there is value in looking beyond the conflict to consider what legislatures are able to accomplish and why. We frame our investigation in terms of "problem solving." David Mayhew, a leading figure of modern congressional studies, has defined problem solving as "a widespread, shared perception that some state of affairs poses a problem and that policymaking should entail a search for a largely agreed upon solution" (2006, 221). Although lawmakers often favor differing policy solutions, they appreciate that many of their supporters are more concerned with whether a perceived problem is addressed than the specifics of how it is addressed (Fiorina 1981; Lenz 2012).

In December 2010, President Barack Obama explained his support for extending the Bush tax cuts in problem-solving terms:

For the past few weeks there's been a lot of talk around Washington about taxes and there's been a lot of political positioning between the two parties. But around kitchen tables, Americans are asking just one question: Are we going to allow their taxes to go up on January 1st, or will we meet our responsibilities to resolve our differences and do what's necessary to speed up the recovery and get people back to work?[1]

In the end, the salience of the issue and a sense of urgency (the new law was passed just two weeks before the old one expired) helped forge an agreement that might not otherwise have emerged in the absence of such pressure. Moreover, the final version of the bill received bipartisan support – most Democrats and Republicans – in both chambers.[2]

A problem-solving perspective recognizes that Americans share common concerns on many issues (Fiorina, Abrams, and Pope 2005; Page and Shapiro 1992; Stimson 1999). They expect the government to defend the nation, reduce crime, promote economic growth, improve transportation, advance health and safety, and ensure access to education – to name a few. Support for these government functions has hardly waivered over the past three decades. Wanting to address problems and successfully addressing them are two different matters however. Lawmakers appreciate that isolating the causes of societal problems can be difficult and that changing conditions alter the effectiveness of existing policies. As one lawmaker put it, "I cannot recall any project of any size that has ever been presented to this committee that came out in the end like the witnesses testified it would at the outset" (Davidson and Oleszek 2004, 9).

We investigate how endogenous structures (committees) and processes (temporary legislation) enhance Congress's ability to address problems in society. We also highlight understudied institutionalized routines and incremental policy adjustments that are important aspects of the legislative playbook (Lindblom 1959; Pressman and Wildavsky 1984). Finally, we turn our attention to the consequences of problem solving for arguably the most important contribution of legislatures – policy change.

---

[1] Statement by President Barack Obama in a press conference, http://www.whitehouse.gov/the-press-office/2010/12/06/statement-president-tax-cuts-and-unemployment-benefits (accessed April 20, 2012).
[2] House (R 139–36; D 138–112); Senate (R 37–5; D 44–14)

IMPLICATIONS FOR LEGISLATIVE STUDIES

Problem solving does not figure prominently in legislative research. If anything, the prevailing theme of existing research is that lawmakers are unable or unwilling to engage in problem solving. "Lost in the political system's focus on conflict and controversy," argue Alan Gerber and Eric Patashnik, "is the tremendous common ground – among ordinary citizens and political elites alike – over government's role in contemporary American society" (2006, 3). There are exceptions. In *Congress and the Common Good*, Arthur Maass argues that "government conducts a process of deliberation that results in decisions that are based on broader community interests, and it designs and implements programs in accordance with these decisions" (1983, 5). In *The Dysfunctional Congress: The Individual Roots of an Institutional Dilemma*, Kenneth Mayer and David Canon document how legislative theories provide little reason to expect legislatures to produce collectively beneficial policies, before observing that "Congress *does* legislate in the national interest and *has* created general benefits at the expense of localized and concentrated interests" (1999, 39; emphasis in original). Still other authors have examined specific instances of lawmakers doing "the right thing" (such as domestic military base closings or reforming Social Security) by enacting policies that serve the public interest (Arnold 1990; Becker 2005; Muir 1982; Weaver 1988). But in the main, the emphasis of research is on the reasons why Congress fails to fulfill its policy responsibilities.

The primary goal of this book is to understand why and how legislators do engage in problem solving on a routine and sustained basis. We see four main contributions to contemporary legislative research. The first is to draw attention to agenda scarcity and limited capacity in legislatures and their implications for policy making. Scarcity receives little attention in existing legislative research. Leading theories of legislative organization implicitly assume that lawmakers' preferences dictate not only the content of the winning policy alternative but also the composition of the legislative agenda (Cox and McCubbins 2005; Krehbiel 1991; Weingast and Marshall 1988). This overly narrow focus neglects important questions about how issues get on the legislative agenda, the considerations influencing what lawmakers prefer in any given debate, and even the substance of the issues that shape a party's "reputation" within the electorate.

The second contribution is to bring an issue perspective to bear on the study of legislative operations and output (Fenno 1973; Lowi 1964). For the better part of a generation, legislative scholars have favored all-encompassing explanations of legislative institutions and behavior. Our work builds upon recent studies demonstrating the value of incorporating policy specific factors into the mix (Clinton and Lapinski 2006; Lapinski 2008; Lee 2009). To a large degree, we confirm what scholars such as E. E. Schattschneider, Theodore Lowi, Frank Baumgartner, Bryan Jones, and others have long noted – that issues often organize activity and conflict in legislatures. Specifically, many issue debates begin with the shared premise that Congress must act. For such "compulsory" issues, lawmakers face considerable pressure to find common ground in timely fashion (Walker 1977). The dynamics of lawmaking are importantly different for other "discretionary" issues where the need for action is less urgent.

Third, this book refocuses attention on the governing contributions of legislative committees. In leading theories of congressional organization, the policy caretaking activities of committees are downplayed or ignored altogether. In partisan theories, committees are portrayed as mere extensions of the majority party leadership. In distributive theories, committees serve limited particularistic purposes. In informational theories, the focus is on the "signaling" contributions of committees. Where are the policy development contributions of committees in these theories? A problem-solving perspective clearly situates committees at the center of governing. It provides a richer account of how committees contribute to the policy-making process than the existing informational perspective. Drawing on original and extensive empirical data on bill referral patterns, we offer new insights into a number of longstanding topics related to committee roles, such as the purposes and effects of committee reforms, patterns of bill-sponsor success, agenda setting, and the dynamics of policy attention.

Fourth, this book advances the study of policy change beyond "major" statutory enactments (i.e., primarily those identified by Mayhew 1991). We lower the threshold for what constitutes a significant enactment to one that encompasses a substantially larger swath of all laws. We then propose a new approach to studying policy changes by exploring those contained within a single law and those that might be part of many different laws. Testing problem-centered explanations for policy change against more familiar preference-centered accounts, we find that policy change in Congress is largely problem driven.

Scarcity, Agendas, and Issue Priorities

A problem-solving perspective emphasizes that "the most important part of the legislative decision process [is] the decision about which decision to consider" (Bauer, Pool, and Dexter 1963, 405). Time and resources are scarce commodities in all legislatures (Cox 2006; Döring 1995, 223). Scarcity means that "even if agreement can be reached on what a problem is and how to solve it, there remains the formidable question of weighing problems according to their importance in the context of scarce time, attention, and money. Which ones should be tackled and solved?" (Mayhew 2006, 222).

Legislative scholars have devoted very little attention to the implications of scarcity for policy making. More commonly, the implicit assumption is that there is no scarcity. For example, gridlock theory portrays policy change solely in terms of the location of the policy status quo and the preferences of policy makers (Krehbiel 1998). Any policy status quo outside of the gridlock interval is immediately reformed – there is no scarcity problem that compels lawmakers to decide which issues should be priorities. Policy studies, in contrast, have long noted that scarcity has important implications for legislative agendas and prospects for policy change. One of the most specific is Jack Walker's 1977 study of the U.S. Senate.

According to Walker, senators "exercise little discretion over the scheduling of items for debate. Much of the business transacted by the Senate is either mandated by the Constitution or required for the maintenance of the vast federal establishment" (1977, 424). Walker then goes on to describe the Senate's issue agenda as made up of a spectrum of items ranging from "required" to "chosen" (Figure 1.1). At the required end of the spectrum are "recurring" legislative issues, such as annual appropriations bills and programs and statutes on short-term authorizations, as well as "politically necessary" issues such as those driven by salient events like the 9/11 terrorist attacks or a massive oil spill. At the opposite "chosen" end of the agenda spectrum are a much smaller set of discretionary issues "selected from the numerous possibilities offered up by the Senate's legislative activists" (1977, 425). Importantly, Walker argues that lawmakers have limited opportunities to take up discretionary issues because mandated or required issues consume much of the available agenda space.[3]

[3] In this book, we will propose a differentiation of issues that is very similar to Walker's. Specifically, we distinguish between "compulsory" and "discretionary" issues, whereas he distinguishes between "required" and "chosen" issues. The main reason for the departure is that we are not just interested in what is on the agenda (i.e., what was "chosen"). We are also interested in comparing what *might* have been on the agenda to the actual agenda.

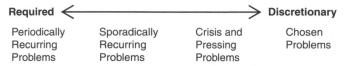

FIGURE 1.1. Walker's Typology of Problems and Agenda Items.
Source: Walker 1977.

John Kingdon (1995) makes a similar point when he portrays policy change as an episodic, event-driven process (see also Baumgartner and Jones 1993). Rather than trying to shift the agenda, policy entrepreneurs recognize that their best opportunities lie in "coupling" their policy ideas to issues that are already on the agenda (1995, Ch. 8). Kingdon specifically references reauthorizations, salient events, presidential attention, and elections as key events prompting policy attention shifts in the face of agenda scarcity. It is easy to appreciate why elected lawmakers would want to respond to publicly salient events or issues that the president highlights. It is harder to appreciate why legislators pass temporary laws requiring reauthorization if one of the consequences is that it limits their opportunities to advance other personal or partisan policy goals.

We argue that decisions to authorize laws and programs on a temporary basis are often attempts to prioritize problem-solving activities. When laws are permanently authorized, inaction has minimal policy consequences. When a law expires, however, the consequence of inaction is often more severe – it is "no policy." Temporary authorizations encourage busy legislators to invest in collectively beneficial problem-solving activities, such as program oversight and policy updating, by altering expectations about whether an issue will make it onto the agenda. As the responsibilities of the federal government have grown, so has the number of programs authorized on a short-term basis.

The Dynamics of Issue Attention and Policy Change

In 2003, a Republican-led Congress and a Republican president passed the Medicare Modernization Act (P.L. 108-173), the "largest expansion of the welfare state since the creation of Medicare" (Fiorina 2006). Media coverage and subsequent scholarly studies of the debates highlighted the differences among the parties, chambers, and even members within the majority party over the details of the reform (Eilperin 2007; Sinclair 2006). But why was a dramatic expansion of the Medicare entitlement on the agenda at all under a Republican government?

Problem solving highlights decisions about policy priorities – what might be termed the *issue agenda*. In contrast, existing legislative theorizing tends to focus on the policy alternatives considered in a given debate – what might be called the *choice agenda*. More often than is generally appreciated, governments have things they must do – crises they must address (rising prescription drug costs) and policies that require updating (reauthorization of the Voting Rights Act) – lest elected officials face retribution from voters at the ballot box. The explanation offered as to why Medicare changes were on the agenda in 2003 was decidedly problem centered. Pollsters advised Republican Party leaders that addressing the salient problem of rising out-of-pocket costs for prescription drugs was critical to the party's prospects in the coming election (Carey 2000, 1436; Oliver, Lee, and Lipton 2004, 307–8). The issue, not the party, drove the agenda.

The fact that Republicans were in control did have important consequences for the choice agenda. The specifics of the Medicare Modernization Act were clearly different than would have been the case under a unified Democratic government. Among other things, the federal government was prohibited from negotiating prices for drugs with pharmaceutical companies. But the policy preferences of the majority party did not explain why the issue was on the agenda in the first place.

We anticipate that policy change in Congress is more often problem driven than preference driven. A limited number of legislative studies have explored the factors influencing legislative policy change by examining variations in legislative output across time (Binder 2003; Brady 1988; Krehbiel 1998; Mayhew 1991) as well as "historic" reforms to existing laws and programs (Berry, Burden, and Howell 2010; Lewis 2002; Maltzman and Shipan 2008; Ragusa 2010). We broaden the investigation of policy change by testing indicators of problem-solving considerations as predictors of not only "historic" statutory changes (which represent a small proportion of all policy changes), but also of policy changes that meet a lower threshold of significance. Indicators of problem-solving motivations appear to be more robust predictors of policy change than are indicators of electorally induced shifts in preferences or partisan control.

PROBLEM SOLVING AND PARTISAN POLITICS

Partisan politics poses important challenges to problem solving. Necessary compromises become more difficult when "every legislative choice by

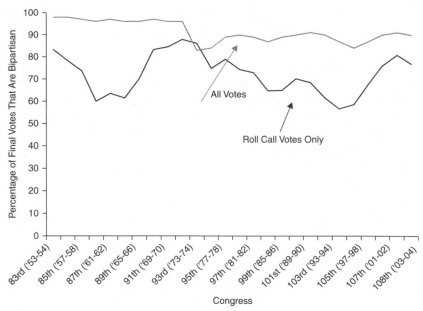

FIGURE 1.2. Bipartisan Voting Behavior on House Final Passage Votes, 1953–2004.

each party is viewed not only in light of what is substantively desirable but also with regard to how it may affect electoral fortunes" (Carson, Finocchiaro, and Rohde 2010, 220; Binder 2006). Some observers conclude that congressional politics has evolved to the point where partisanship and conflict are all-consuming. Yet it is one thing to draw attention to the increasing role of partisanship in congressional deliberations, and another to conclude that partisanship is the driving force of legislative operations. Partisan politics does not infuse every legislative issue – far from it. The vast majority (about 80%) of House bills in the modern era have passed with bipartisan support – a majority of Republicans aligning with a majority of Democrats (Figure 1.2; see also Lynch and Madonna 2008; Lee 2005, 308). As well, nearly three-fourths of the historic laws identified by Mayhew adopted in the postwar era were passed with bipartisan majorities or by voice vote (Mayhew 1991).

Laurel Harbridge similarly finds high levels of bipartisanship when analyzing a different facet of lawmaking – publicly expressed support for legislative proposals through bill cosponsorship from 1973 to 2004. More than half of all bills in the House of Representatives that have multiple cosponsors receive significant support from lawmakers of both parties. Important legislation is the most likely to attract bipartisan cosponsors (Harbridge 2011).[4]

That decision making in Congress has become dramatically more partisan is also less evident in the data than is generally believed. Jamie Carson and colleagues carefully examine four different congressional terms from the late-1970s through the mid-2000s and report that the proportion of conflictual bills has, if anything, decreased (Carson, Finocchiaro, and Rohde 2010, Appendix). The percentage of these conflictual bills that involved partisan conflicts did increase by about 15 percent, but the total number of partisan bills decreased by more than 40 percent over the three decades of their analysis.

These patterns underscore that congressional policy making is not simply a zero sum struggle between the political parties. The congressional "agenda is diverse and multifaceted, and only a portion of it relates to matters that provoke disagreement between the parties.... Sometimes controversy will arise from sources other than party, such as regional or urban-rural conflicts" (Rohde 2005a, 208). For example, conflicts between the House and Senate seem to elicit as much media attention as do partisan conflicts (Baker 2008).

A problem-solving perspective helps to explain why lawmakers cooperate more often than existing perspectives lead us to expect. Majorities of Americans in both parties continue to express support for government programs and deep disapproval of lawmakers' inability to find common ground on some of the pressing issues of the day. Problem solving helps to explain why lawmakers often pursue workable solutions when doing so requires compromising strongly held values. At the very least, this suggests that many lawmakers do not always view choices in purely partisan terms, and that party agendas are not as distinct as many would assume.

Overall, we hope that readers agree that *Congress and the Politics of Problem Solving* provides a refreshing and provocative perspective that draws renewed attention to the policy contributions of legislatures and the underlying structures, particularly committees, that help them to fulfill their governing responsibilities. We make a compelling case that, to a very large degree, the legislative process is problem driven. Citizens often share common concerns about societal problems and expect their representatives to do more than stake out ideologically motivated positions. Lawmakers appreciate that voters value problem solving and that

---

[4] Harbridge defines *bipartisan cosponsorship* as bills that have at least 20% of the cosponsors from the party other than the original sponsor.

they have an electoral interest in responding to such concerns. Congress is not merely a venue for expressing partisan or ideological divisions; it is an operational governing body.

Data Sources

Roll call voting has been an important and valuable source of information in contemporary congressional studies. However, roll call votes capture only one limited aspect of lawmaking that is not necessarily representative of the issues considered or policy changes adopted by Congress (Carrubba, Gabel, and Hug 2008; Krehbiel and Woon 2005). Prior studies rightly question whether conclusions drawn from floor voting behavior extend to other contexts, such as committee politics (Carson, Finocchiaro, and Rohde 2010; Mayhew 2006; Potoski and Talbert 2000). Lawmakers sponsor bills, committees engage in oversight and policy development, leaders make decisions about issue priorities and agendas, and the institution enacts policy changes that vary widely in terms of significance. In addition, studies of roll call voting have generally found that lawmakers exhibit stable patterns of voting over time, which has been used to suggest that electoral replacement is the primary driver of policy change in Congress (Asher and Weisberg 1978; Brady and Sinclair 1984; Brady and Volden 1998; Poole and Rosenthal 2007). Moving beyond roll call votes as a testing ground for legislative theories can produce significantly different perspectives on lawmaking and policy change (Harbridge 2011; Lee 2009).

Valuable data sources tapping many different aspects of legislative policy making are now widely available. The data used in this book come from every corner of American politics. We investigate the electoral foundations of problem solving by examining more than two decades worth of American National Elections Studies surveys, as well as a unique survey of former members of Congress. To test hypotheses related to legislative organization and agenda setting, we exploit other novel data sources spanning decades of policy making. These include our Congressional Bills Project, an archive of information about more than four hundred thousand public and private bills introduced since 1947. In addition, we construct an important new database of expiring provisions of law over two decades. These original data sets are further supplemented by other valuable resources, including the Policy Agendas Project, the Congressional Districts Data Set, the PIPC Roll Call Voting database, Keith Poole and Howard Rosenthal's NOMINATE scores, Sarah Binder's compilation of newspaper editorials, James Stimson's policy mood measures, Andrew

Rudalevige's presidential statements, Harold Spaeth's Supreme Court decisions, Gallup's "most important problem" surveys, and a congressional staff survey by the Annenberg Public Policy Center. Exploiting such a wide array of sources has its own limitations. Foremost among them is that different data sources span different time periods. This inevitably means that the periods of study vary for different aspects of our investigation. To address this source of concern, we make every practical effort to ensure that the years or congressional terms examined minimize the potential for bias. In our view, the considerable advantages stemming from this exploitation of diverse data sources outweigh the potential pitfalls.

OVERVIEW OF THE BOOK

Congress and the Politics of Problem Solving offers important insights into electoral accountability, institutional design, agenda-setting processes, and policy-change dynamics in legislatures. The first part of the book investigates the electoral foundations of problem solving. In Chapter 2, *Problem-Focused Voters and Congressional Accountability*, we propose that reelection-motivated lawmakers have incentives to respond to publicly salient events in a timely manner and to ensure that existing government programs perform to the satisfaction of voters. Support for these assertions is found in existing congressional elections research and in voter and elite surveys. Electoral studies indicate that voters care about problem solving and that it influences their vote choices. Elite surveys also indicate that lawmakers believe that their personal and collective legislative accomplishments influence their reelection prospects. Chapter 3, *Congressional Approval and Incumbent Accountability*, extends the theme of Chapter 2 by systematically testing the hypothesis that incumbent legislators have electoral incentives to be concerned about Congress's collective performance. Analyzing voter decisions and district-level incumbent vote shares over several decades, we find that approval of Congress is significantly related to support for individual incumbents, whether support is measured in vote share, probability of reelection, or probability of returning to office (to account for strategic retirements). The importance of collective performance also varies by political conditions. Under unified governments, we find that only incumbents of the majority party are held to account for Congress's collective performance. Under divided government – the more common condition – collective accountability extends to incumbents of both political parties.

The second part of the book turns to the question of how electoral incentives to address problems in society impact the organization and activities of Congress. Chapter 4, *Problem-Solving Constraints and Legislative Institutions*, argues that committee systems can be viewed as institutional responses to two important constraints to problem solving – scarcity and shirking. Committees increase legislative problem-solving capacity through (among other things) a division of labor and nearly exclusive issue jurisdictions that promote specialization and accountability. However, as the scope of federal government responsibilities have expanded in recent decades, Congress has faced increasing challenges in terms of its ability to address problems in an effective and timely manner. Chapter 5, *Agenda Scarcity, Problem Solving, and Temporary Legislation*, proposes that a central reason for the increasing use of short-term authorizations in Congress has been to encourage problem-solving activities in an environment of limited legislative capacity. The challenge that lawmakers face is that promises of side payments or policy influence for engaging in collectively beneficial problem-solving activities are less effectual rewards to the extent that proposals are unlikely to make it onto the agenda. When Congress authorizes a program on a temporary basis, expectations that Congress will revisit the issue in the foreseeable future are considerably enhanced, as are members' incentives to invest in that issue.

The third part of the book tests some institutional implications of the theoretical arguments presented in the previous chapters. Chapter 6, *Rethinking Committee Reform*, investigates the institutional consequences of the largest set of committee jurisdictional reforms of the postwar period. Prior research concludes that the Bolling-Hansen reforms of the 1970s had no appreciable impact on congressional policy-making activities. A problem-solving perspective offers specific and unique predictions about their consequences. We find that the reforms substantially clarified committee issue responsibilities in ways that served to promote information sharing and reduce policy duplication. Significantly, these findings match the stated objectives of the reformers of the time – objectives that have been largely rejected by scholars. Chapter 7, *Agenda Setting in a Problem-Solving Legislature*, examines the legislative issue agenda with the goal of assessing the extent to which it is problem driven. After developing an original methodology for distinguishing compulsory issues from discretionary ones, we find that compulsory issues make up an increasing proportion of the agenda as legislation moves through the process. Committees play a much more central role in managing compulsory issues both in terms of who sponsors the bills that pass the chamber and in terms of whose policy positions prevail on the floor.

The fourth part of the book shifts from testing institutional implications of a problem-solving perspective to testing its policy implications. Are legislative activity and policy change within issue areas shaped by problem-solving considerations? We anticipate that agenda scarcity means that compulsory issues will serve as important focal points for policy change. Chapter 8, *Problem Solving and Policy Focal Points*, investigates changing attention to issues across time, as measured by member bill-sponsor activity. Whereas previous research portrays bills sponsorship as a means for shaping the legislative agenda, we find that lawmakers sponsor bills in anticipation of congressional action. The best explanations for variations in legislative attention to issues are problem centered.

Chapter 9, *Problem Solving and the Dynamics of Policy Change*, addresses what is arguably the core question of governmental studies: what considerations best explain policy change? An investigation of statutory changes builds on existing research to shed additional light on why "major laws" are reformed. An investigation of cumulative policy changes takes the study of policy change a step further by acknowledging that a single law may address multiple policies (e.g., an omnibus law) and that a policy can be a product of multiple laws (e.g., airline safety policy).

Although several different dependent variables are examined in Chapters 8 and 9 – bill sponsorships, statutory changes, and cumulative policy changes – our findings regarding key explanatory variables are similar. Expiring provisions of law and indicators of public issue salience – variables capturing problem-solving motivations – are robust predictors of all three. Indicators of the changing preferences of lawmakers and changes in partisan control (measured in a variety of established ways) are not.

The concluding chapter reflects on these findings and their boundaries. A problem-solving perspective constitutes an important and refreshing departure from existing approaches to the study of lawmaking. It connects the policy-making activities of Congress to the electoral arena. It fills in details about how committees contribute to lawmaking and why lawmakers engage in committee work. It offers the most specific insights into the composition of the legislative agenda of any study to date and demonstrates the value and importance of distinguishing among the different types of issues legislatures address. Perhaps most importantly, it offers a new account of congressional policy change that focuses scholarly attention on the question of why legislatures take up issues, emphasizing the important role of problems as opposed to preferences in explaining legislative agendas. This account helps to explain why seemingly "broken" legislatures nevertheless continue to engage in important lawmaking activities and often address important issues when circumstances would otherwise suggest little possibility of change. Recurring policy items and matters propelled onto the agenda by public or presidential salience tend to drive Congress's lawmaking activity.

2

Problem-Focused Voters and Congressional Accountability

> What [voters are] looking for is someone who solves the problem, not for a
> solution that happens to be halfway between the two parties.
>
> Rep. Tom Perriello (D-VA; Dionne 2010)

A problem-solving perspective on legislative organization and behavior starts from the same assumption as many legislative theories – that lawmakers are primarily motivated by reelection. Lawmakers may not always be "single-minded" seekers of reelection, but for most getting reelected is paramount to the pursuit of other policy and career goals (Fiorina 1989; Mayhew 1974). Significantly, prior research often portrays lawmakers' pursuit of reelection as corrosive to the institution's broader goals. For example, Mayhew argues "if all members did nothing but pursue their electoral goals, Congress would decay or collapse" (Mayhew 1974, 141). A central difference between a problem-solving perspective and many other perspectives is the assumption that voters also care about collective outputs and are willing to hold lawmakers accountable for whether problems in society are addressed. This means that incumbent legislators do have electoral incentives to be concerned about Congress's collective performance and to support institutions and processes that promote problem solving.

In this chapter and the next, we consider the evidence for this assumption. Until recently, relevant academic research offered little reason to think that the collective performance of Congress mattered to electorally minded lawmakers. However, more recent research suggests that congressional performance has a significant effect on support for the majority party in Congress. In the current chapter, we argue that voters care about problem solving and that their representatives perceive this concern. In Chapter 3, we then build on existing studies to examine the nature of collective congressional accountability. We offer evidence, both in terms of vote share and lawmaker turnover, that incumbents of the majority and minority parties have electoral reasons to be concerned about Congress's collective performance. Later we will argue that such concerns are central to appreciating why lawmakers support institutions and processes that promote problem solving.

WHERE'S CONGRESS IN PRIOR CONGRESSIONAL ELECTIONS RESEARCH?

Theories of legislative organization often assume that voters care about Congress's performance. For example, in distinguishing between policies and outcomes, Keith Krehbiel assumes that lawmakers pursue information because it reduces their uncertainty about a policy's future credit-claiming or blame-avoiding consequences when the outcomes obtain (1991, 62). Gary Cox and Mathew McCubbins assume that the goal of party leaders is to protect the party's "reputation" in the electorate: "If a party's reputation improves or worsens, all members of the party benefit or suffer together, regardless of whether they contributed to the improvement or worsening" (2005, 21; see also 1993).

Yet, congressional elections research has traditionally offered little reason to think that the collective or even individual policy performance of lawmakers has much impact on their reelection prospects. As R. Douglas Arnold once put it, "If legislators consulted the scholarly literature on congressional elections, they might conclude that they need not worry much about either the positions that they take or the effects that they produce, because these are not the major determinants of electoral outcomes" (Arnold 1990, 37; see also Binder 2003; Fiorina 1980).

In general, scholars have treated congressional elections as a specialized area of the broader voting literature (Burden and Wichowsky 2010). Two strands of this research are of particular interest here. The first investigates the considerations shaping voter preferences. The second, very much related to the first, investigates how macroconditions, such as the state of the economy or presidential popularity, affect congressional election outcomes.

Early studies of individual voter decisions in the United States concluded that partisan attachments developed early in life were the single most important predictor of vote choice (Bartels 2000; Campbell et al. 1960; Stokes and Miller 1962). Subsequent research challenged this socialization perspective, suggesting that voter preferences changed in response to information. Voters are more likely to support candidates who share their ideological or policy preferences (Abramowitz 1984; Erikson and Wright 1993, 2009; Johannes and McAdams 1981; Serra and Moon 1994; Stone and Simas 2010; Wright 1978). In addition, when voters vote for a candidate of the other party, it is almost always to support the incumbent. Research on this "incumbency advantage" associates party switching with many different causes, including simple name recognition, perceptions of competence, personal contact, and constituency service (Bond, Covington, and Fleisher 1985; Cain, Ferejohn, and Fiorina 1987; Cover 1977; Fenno 1978; Ferejohn 1977; Fiorina 1977; Johannes and McAdams 1981; Nelson 1978; Serra and Moon 1994; Yiannakis 1981).

Research on national-level congressional election trends has emphasized the importance of macroconditions, such as the president's popularity and the state of the economy (Born 1984; Calvert and Ferejohn 1983; Campbell and Sumners 1990; Ferejohn and Calvert 1984). Midterm elections studies have highlighted variations in voter turnout, a party's "exposure," and strategic candidate behavior in explaining seat losses and gains by the president's party in Congress (Campbell 1991; Jacobson 1989).

Thus, although "retrospective" issue accountability is a core concept of almost every theory of congressional organization, little in the historical congressional elections literature suggests that lawmakers should be concerned about their performance in office (Fiorina 1981). Even economic conditions are portrayed as having indirect effects through their impact on public approval of the president's performance (Abramowitz, Cover, and Norpoth 1986; Alesina and Rosenthal 1995; Born 1990a; Burden and Kimball 2004; Kernell 1977; Kiewiet 1983; Kramer 1971; Tufte 1975, 1978); on candidate entry and exit decisions (quality candidates enter races when their party is favoured; Jacobson 1989; Jacobson and Kernell 1983; Wolak 2007); or through ambiguous general voter satisfaction or dissatisfaction with the economy (voting based on general, national economic circumstances; Hibbing and Alford 1981; Kinder and Kiewiet 1979; Mann and Wolfinger 1980).

A small number of recent studies have begun to link roll call voting positions and support for individual congressional candidates (Ansolabehere and Jones 2010; Canes-Wrone, Brady, and Cogan 2002; more on this later). Additional research finds that voters favor "quality"

candidates – that is, those that exhibit higher levels of legislative competence and integrity (McCurley and Mondak 1995), and that incumbents
who can tout policy specialization and legislative accomplishments fare
better at the polls (Sellers 1998). Students of Congress are also familiar
with the fact that the public evaluates their representatives much more
positively than they evaluate Congress (Fenno 1975). This has been interpreted as evidence that incumbents have little to fear where public disapproval of Congress is concerned. Richard Fenno argues that voters evaluate
incumbents in terms of constituent service, whereas Congress is evaluated
in terms of national policy making, once again offering little support for
the retrospective accountability that is central to leading theories.

Yet, it turns out that the love-hate pattern that Fenno highlighted is
not unique to Congress: "Positive evaluations of things personal and
local are very consistently coupled with negative evaluations of those
very same entities as large scale collectives" (Mutz and Flemming 1999).
People offer more negative opinions when asked to evaluate "doctors in
general" versus their "own doctor" (Jacobs and Shapiro 1994). Diana
Mutz and Gregory Flemming argue that the discrepancy stems from
"negative perceptual biases" of abstract entities, such as "Congress" or
"doctors" (1999, 88). It should not be interpreted as indicating that voter
assessments of incumbent lawmakers are divorced from their assessments
of Congress.

Scholars surveying the congressional elections literature have also
noted that this work lacks a unifying theory of either individual voter
preference formation or collective choice (Burden and Wichowsky 2010;
Ragsdale 1994). Focusing specifically on economic voting research, Lyn
Ragsdale observed:

Since 1983, scholars' fascination with the electoral consequences of the economy has continued, as has confusion about what those consequences are. The
confusion stems at least partly from the field's limited theoretical development
and heavy empiricism. Researchers generally accept a simple theory of economic
voting, which states that the economy affects elections. Debate in the field is often
less about how valid the theory is than about how best to test it. (1994, 539)

In her theory, Ragsdale proposes that voters consider broader government performance (e.g., its foreign and domestic policy accomplishments)
and not just the economy: "The referendum notion, so often discussed
as a matter of satisfaction or dissatisfaction with economic conditions,
becomes a more intricate statement about government performance on
economic and noneconomic matters" (1994, 546). The notion that public

assessments of broader government performance are related to support for individual candidates also receives support in other studies. Richard Born (1990b) carefully concludes that voters who approve of Congress are more likely to approve of their incumbent lawmaker's performance in office. In a well-researched book, David Jones and Monika McDermott (2009) link congressional approval to election outcomes. They find that candidates of the majority party in Congress fare better when public approval of Congress is higher.

IS CONGRESSIONAL APPROVAL RELATED TO CONGRESSIONAL PERFORMANCE?

Perhaps congressional approval is driven by factors that have little to do with the performance or accomplishments of Congress – such as attitudes toward the president, partisan affiliation, or broader economic conditions. A 2006 Indiana University survey provides a unique opportunity to examine whether judgments of congressional performance are related to congressional approval. Along with the standard battery of questions about partisan identification, ideology, presidential job approval, congressional job approval, and economic conditions, the Indiana survey asked respondents to grade ten aspects of Congress's performance. Our goal here is to explore whether respondent congressional performance evaluations are related to approval or disapproval of Congress more generally.

Table 2.1 correlates each performance grade with respondents' overall approval of Congress. Overall performance does correlate with overall approval, but modestly (Pearson's $r = 0.54$), indicating that the two questions are not tapping into the same voter considerations. Turning to questions addressing more specific aspects of congressional performance: opinions about policy making – congressional oversight of the executive, whether Congress is tackling the key issues facing the country, and whether it is carrying on a productive discussion on important issues – seem to be more strongly related to approval of Congress (Pearson's $r = 0.45$, average correlation) than opinions about membership and process – ethics, transparency, and interest group influence (Pearson's $r = 0.33$, average correlation).

The findings of Table 2.1 suggest that the performance/approval distinction is meaningful. Performance assessments are not simply proxies for approval. In addition, policy performance assessments appear to affect

TABLE 2.1. *Impact of Congressional Performance on Congressional Job Approval*

	Correlation with Job Approval Rating
Overall congressional performance grade (A to F)	0.544
How well do you think Congress has done recently in overseeing the activities of the president and the executive branch?	0.482
What grade would you give Congress for encouraging its own level of bipartisan cooperation?	0.407
What grade would you give Congress for conducting its business in a careful, deliberate way?	0.404
What grade would you give Congress for representing all of America's diverse groups and interests?	0.358
What grade would you give Congress for tackling the key issues facing the country?	0.455
What grade would you give Congress for holding its members to high standards of ethical conduct?	0.342
What grade would you give Congress for carrying on a productive discussion on important issues?	0.426
What grade would you give Congress for making its workings and activities open to the public?	0.333
What grade would you give Congress for controlling the influence of special interests groups?	0.333

Source: Indiana University, Center for Congress 2006.

approval more strongly than process performance assessments. However, these findings also do not directly address the question of whether congressional approval is driven by perceptions of congressional performance, or by other (unrelated) factors. Addressing this question requires a multivariate approach.

Table 2.2 reports results from two ordered logistic regressions drawing on the same Indiana University survey. The dependent variable in both models is the respondent's approval of Congress (4-point scale). If approval of Congress is based on partisan or ideological congruence, then we would expect Republican and right-leaning voters (7-point ideological scale) to express higher levels of congressional approval in 2006. As well, voters who approve of Republican President George W. Bush's performance will be more likely to approve of the Republican Congress's performance. Public approval of Congress should also be higher among respondents with more positive assessments of their personal or national

TABLE 2.2. *Factors Influencing Congressional Job Approval, 2006*

	Model 1		Model 2	
	Coefficient	S. E.	Coefficient	S. E.
Congressional Performance	–	–	1.69*	.11
Ideology	.033	.06	.027	.06
Party ID	–.016	.04	–.027	.04
Presidential Approval	.491*	.06	.337*	.06
Economic Conditions (personal)	.002	.07	–.021	.07
Economic (sociotropic)	.119*	.06	.062	.06
Number of Cases	1,105		1,105	
Log Likelihood	–.1178		–.1032	
Pseudo R^2	.08		.19	

Source: Indiana University, Center for Congress 2006; $*p < .05$.

economic conditions. Finally, voters who positively assess Congress's performance (overall) should be more approving of Congress.

Model 1 (first column) excludes the congressional performance variable. Model 2 then asks whether the addition of this factor substantially improves the model's explanatory power and/or alters the findings. Partisan and ideological congruence – whether the voter's political leanings place him closer to the majority (Republican) party – are not significant predictors of congressional approval in either model. This finding accords with prior research that concludes that "for large portions of the populace, partisan control does not determine their attitudes toward Congress" (Hibbing and Larimer 2008). Congressional approval is not merely a proxy for shared preferences with the party in power. Personal economic circumstances also have no meaningful impact on whether respondents approve of Congress (Kiewiet 1983). Presidential approval and national economic conditions are important predictors of approval. Specifically, respondents who approved of the president's job performance, and those who viewed national (sociotropic) economic conditions more positively, were more likely to approve of the Republican-controlled Congress.

Turning to model 2, adding respondents' overall congressional performance ratings does substantially improve the model's fit to the data (the log-likelihood ratio declines and the pseudo R-squared doubles). Congressional performance evaluations are meaningful and significant predictors of approval. Approval of the president continues to be an important predictor while partisan and ideological congruence remain unimportant. The main substantive change is that economic evaluations are no longer predictive. This finding appears to confirm Ragsdale's proposition that assessments of government performance are about more than the economy. The congressional performance variable not only captures the impact of respondent assessments of economics on approval. It provides additional explanatory power, suggesting that other performance considerations are influencing congressional approval as well.

CONGRESSIONAL PERFORMANCE AND PROBLEM SOLVING

A problem-solving perspective emphasizes commonly perceived problems, shared desires to see those problems addressed, and the electoral consequences of failing to do so. A common assumption of political science theorizing is that well-informed voters with clearly formed policy preferences hold lawmakers accountable for their positions on legislative proposals (Ansolabehere and Jones 2010; Ansolabehere, Rodden, and Snyder 2008; Canes-Wrone, Brady, and Cogan 2002). If lawmakers only expect to be punished or rewarded for their policy positions, then there might be little reason to expect anything other than stalemate on many issues. However, elections scholars have long doubted that voters possess the solid engagement and rich knowledge required for informed policy voting (Delli Carpini and Keeter 1996; Miller and Stokes 1963). Similarly, legislative scholars studying particular issues have found that voters often lack strong policy preferences (Ainsworth and Hall 2011; Berinski 2004). Instead, a more plausible view of electoral accountability asserts that many constituents hold incumbents accountable for broader "conditions in society" and broader governmental performance (Arnold 1990). Recent empirical research confirms that there is little evidence to indicate that voters judge candidates based on their policy stances (Lenz 2009).

Surveys report that the American public prefers a member of Congress who is willing to find practical solutions to the country's problems to one who has strong values and convictions (by a 2–1 margin).[1] Gary Jacobson finds that perceptions of which candidate would do a better job of "dealing with the most important problems facing the nation" are better predictors of incumbent support than agreement with the incumbent's policy positions, "satisfaction" with voter-initiated contact, or approval

---

[1] George Washington University Battleground Survey, conducted in February 2006 and July 2007.

of the incumbent's job performance (Jacobson 2009, Table 5–11). John Hibbing and Elizabeth Theiss-Morse find that an overwhelming majority of Americans (86%) agree that elected officials would help the country more if they would "stop talking and just take action on important problems" (Hibbing and Theiss-Morse 2002, 135–6). They conclude that most Americans want "a system that is instinctively in touch with the problems of real Americans and that would respond with every ounce of courtesy and attentiveness imaginable if those real Americans ever did make an actual request upon the system" (2002, 131).

The fact that Americans agree that their representatives should be addressing important problems does not necessarily mean that voters are in agreement with respect to the problems that need addressing. However, there seems to be more public consensus than is generally appreciated. Partisans are not as divided on moral issues as many argue (Ainsworth and Hall 2010; Fiorina, Abrams, and Pope 2005). But voters share common concerns about other issues as well. The General Social Survey has posed the "most important problem facing the nation" question twenty-one times between 1960 and 2004. Responses to this open-ended question are collapsed into eight or nine larger categories (e.g., economy, crime, health care). Majorities of Democratic, Republican, and Independent voters have agreed on the top three most important problems facing the nation in sixteen out of twenty-one years (76%). In eleven of the twenty-one years (more than 50%), Democrats, Republicans, and Independents also agreed on the rank ordering of the top three problems. In five of those remaining ten years, all three groups agreed on the top two problems facing the nation. Since 1970, partisans have disagreed about the top three problems facing the nation just once (in 1998).

Not all voters care about problem solving more than positions. Moderates are more likely to favor compromise than extreme partisans (Harbridge and Malhotra 2011). Our argument is that lawmakers have electoral reasons to care about whether problems get addressed, in addition to any electoral reasons they may have to stick to their guns. Asked which would be worse, a Congress that passed too many costly government programs and increased the deficit, or a Congress that failed to take strong and aggressive action to deal with the problems of the day (the economy, health care, energy, etc.), significantly more respondents (48% vs. 41%) wanted lawmakers to deal with the problems of the day.[2] Voters also indicate willingness to factor problem solving into

---

[2] Survey by Women's Voices. Women Vote. January/February 2009.

their evaluations of lawmakers. Asked what they thought their friends and neighbors would do "If Congress does not deal this year with the most pressing problems facing the nation," two-thirds of respondents in a George Washington University poll believed that their friends and neighbors would not vote for the incumbent or would not vote at all.[3] This suggests that incumbents do have electoral incentives to be concerned about Congress's decay or collapse.

LAWMAKERS' PERCEPTIONS OF THE LINKAGE BETWEEN PROBLEM SOLVING AND VOTE CHOICE

If there is evidence to indicate that voters are prepared to credit or blame Congress for addressing problems, do lawmakers also perceive that problem solving is important for their reelection prospects? This question has received limited attention as well. Studies of lawmaker behavior in the district have found that credit claiming and explanations of policy choices are important components of "home styles" (Fenno 1978, 141–6; see also Kingdon 1989, 47–54; Mayhew 1974). In addition, researchers emphasize that lawmakers try to avoid taking controversial positions out of fear that those positions will attract opposition (Arnold 1990, 38). But these studies do not directly address whether lawmakers perceive that the accomplishments of Congress, as well as their own accomplishments, matter to voters.

Accordingly, we conducted our own survey of former members of Congress to gauge lawmaker perceptions directly.[4] A mail survey was sent out in two waves – the first in July 2008 (163 surveys), and the second in November 2008 (40 surveys). Twenty-eight surveys were returned (a response rate of 13.5%) by a diverse set of former legislators, who served on Capitol Hill from the 1950s through the mid-2000s. Slightly more than half (15) were Democrats. Average tenure was just more than five congressional terms. Most retired voluntarily, but seven of the twenty-eight were defeated in their last reelection bid.

The primary question asked: "Thinking of the last time you faced reelection, what do you believe were the most important factors for your constituents when deciding which candidate to vote for?" Nine possible

---

[3] George Washington University Battleground Survey, conducted in September 2006.
[4] We obtained our sample of respondents from the U.S. Association of Former Members of Congress and through Internet searches for contact information. The survey was initially part of Bustamante 2008.

TABLE 2.3. *Former Members' Views of the Factors Shaping Constituents' Voting Decisions*

Factor	Mean Rating (1–10 scale)
Constituent service	7.32
Your legislative accomplishments	6.54
The economy	6.14
The policy positions you took during the campaign	5.96
Your partisan affiliation	5.75
Approval of the overall performance of the president	4.68
Qualities of your challenger	4.64
Approval of the overall performance of Congress	4.29
Congress's legislative accomplishments	4.07
Your ability to bring federal funds to the district	3.04

Source: Bustamante 2008.

options were presented, and lawmakers were asked to rate each on a 1–10 scale from not at all important (1) to extremely important (10).[5] Table 2.3 provides the average ratings for each option. Perhaps not surprisingly, lawmakers ranked constituent service at the top (Cover and Brumberg 1982). The lawmaker's legislative accomplishments ranked second. (To avoid possible confusion between legislative accomplishments and delivering federal benefits to the district (pork), we included a separate option for each.) On average, Congress's performance was more important for the representatives' reelections than district-directed federal benefits and not far behind perceptions of the president's performance. Despite of the long research lineage extolling its virtues (see, e.g., Ferejohn 1974; Levitt and Snyder 1997), federal pork ranked at the bottom of importance for lawmakers. This finding accords with research casting doubt on the empirical relevance of distributive accounts of legislative organization and behavior (Lee 2003; Maass 1983; Stein and Bickers 1994, 1995).

Lipinski found that a very sizable percentage (75%) of the eighty sitting members of the 105th Congress (1997–8) he interviewed expressed the view that "overall congressional approval" was meaningful for their reelection prospects (2004, 29). We also asked former legislators a similar question: "To what extent do you believe that the overall legislative

---

[5] An "other" option, with a space to fill in a description, was provided for respondents but its ratings are not included in Table 2.3.

performance of Congress was an important factor in the voting decisions of constituents in your last reelection?" In our survey, former members clearly indicated that they believed Congress's performance mattered. On average, they gave it a 2.4 on a 1- to 5-point scale.

CONCLUSION

The congressional elections literature has historically offered little reason to think that what happens in Congress affects the reelection prospects of congressional incumbents. However, more recent findings are starting to tell a different story. Existing elections research has also been criticized as heavy on empiricism and light on theorizing. Following the lead of Ragsdale and others, we theorize that voters care about problems in society and are willing to hold Congress accountable for whether problems get addressed. Supporting evidence was found in survey research indicating the public approval of Congress is linked to judgments about policy-related congressional performance, that there has been widespread consensus regarding the "most important problems facing the nation" over time, and that former lawmakers view their own accomplishments and the accomplishments of Congress as having important electoral consequences.

In the next chapter, we take a closer look at the impact of congressional approval on vote choice in congressional elections. A central purpose of this investigation is to ask whether collective accountability is restricted to members of the majority party, or whether incumbents of both political parties sometimes have shared incentives to be concerned about Congress's collective performance.

3

Congressional Approval and Incumbent Accountability

with Michael J. Ensley

> Voting will be easy this year. Incumbents: out. Non-incumbents: in.
>
> A voter (*Rochester Business Journal* 2010)

Surveys indicate that voters are willing to blame or credit both parties for Congress's job performance. Pundits and lawmakers warn of the electoral consequences of legislative gridlock for incumbents of both parties (Capehart 2010). Yet, within legislative studies, the notion that public attitudes toward Congress influence congressional election outcomes, or that electoral credit or blame extends to incumbents of both parties, is not widely accepted. Evaluations of Congress, according to the conventional view, "have very little influence on how Americans vote in congressional elections. When it comes to choosing candidates for Congress, it is opinions of the president's performance that matter" (Abramowitz 2010).

In this chapter, we propose and test a theory of collective congressional performance accountability. Voters, armed with basic knowledge of who the incumbent is and a sense of current social and economic conditions, decide whether to support the incumbent or vote for change. This *congressional performance rule* better accords with what voters know about candidates and Congress than existing retrospective voter theories that assume *partisan performance accountability*. We then test the evidence for these competing theories by examining the impact of congressional approval in House elections in four different ways: at the microlevel of the individual voter and at the macrolevel of district-wide incumbent vote share, probability of reelection, and retirement rates. We find that congressional approval significantly affects support for incumbents of the majority and minority parties and that its impact is similar to other centerpiece variables of congressional elections research, such as challenger quality, candidate ideology, and incumbency status.

A THEORY OF CONGRESSIONAL PERFORMANCE ACCOUNTABILITY

As discussed in Chapter 2, congressional election outcomes have traditionally been explained in terms of the characteristics of candidate and voters, district-specific factors, and national conditions (Abramowitz, Cover, and Norpoth 1986; Basinger and Ensley 2007; Jacobson 2009; Jacobson and Kernell 1983; Tufte 1975). Legislative actions deemed to be electorally meaningful are almost uniformly individual in nature – personal contact, constituency service, or scandal (Cain, Ferejohn, and Fiorina 1987; Fenno 1978; Jacobson and Dimock 1994; Mayhew 1974). The collective performance of Congress is not among the factors deemed to be central to appreciating congressional election outcomes.

We argued that voters also care about problem solving and found that public ratings of Congress's performance are better predictors of congressional approval than are opinions about the president's performance, assessments of economic conditions, or identification with the majority party in Congress. Several more recent studies also raise important questions about the conventional view that members of Congress need not be concerned about the institution's performance. Born not only finds that congressional approval is a significant predictor of voter approval of individual incumbents, he also finds that majority party identification "never came close to being statistically significant" in explaining that approval (1990b, 1227). Jones and McDermott examine election outcomes and find that "congressional approval has a positive and a significant effect on voting for candidates from the majority party in the House regardless of incumbency status" (Jones and McDermott 2004; see also 2009; McDermott and Jones 2003), while Jones (2010) reports opposite effects for majority and minority party incumbents.[1] Finally, Jennifer Wolak (2007) finds that congressional approval significantly predicts House retirement rates, but does not ask whether approval has similar or differing effects for majority and minority party incumbents.

---

[1] Majority party incumbents are more likely to be reelected when the public approves of Congress's job performance while minority party incumbents are less likely to be reelected.

Although these recent studies draw differing conclusions about the nature of congressional accountability, majority party accountability is clearly the more common assumption of institutional theories. It is also thought be the most accessible option for voters. In *The Logic of Congressional Action*, Arnold proposes that voters can hold Congress retrospectively accountable in two ways.[2] First, they may judge incumbent lawmakers based on the performance of the majority party. This *party performance rule* requires just two things of voters: a judgment about whether conditions in society are improving or deteriorating and knowledge of which party controls the government (Arnold 1990, 41). Second, voters may hold incumbents retrospectively accountable for their actions as individuals. This *incumbent performance rule* requires that voters link specific actions by the incumbent to improving or deteriorating conditions in society – typically a higher bar than knowing which party controls Congress (Arnold 1990, 42–3).

We propose a third type of retrospective voting – *congressional performance accountability*. Applying this rule requires only that voters recognize the incumbent's name on the ballot and make a judgment about conditions in society. Such a rule predicts bipartisan rather than partisan congressional accountability. It also more accurately captures two important findings related to voter knowledge. The first is that the vast majority of voters (consistently above 90%) are able to recognize the incumbent's name on the ballot (a central requirement of the congressional performance rule; Jacobson 2009, 123). The second is that the same voters are less able to correctly name the party in power (a central requirement of the party performance rule). Specifically, for the 1978–1994 time period, American National Election Studies (ANES) respondents had a 50/50 chance of correctly identifying which party controlled the House of Representatives (Nicholson and Segura 1999, 614–15). Under divided government, just 38 percent of respondents correctly identified which party controlled the House.

If voters do not know which party controls Congress, it is hard to see how they can hold the majority party accountable. Additional research also questions whether voters evaluate the performance of Congress in partisan terms: "Seeing congressional approval as primarily a function of partisanship is a common practice" observes Hibbing, "[but] is also incomplete if not misleading" (2005, 477). In the 2002 and 2006 elections,

---

[2] Arnold also proposes that prospective evaluations of Congress come in two varieties – the party position on issues and the candidate position.

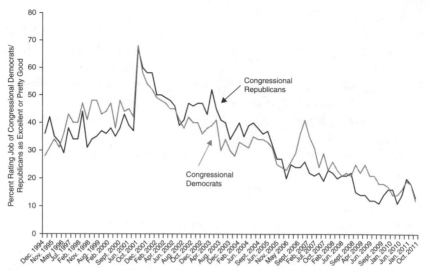

FIGURE 3.1. Trends in Job Approval for Congressional Democrats and Republicans. Figure generated from Harris Poll data by Christopher Larimer.

public dissatisfaction with "congressional Democrats" (the minority) was nearly as high as dissatisfaction with "congressional Republicans" (the majority; Mitchell and Mondak 2009). This similarity in satisfaction between congressional Democrats and Republicans is fairly consistent (see Figure 3.1). According to John Hibbing and Christopher Larimer, "Despite the assumptions by strong partisans, it is not the case that when evaluation of one of the major parties in Congress goes up, evaluation of the other major party goes down. For the most part, when it comes to evaluations of Congress, the parties are in it together" (2008, 8; see also Stimson 2004).[3]

The 2009 Cooperative Congressional Election Study found that, by a margin of 46–42 percent, respondents assigned credit or blame for Congress's performance to both parties over the majority party (Table 3.1). Self-described independents, often key to electoral shifts, were almost twice as likely to assign credit or blame to both parties than to the major- ity party alone (57% vs. 32%). The willingness of voters to cast bipartisan credit or blame extended to party identifiers as well, with 27 percent of minority party identifiers saying that their own party's representatives were equally responsible for how Congress was handling its job. As one

[3] The correlation is a "whopping .78" for the 1994–2008 time period (Hibbing and Larimer 2008, 8).

TABLE 3.1. *Voter Perceptions of Responsibility for Congressional Performance*

Respondent Partisan Identification	"Party most responsible for how Congress has handled its job"			
	Democratic Party	Republican Party	Both Parties Are Equally Responsible	Total %
Democrat	30	20	50	34
	(104)	(67)	(170)	(341)
Republican	67	5	27	27
	(183)	(15)	(74)	(272)
Independent	32	10	57	28
	(90)	(28)	(158)	(276)
Other, Not Sure	35	9	56	11
	(38)	(10)	(61)	(109)
Total	42	12	46	100
	(415)	(120)	(463)	(998)

Note: Cell entries are percentages among each type of partisan identifier. The total number of respondents is in parentheses. In 2009 Democrats controlled Congress.
Source: Cooperative Congressional Election Study 2009.

New Hampshire voter put it when asked why she would be voting against Republican (minority party) Senator John Sununu in 2008: "I don't think he's too bad, but with the economy going the way it has been going the last few years, nobody in office looks too good right now" (Herszenhorn 2008).

We are not suggesting that partisanship is unimportant in congressional elections. Its greatest impact derives from evaluations of the president and his policies (Jacobson 2009, Ch. 6). The largest partisan swings in congressional seats of recent times (1994, 2006, and 2010) have occurred during periods of unified government. However, most elections (about two-thirds since World War II) occur during periods of divided government. It is these elections where we anticipate that incumbents of both parties have the greatest reasons to be concerned about shared congressional performance accountability.

TESTING THE CONGRESSIONAL PERFORMANCE HYPOTHESIS

The congressional performance rule predicts that congressional approval will have positive electoral benefits for incumbents of both parties, whereas partisan performance accountability predicts that approval will have positive consequences for incumbents of the majority party only, and even negative consequences for minority party incumbents (Jones 2010; Jones and McDermott 2004). We test these competing hypotheses by examining House election outcomes from four directions: individual voters' decisions (1980–2004), incumbent vote share at the district level (1974–2010), incumbent probabilities of reelection, and incumbent retirement rates (1974–2010). Individual-level surveys tap into specific voter considerations but are not representative at the district level. District vote shares provide an opportunity to examine effects of approval for vote share, but do not directly assess the impact of approval on incumbent reelection rates. Finally, reelection probabilities are also potentially incomplete indicators of vulnerability to the extent that incumbents are less likely to seek reelection when public approval of Congress is lower (Jacobson and Dimock 1994; Jacobson and Kernell 1983).

Congressional Approval and Incumbent Support among Individual Voters

Does congressional approval have a measurable impact on voting decisions at the individual level? The dependent variable in this analysis is a dichotomous indicator of whether a respondent voted for the candidate who we determined was the incumbent in incumbent-ran House elections (1974–2004). The primary independent variable (*Congressional Approval*) indicates whether this respondent approves (1), has no opinion (0), or disapproves (–1) of how Congress performs. The question, "Do you approve or disapprove of the way the U.S. Congress has been handling its job?" was first included in the ANES in 1980 and has been included in every subsequent survey through 2004 (there was no ANES survey in 2006). A positive coefficient for this variable indicates that voters who evaluate Congress positively are more likely to have voted for the incumbent.

To test whether congressional approval has differential effects for incumbents of the two parties, we also interact *Congressional Approval* with the party affiliation of the incumbent (*Majority* × *Congressional Approval*). A positive coefficient for this interaction variable indicates that voters are more likely to hold majority party incumbents accountable for the performance of Congress than minority candidates.[4] Thus,

---

[4] Respondents who did not vote for either major party candidate are excluded as are open-seat races.

the party performance rule predicts an insignificant or negative *Congressional Approval* coefficient and a positive and significant *Majority × Congressional Approval* coefficient. The congressional performance rule predicts a positive *Congressional Approval* coefficient, and a positive or insignificant *Majority ×Congressional Approval* coefficient.

We control for established predictors of candidate support at the individual level. These predictors can be grouped into three categories:

Voter Effects

Partisan identification (7-point scale; *Partisan Identification*) and ideology (7-point scale; *Ideology*) captures the voter's political leanings. An additional dummy variable further distinguishes ideologically unidentified voters from ideological centrists (*Unidentified*).[5] Interactions between *Partisan Identification* and *Ideology* and the incumbent's party (*Republican Incumbent*) capture whether the voter leans toward the incumbent. An *Unidentified × Republican* interaction term controls for whether nonideological voters were nevertheless more supportive of one party's candidates.

National Conditions

Voters with more positive presidential and economic assessments should be more likely to support a candidate of the president's party. Approval of the president's performance (5-point scale; *Presidential Approval*) should lead to greater support for an incumbent of the president's party. Economic conditions are measured on a 5-point scale from "gotten much worse" to "gotten much better" (*Retrospective Economic Evaluation*).

Candidate and District Effects

The specifics of the race should also affect candidate support. Research indicates that candidate awareness tends to leave a favorable impression (Basinger and Lavine 2005; Jacobson 2009; Jones and McDermott 2009). *Net Recall* controls for whether the respondent is able to "recall" the name of the incumbent (+1), both or neither candidates (0), or only the challenger (−1). To control for other, unmeasured, candidate- and campaign-specific effects, the model also incorporates fixed-effects for each congressional district in each election year.

---

[5] Treating "unidentified" individuals as moderates does not affect the results presented in Table 3.2.

TABLE 3.2. *The Impact of Congressional Approval on Incumbent Support at the Individual Voter Level, 1980–2004*

Independent Variable	Coefficient	S. E.	exp(Coeff.)
Net Recall	0.85*	0.09	2.344
Unidentified	−0.08	0.14	0.921
Unidentified × Republican Incumbent	−0.08	0.20	0.920
Ideology	−0.37*	0.05	0.691
Ideology × Republican Incumbent	0.60*	0.07	1.828
Partisan Identification	−0.53*	0.03	0.586
Partisan Identification × Republican Incumbent	1.11*	0.05	3.031
Presidential Approval	−0.46*	0.06	0.633
Presidential Approval × President's Party	0.86*	0.09	2.355
Retrospective Economic Evaluation	−0.04	0.05	0.959
Retrospective Economic Evaluation × President's Party	0.16	0.08	1.169
Congressional Approval	0.16*	0.07	1.169
Congressional Approval × Majority Party	0.15	0.08	1.157
Number of Observations	6,804		
Number of Groups (races)	804		
Pseudo R^2	0.43		

Notes: Fixed-effects logistic regression of vote for the incumbent (1 = vote for incumbent, 0 = vote for challenger); *$p < .05$.
Source: American National Election Studies.

Findings for Individual Voters and Incumbent Support

Table 3.2 indicates that the coefficients for both *Congressional Approval* and *Congressional Approval × Majority* are positive and significant – consistent with the predictions of the congressional performance rule. A voter who approves of Congress's job performance is more likely to approve of the incumbent's performance, whether the incumbent is a member of the majority or minority party. Approval of Congress leads to an 8 percent increase in support if the candidate is a minority party incumbent, and a 15 percent increase in support for an incumbent of the majority party.

Table 3.2 further indicates that the effects of the control variables accord with prior expectations. Conservative and Republican voters are more likely to support the incumbent if she or he is a Republican. Voters who identify with the president's party and approve of the president, and voters who view the economy more favorably, are much more likely to vote for the incumbent if she or he is of the president's party. (The coefficients for Republican incumbent, president's party, and majority party are not reported because they are absorbed by the fixed-effects specification.[6])

How do these findings compare to prior research in this area? McDermott and Jones (2003) analyze the ANES (1980–2002) but find that approval only affects support for majority party candidates. We control for the voter's ideology, plus year-to-year and incumbent-specific variations through fixed effects whereas they include approval of the incumbent's job as an additional control and do not control for fixed effects. In Appendix A we show how these differences matter. Briefly, congressional approval no longer predicts support for incumbents of either party if incumbent approval is included and voter ideology and incumbent fixed effects are excluded from our model (Table A.1). Incumbent approval is highly correlated with incumbent support (the gamma statistic between these two ordinal variables is 0.83). If we substitute incumbent approval for our original dependent variable (incumbent support) the findings mirror Born's (1990b) earlier study of incumbent approval (Table A.2). That is, congressional approval has bipartisan consequences. Although it is possible that this pattern indicates that voters approve of Congress because they approve of their incumbent, we are not aware of any theory that predicts such a relationship. If anything, existing perspectives argue that incumbents and the institution are evaluated according to very different standards (Hibbing 2005).[7]

Accountability at the District Level (1974–2010)

If individual voters are more likely to vote for incumbents when they approve of Congress, is this behavior detectable at the district level? Do incumbents win by larger electoral margins when national polls register higher levels of congressional approval? The dependent variable in this

---

[6] A potential drawback of using fixed effects is that races where everyone in the district votes for the incumbent are excluded from the analysis (approximately 2,000 respondents). We also estimated the model with random effects, including dummy variables for incumbent party affiliation, majority party status, and same party as the president. We also included election-year dummies, and interacted election year with party of incumbent to control for any national partisan swings. The results for congressional approval are very similar, but a Hausman test of the difference in the estimates of the fixed-effects and random-effects models is statistically significant. Thus, we opted to present the fixed-effects results.

[7] Testing this would require an instrumental variables or system of equations approach and convincing (ANES provided) instruments for congressional approval. Such an approach is unlikely to resolve any lingering doubts about our findings.

analysis – the incumbent's share of the two-party vote (incumbent-ran races only) – is continuous and well behaved thus warranting an ordinary least squares (OLS) regression analysis.[8] The central independent variables examined are the same as before (*Congressional Approval* and *Congressional Approval × Majority*) except that approval is measured using average approval ratings across a series of polls rather than at the individual voter level (*Congressional Approval*; Durr, Gilmour, and Wolbrecht 1997).[9] The different unit of analysis (the congressional district rather than the individual voter) implies a somewhat different set of control variables, once again drawn from prior research in this area.

District and Candidate Effects

Normal Vote controls for the expected vote share of the incumbent based on the district's average deviation from the most recent nationwide presidential vote. Three additional variables control for the intensity or competitiveness of the campaign, including whether the challenger previously held an elective office (*Quality Challenger*), the natural log of the ratio of the incumbent and challenger's spending (*Spending Ratio*; Canes-Wrone, Brady, and Cogan 2002), and whether the district was redrawn after the previous election (*Redistricted*; Desposato and Petrocik 2003). Finally, we control for incumbent-specific variations by incorporating incumbent fixed effects and clustered standard errors.

National Conditions

Presidential popularity in this analysis is based upon the last Gallup poll prior to the election (*Presidential Approval*). As before, we allow the effect of this variable to vary depending on whether the incumbent is a member of the president's party (*Presidential Approval × President's Party*). Economic conditions are measured by gross domestic product (GDP) per capita and are also allowed to vary by the incumbent's party (*Change in GDP*; *Change in GDP × President's Party*).[10]

[8] We exclude open-seat races, those where the incumbent did not face a challenge, and those where redistricting had two incumbents competing for the same seat.

[9] The variable was obtained from Christina Wolbrecht (http://www.nd.edu/~cwolbrec/research.html; accessed September 1, 2010) and was originally created using Jim Stimson's WCALC program http://www.unc.edu/~jstimson/; accessed September 1, 2010). Updates through 2010 were provided by Jennifer Wolak. There are not enough survey respondents in each congressional district to reliably construct such a district-level measure of approval.

[10] The data on GDP per capita were obtained from the Bureau of Economic Analysis (http://www.bea.gov/bea/dn/nipaweb/index.asp; accessed May 28, 2010). Using the percentage change in disposable income per capita yields similar results.

We rely on candidate fixed effects (a dummy for each incumbent) to control for candidate-specific factors because we are analyzing panel data. Jones and McDermott (2009) and Jones (2010) control for candidate-specific effects with a lagged dependent variable (the incumbent's vote share in the previous election; LDV). Fixed-effects and LDV models are not equivalent strategies of controlling for omitted variable bias. In this case, fixed effects control for time-invariant aspects of incumbency, whereas an LDV controls for incumbent-specific but dynamic elements of incumbency. If there are variables that affect an incumbents' performance that are time-invariant such as the incumbent's race, gender, religion, charisma, or ideology (which does not vary much over time according to Poole and Rosenthal 2007), failure to control for these individual-specific attributes will produce omitted variable bias if the omitted factors are correlated with observed covariates. Similarly, ignoring dynamic elements could also introduce bias. There are several options for appropriately combining a LDV and fixed effects, which are well documented by Gregory Wawro (2002). We followed the advice offered by Wawro for estimating fixed effects models with an LDV and found that an LDV is not a significant predictor of district vote share in a combined model and that our findings are very similar (not shown).

Findings for District-Level Incumbent Support

Once again, the effects of the control variables for incumbent vote share are in the expected directions (Table 3.3). More importantly, the effects of congressional approval closely mirror what was observed at the individual voter level. When national polls register higher levels of congressional approval, incumbents of both political parties receive significantly larger shares of the district-wide vote. Remarkably, the size of these effects is comparable to other widely recognized predictors of candidate support, such as candidate ideology, incumbency, and challenger quality. Specifically, as congressional approval increases from the minimum (25%) to the maximum (49%) levels observed across the period of study, expected vote share increases by 2.5 percent for minority party incumbents and by 7 percent for majority party incumbents.[11] In the same model, facing a quality challenger reduces expected vote share by 2.2 percent. Prior studies of incumbency effects estimate an added average advantage of 2.7 percent (Carson et al. 2007). The impact of ideology is also similar. Brandice Canes-Wrone and colleagues (2002) report that a 25-point shift in the incumbent's Americans

---

[11] The range between the minimum and maximum of congressional approval is 12 percentage points over this time period.

TABLE 3.3. *The Impact of Congressional Approval on House Incumbent District Vote Share, 1974–2010*

Independent Variable	Coefficient	S. E.[a]
Spending Ratio	6.35*	0.32
Challenger Quality	−2.28*	0.26
Normal Vote	0.42*	0.03
Redistricted	−0.44*	0.23
President's Party	−13.93*	0.79
Presidential Approval	−0.17*	0.02
Presidential Approval × Presidential Party	0.20*	0.02
Change in GDP	−0.39*	0.06
Change in GDP × Presidential Party	0.82*	0.07
Majority Party	−8.53*	1.06
Congressional Approval	0.11*	0.03
Congressional Approval × Majority Party	0.21*	0.03
Constant	61.79*	0.94
Number of Observations	5,957	
Number of Incumbents	1,477	
R^2	0.81	

[a]Robust Clustered Standard Errors; *= $p < .05$.

Notes: Fixed-effects regression of incumbent share of two-party vote.

Source: Compiled by authors.

for Democratic Action (ADA) score (one standard deviation) produces a 1 to 3 percent shift in vote share.

Accountability under Divided and Unified Governments

Our *congressional performance rule* is rooted in two important observations: polls indicate that voters are willing to assign credit or blame for congressional performance to both parties, and voters are much more likely to recognize the incumbent's name on the ballot than they are to correctly identify which party controls the House. However, voter knowledge of congressional control is substantially worse under a divided government. This suggests that voters are more likely to apply the congressional performance rule during the more common situation of a divided government. Furthermore, some scholars have argued that in contrast to the case of a unified government, the minority party in Congress can less credibly claim immunity from the actions of Congress (Trubowitz and Mellow 2005). For the period from 1974 to 2010, government was divided in thirteen out of nineteen elections (68%). To test

TABLE 3.4. *The Impact of Congressional Approval on House Incumbent District Vote Share under Divided and Unified Governments, 1974–2010*

Independent Variable	Divided Government		Unified Government	
	Coefficient	S. E.[a]	Coefficient	S. E.[a]
Spending Ratio	7.39*	0.42	3.82*	0.66
Challenger Quality	−1.97*	0.34	−2.52*	0.66
Normal Vote	0.41*	0.03	0.48*	0.07
Redistricted	0.09	0.27	−1.17	1.49
President's Party[b]	−3.57	5.20	–	–
Presidential Approval	−0.15*	0.05	0.17	0.17
Presidential Approval × Presidential Party	0.02	0.08	−0.27	0.34
Change in GDP	−0.45*	0.07	−0.54	0.39
Change in GDP × Presidential Party	1.12*	0.10	1.08	0.69
Majority Party	−0.36	4.79	−22.51*	3.97
Congressional Approval	0.28*	0.07	−0.22	0.17
Congressional Approval × Majority Party	0.06	0.10	0.81*	0.33
Constant	50.42*	5.18	61.19*	2.72
Number of Observations	4,017		1,940	
Number of Incumbents	1,351		1,044	
R^2	0.83		0.91	

[a]Robust Clustered Standard Errors; [b]Variable is dropped because under a unified government President's Party is equivalent to Majority Party; Divided Government exists when the House is controlled by a different party than the presidency.

Notes: Fixed-effects regression of incumbent share of two-party vote; *$p < .05$.

Source: Compiled by authors.

this hypothesis, we replicate the previous district-level analysis separately for elections that occurred during periods of unified and divided governments.

Table 3.4 demonstrates striking differences in collective accountability. During times of unified government,[12] the *partisan performance rule* offers the best explanation for the impact of congressional approval on district-wide incumbent vote share (model 1 of Table 3.4).[13] *Congressional Approval × Majority* is significant while *Congressional Approval* is not. During times of divided government, however, the *congressional*

[12] The years: 1978, 1980, 1994, 2004, 2006, and 2010.
[13] *President's Party* is excluded from this model because under unified government it is equivalent to majority party.

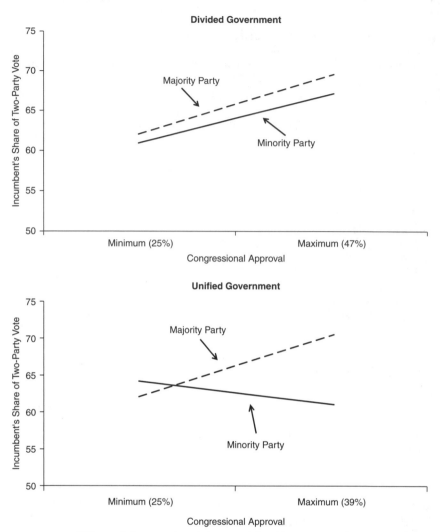

FIGURE 3.2. Effect of Congressional Approval for House Incumbent Vote Share under Unified versus Divided Government.
Note: Marginal effects are estimated by varying Congressional Approval from its minimum to maximum value while holding all other variables at their mean values.

performance rule offers the best explanation. In model 2 of Table 3.4, *Congressional Approval* significantly predicts the incumbent's vote share whereas *Congressional Approval* × *Majority* is not. Other things equal, voters hold incumbents of both parties in the House equally account-able under the more common case of a divided government. Figure 3.2

illustrates these differences by presenting marginal effects as congressional approval varies under each condition.

ACCOUNTABILITY AND THE INCUMBENT'S PROBABILITY OF REELECTION

Are the effects of congressional approval large enough to influence whether incumbents return to office? What effect does congressional approval have on an incumbent's probability of losing his seat? To assess the impact of congressional approval on probability of victory, we replicated the analysis reported in Table 3.3 using a fixed-effects logit where the dependent variable indicates whether or not the incumbent won reelection. Only incumbents who lost an election at some point can be included in this analysis (representing 16% of the cases of our earlier analysis).[14] These are also a biased set of lawmakers, given that most incumbents are never defeated. Nevertheless, knowing whether congressional approval matters for the most vulnerable incumbents is informative, because they are often the keys to party control and policy decisions.

The coefficients for *Congressional Approval* and *Congressional Approval × Majority* in Table 3.5 are positive and significant, indicating that "vulnerable" incumbents of both parties are more likely to be reelected when the public expresses greater approval for Congress's job performance. Figure 3.3 presents marginal probabilities for different levels of approval. To calculate predicted probabilities for a fixed logit, we chose a baseline equal to the marginal probability of winning when all variables in the model are held at their mean values (70% in this sample). As congressional approval increases from 30 to 40 percent, a minority party incumbent's probability of winning reelection increases from .54 to .87. A similar shift in approval increases the probability of reelection for majority party incumbents even more – from .33 to .89. Public attitudes toward Congress do not just affect vote shares; they affect reelection rates for incumbents of both parties.

Accountability and Strategic Decisions to Retire

Lastly, we ask: does congressional approval affect not only incumbents' probability of reelection but also their decisions to seek reelection? If so,

[14] We are using a "within" estimator and therefore cannot assess the effect of independent variables measured in deviations from the mean value if there is no variation in the dependent variable.

TABLE 3.5. *The Impact of Congressional Approval on House Incumbent Reelection Rates, 1974–2010*

Independent Variable	Coefficient	S. E.
Spending Ratio	14.66*	2.16
Challenger Quality	−0.37	0.29
Normal Vote	0.21*	0.04
Redistricted	0.01	0.41
President's Party	−7.89*	2.00
Presidential Approval	−0.16*	0.05
Presidential Approval × Presidential Party	0.12*	0.05
Change in GDP	−0.14	0.10
Change in GDP × Presidential Party	0.25*	0.12
Majority Party	−4.19*	1.98
Congressional Approval	0.17*	0.06
Congressional Approval × Majority Party	0.11*	0.06
Number of Observations	941	
Number of Incumbents	209	
Pseudo R^2	0.62	

Notes: Fixed-effects logistic regression of incumbent's probability of reelection (1 = incumbent wins, 0 = incumbent defeated); *$p < 0.05$.
Source: Compiled by authors.

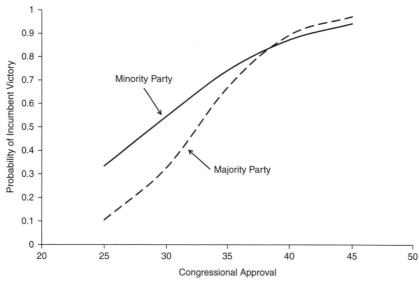

FIGURE 3.3. Effect of Congressional Approval on the Probability of Incumbent Victory, 1974–2010.
Note: Marginal effects are estimated by varying Congressional Approval from its minimum to maximum value while holding all other variables at their mean values. Only includes incumbents who lost their last general election.

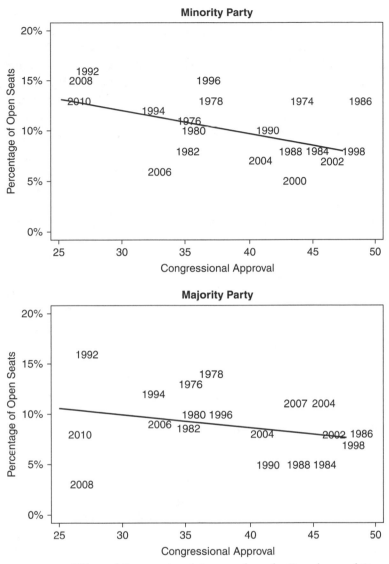

FIGURE 3.4. Effect of Congressional Approval on the Prevalence of Open Seats, 1974–2010.

a focus on election outcomes may underestimate the full consequences of congressional approval. For example, Gary Jacobson and Michael Dimock (1994) find that turnover resulting from the "check kiting" scandal of 1992 was more likely to stem from strategic retirements than from electoral defeats (see also Groseclose and Krehbiel 1994). Prior research also finds that congressional approval predicts retirement rates in the

House (Stone et al. 2010; Wolak 2007). Jones and McDermott (2009) find that congressional approval predicts voluntary retirements among majority party incumbents, but not among minority party incumbents.

Figure 3.4 indicates fairly robust correlations between congressional approval and open seats in the House.[15] For the period from 1974 to 2010, the correlation between congressional approval and the percentage of seats vacated by majority party incumbents is −0.27. For minority party incumbents, the correlation between congressional approval and open seats is −0.50.

Next we estimate a Cox proportional-hazards model that predicts whether a given House incumbent ran for reelection (Box-Steffensmeier and Jones 1997). The model is similar to the earlier district-level analysis, with a few differences. Because there was no campaign, the campaign spending and challenger quality variables are excluded. However, prior outcomes should affect expectations about reelectability; therefore we include the incumbent's prior election result (*Lagged Vote Share*), as well as a dummy controlling for whether that election was contested by a candidate of the other major party (*Previously Contested*). We also hypothesize that an incumbent of the majority party has more reason to seek reelection, particularly under a unified government, and therefore we control for *Unified Government* and *Unified Government* × *Majority Party*. Finally, *Ideological Extremity* is measured by the absolute value of the incumbent's DW-NOMINATE score (Poole and Rosenthal 2007).[16]

Findings for Strategic Retirements

Table 3.6 reports hazards ratios in order to interpret the substantive effects of the independent variables more easily. A hazard ratio represents the increase in the odds of surviving another period for a unit increase in the independent variable. Model 1 confirms that congressional approval is significantly and negatively related to the decision to retire. Specifically, the hazard ratio for *Congressional Approval* (0.96) indicates that each 1 percent increase in congressional approval reduces the incumbent's probability of retirement by 4 percent as compared to the baseline retirement

---

[15] Open seats captures all incumbent departures, including decisions to pursue higher office. However, we exclude instances where the incumbent was replaced through an appointment or special election (as these latter events are unlikely related to congressional approval).

[16] DW-NOMINATE scores are dynamic measures of incumbent ideology based on the analysis of roll call votes using a scaling algorithm developed Keith Poole and Howard Rosenthal.

TABLE 3.6. *The Impact of Congressional Approval on Retirement Decisions in the House, 1974–2010*

Independent Variable	Hazard Ratio	S. E.[a]	Hazard Ratio	S. E.[a]
Time × Lagged Vote Share			3.16*	2.06
Time × Previously Contested			0.98*	0.01
Time × Normal Vote			1.02	0.01
Time × Ideological Extremity			0.43*	0.19
Lagged Vote Share	0.97*	0.01	1.01	0.02
Previously Contested	8.03*	3.25	1.08	1.31
Normal Vote	1.00	0.01	0.97	0.02
Ideological Extremity	0.37*	0.10	1.67	1.32
Redistricted	1.11	0.12	1.11	0.12
President's Party	0.82	0.83	0.78	0.80
Presidential Approval	1.01	0.01	1.01	0.01
Presidential Approval × Presidential Party	1.01	0.02	1.01	0.02
Change in GDP	1.05	0.03	1.05*	0.03
Change in GDP × Presidential Party	0.95	0.04	0.95	0.04
Unified Government	0.74	0.29	0.73	0.28
Majority Party	0.46	0.46	0.47	0.46
Unified × Majority	1.84	1.35	1.93	1.42
Congressional Approval	0.96*	0.02	0.96*	0.02
Congressional Approval × Majority Party	1.01	0.02	1.01	0.02
Number of Observations	6,580		6,580	
Number of Incumbents	1,425		1,425	
Number of Failures	693		693	

[a] Robust Standard Errors; Efron method for ties; *$p < 0.05$.

Notes: Cox-proportional hazards regression model of incumbent retirement (1 = incumbent retirement, 0 = otherwise).

Source: Compiled by authors.

rate. The hazard ratio for the interaction between congressional approval and majority party status (*Congressional Approval × Majority*) is not statistically significant, indicating that, other things equal, congressional approval has similar retirement consequences for incumbents of both parties.

The variables with nonproportional hazards, based on the Schoenfeld residuals, are *Lagged Vote Share, Previously Contested, Normal Vote,* and *Ideological Extremity*.[17] Following the recommendations of Janet

---

[17] The global test has a *p* value of .03.

Box-Steffensmeier and Brad Jones (2004), we test a second model (model 2 of Table 3.6) that includes an interaction between time and these variables. The substantive conclusions for this second model are the same. As congressional approval increases, incumbents of both parties are less likely to retire. This confirms that the actual consequences of congressional approval are likely larger than those reported in our earlier analyses of electoral effects.

CONCLUSION

The purpose of this chapter has been to test a central tenet of the problem-solving perspective – that incumbents have reasons to think that voters may hold them individually accountable for Congress's collective performance. Examining incumbent accountability from several angles (individual voter decisions, district-wide vote shares, probability of reelection, and retirement decisions) we found a consistent pattern – congressional approval is related to electoral support and reelection rates for incumbents of both parties. Under a unified government, the burden falls on the president's party. However, under the more common case of divided government, incumbents of both parties in Congress have reasons to be concerned about public approval of Congress's performance.

The findings reported in Chapters 2 and 3 offer evidence suggesting that incumbents do have electoral incentives to be concerned about institutional effectiveness. In the chapters that follow, we first consider some implications of a problem-solving electoral imperative for congressional organization and behavior. A problem-solving perspective helps to explain why lawmakers support committee systems and deliberative processes that limit their own access to the legislative agenda. Chapter 4 draws attention to two important constraints to problem solving – scarcity and shirking. Committee systems address these constraints through the creation of largely exclusive jurisdictions that promote parallel processing, information sharing, and specialization, and that create enhanced credit-claiming opportunities for individual committee members. Chapter 5 focuses on another institutional development – short-term authorizations – that reflects more recent challenges to problem solving. Although members of Congress value the oversight and policy-updating activities of committees, limited plenary time raises doubts about whether a committee's recommendation will be taken up by the legislature. When Congress authorizes a program on a temporary or short-term basis, it promotes problem solving by giving committee members more reason to invest in the issue.

PART II

4

Problem-Solving Constraints and Legislative Institutions

> The role of the federal government has dramatically expanded as it attempts to find solutions to the range of complex problems facing our society. In particular, the demands placed upon the legislative branch have grown to staggering proportions. Both the expanded government agenda and the complexity of the issues before our lawmakers have severely challenged the ability of the legislature to perform its functions responsibly and productively. The way the Congress structures and uses its time is of critical importance to the quantity and quality of legislation emanating from the institution.
>
> Thomas J. O'Donnell, summarizing the findings of the 1977 Obey Commission (1981)

The previous chapters offered evidence that voters expect lawmakers to address problems in society and are willing to hold them collectively accountable. Members of Congress report that they believe congressional accomplishments have implications for their own reelection prospects. Lawmakers have collective incentives to engage in problem solving because voters' perceptions of congressional performance have demonstrable electoral consequences. How then do problem-solving incentives in the electoral arena affect organization and behavior in the legislative arena?

When it comes to addressing the many and varied problems and policy demands of voters, members of Congress rely upon the body's primary governing institution – its committee system. This is certainly not a novel point of emphasis. Scholars and lawmakers alike draw attention to the central roles of committees in lawmaking. Scholars have portrayed the legislative work of Congress as primarily committee centered as far back as Woodrow Wilson (1981 [1885]), Lauros McConachie (1898), and George Galloway (1946), and this view still largely persists today.

Longtime representative Henry Waxman (D-CA) describes the normal functioning of Congress as a "bottom-up" process where "committees with relevant expertise [write] the nation's laws" (2010, 132).

This chapter proposes that two important constraints to problem solving explain key features of congressional organization. The first constraint – agenda scarcity – has received limited attention in legislative studies. Simply put, legislatures face more policy demands than they can accommodate. The second constraint – what we term the "problem-solving paradox" – is more familiar to legislative scholars. Individual lawmakers have incentives to underinvest in problem-solving activities such as oversight and policy updating because the electoral benefits of those activities are broadly distributed. We portray the committee system as an institutional response to these two constraints. Committees and the division of labor they embody are fundamental to lawmakers' collective electoral welfare, not because they serve narrow district interests or because they facilitate biased partisan agendas, but because they enhance the body's lawmaking capacity (Krehbiel 1991). Jurisdictional arrangements, committee hierarchies, and policy-making property rights are deliberate arrangements that encourage lawmakers to contribute to the problem-solving efforts of Congress. In the next chapter (Chapter 5), we highlight another important institutional development that steers scarce legislative resources toward problem-solving activities – "temporary legislation." In succeeding chapters, we then draw on many decades of data on legislator behavior, congressional organization, and output to test different implications of this perspective.

AGENDA SCARCITY

A common feature of legislatures is "the constant pressure on their time" (Döring 1995, 223). Lawmakers, staff, and almost anyone who interacts with Congress on a regular basis have long lamented that Congress faces many more demands than it can accommodate. In the 1920s, "Congress would scarcely have three or four issues of consequence besides appropriations bills" (Speaker Joseph Martin [R-MA] quoted in Donovan 1960, 49). By the 1940s, Congress's calendars and committee schedules had become "increasingly congested, its councils confused, and its members bewildered and harassed by multiplying complex problems and local pressures" (Galloway 1946, 43). Reforms in the 1940s and 1970s that expanded congressional staff and increased the number of congressional subcommittees provided only limited relief (O'Donnell 1981, 127). Studying the 1980s House of Representatives, Richard Hall observed that "congressmen in committees simply have too much to do legislatively and too little time, energy and other legislative resources to do it" (Hall 1996, 24). Said one lawmaker, "Every day that Congress is in session, members are constantly being barraged by problems ... that demand their urgent attention. The number of these competing claims unfortunately far outstrips the time and resources that Congress can apply to them" (Waxman 2010, 55). *Congressional Quarterly Weekly Report* typically kicks off its coverage of contemporary legislative sessions by highlighting the time-related pressures on lawmakers, namely: "So much legislation to pass, so little time in which to do it"[1] (see also Quirk 2006, 327–8).

Agenda scarcity is rooted in the fact that plenary time is a scarce resource. In referring to legislative time, Peter Drucker notes, "No matter how high the demand, the supply will not go up. There is no price for it and no marginal utility curve for it" (1985, 26). Scarce agenda time raises two related issues for legislatures. The first is the general matter of how much the legislature can accomplish – its policy-making capacity. Assuming that there is not enough time and resources to do everything, the second is, how will a legislature's limited time and resources be allocated?

Limited capacity forces decisions about issue priorities. Although agenda scarcity is receiving increased attention in legislative studies, much of the focus has been on the value of preserving time (Ainsworth and Flathman 1995; Bach and Smith 1990; Cox 2006; Den Hartog and Monroe 2011). Its implications for policy choices in the face of competing demands have received substantially more attention from public policy scholars (Baumgartner and Jones 1993; Birkland 1997; Donovan

---

[1] Carney, Dan. "Time Beginning to Run Out on Crowded GOP Agenda." *CQ Weekly Online* (November 25, 1995): 3586–8. Other examples from *Congressional Quarterly* include, Blakely, Steve. "Congress Returns to Crowded Fall Agenda." *CQ Weekly* (August 31, 1985): 1695; "What's Ahead: Returning Members Face Full Agenda." *CQ Weekly* (September 2, 1989): 2239; "What's Ahead: Congress Returning to Full Agenda." *CQ Weekly* (January 20, 1990): 134; Hook, Janet. "Legislative Schedule: Changed World, Full Agenda Face Returning Congress." *CQ Weekly* (September 7, 1991): 2547; Rubin, Alissa J. "Extension of Debt Limit Tops Crowded Agenda." *CQ Weekly* (February 24, 1996): 500; Cassata, Donna. "Housing Programs Top Full Agenda." *CQ Weekly* (May 31, 1997): 1265; Nather, David. "GOP Sees Best Bet in Stuffed Agenda." *CQ Weekly* (September 4, 2006): 2300–1; Schatz, Joseph J., and Jonathan Allen. "New Items Crowd Out Old in Fall Agenda." *CQ Weekly* (July 25, 2005): 2042.

2001). As discussed in Chapter 1, Walker (1977) asserts that limited agenda space and the imperative to address compulsory issues leave limited opportunities for the Senate to address discretionary issues (discussed in more detail in the next chapter). Kingdon observes that with so many problems "pressing down on the system," predictable and unpredictable "windows of opportunity" offer the best prospects for policy entrepreneurs seeking to advance policy solutions (1995, 16). In contrast, legislative agenda-setting research typically focuses on how procedures and behavior shape available policy alternatives (e.g., which minimum wage proposal prevails) rather than a legislature's issue priorities (i.e., will the minimum wage or tax reform be on the agenda?).

THE "PROBLEM-SOLVING PARADOX"

In *Congress: The Electoral Connection*, David Mayhew argued that legislators – as single-minded seekers of reelection – have little incentive to invest in activities such as program oversight ("scrutiny of impact") or policy development. From the individual legislator's perspective, "It is a misallocation of resources to devote time and energy to prescription or scrutiny of impact unless ... credit is available for legislative maneuvering. On matters where credit claiming opportunities are thin, therefore, we should not be surprised to find that members display only modest interest in what goes into bills or what their passage accomplishes" (Mayhew 1974, 122).

The disincentives for collective action that existed when *Congress: The Electoral Connection* was first published in 1974 have arguably become even more pronounced over time. Recent research offers little reason to think that lawmakers are capable of problem solving at all (Gerber and Patashnik 2007; Mann and Ornstein 2006; Mayer and Canon 1999). Yet, Congress continues to engage in problem solving and continues to produce general-interest policies. Any problem-solving account of congressional behavior and organization must therefore address the question of why rational, reelection-driven individuals would want to invest in such activities.

THE LIMITED CONTRIBUTIONS OF COMMITTEES
IN CONTEMPORARY LEGISLATIVE THEORIES

Every democratic system of government has a legislature with a committee system (Yamamoto 2007, 15). Comparative public law research examining the expanding roles of committees in parliaments in the twentieth century points to the challenges that legislatures face in terms of expanded public functions and services, increased statutory activity, the increasingly technical nature of lawmaking, and efforts to check the executive (Fasone 2011). Some studies of the congressional committee system highlight the importance of such objectives (Cooper 1970; Longley and Davidson 1998; Maass 1983). However, contemporary theories of legislative organization ascribe more limited roles to committees. The ongoing debate among proponents of distributive, partisan, informational theories of legislative organization arguably skirts, or at least deemphasizes, important questions about the contributions that committees make to the lawmaking process. One of these theories – distributive theory – ironically implies that a committee's influence is inversely related to broader legislative interest in its policy affairs.

Distributive theory depicts the congressional committee system as a calculated choice of lawmakers (Krehbiel 1991; Shepsle and Weingast 1987; Weingast and Marshall 1988). The main benefit of committee structures is to promote stable legislative outcomes by reducing an unstable multidimensional decision space to stable single-dimensional choices. Committees therefore lower the transaction costs of lawmaking while promoting "gains from trade" by enabling the small number of lawmakers who have the most to gain electorally on a given issue to set the agenda on that issue. This structure is self-sustaining so long as lawmakers are willing to defer to the preferences of others on issues not central to their own reelection prospects. Thus, distributive theory predicts that committees will exercise their least influence when issues impact the electoral prospects of most lawmakers (e.g., education, transportation, and defense).

In other models of congressional organization, committees are not functional necessities to normal legislative operations. Partisan and informational theories provide roles for committees, but committees are not essential features of the theories. As Krehbiel notes, "with the possible exception of Weingast and Marshall's (1988) industrial organization [distributive] approach, none of the theories [informational and partisan] ... meets a strict analytical definition of a theory of legislative organization. That is, the models characterize institutional features as exogenous – not as objects of calculated choice by players in the game" (2004, 122). In the partisan cartel theory (Cox and McCubbins 1993, 2005), majority party members delegate procedural control to party leaders, who then exercise agenda control to advance the party priorities. Committees are portrayed as an arm of the party leadership – one component of a "redundancy" system that ensures that the floor agenda reflects the party's preferences (Cox and McCubbins 2005, 42). In the conditional party government approach, committees are also portrayed as promoters of majority party policy priorities, but only under specific conditions; namely (1) deep ideological divisions between the two parties, (2) ideological homogeneity within each party, and (3) a relatively limited set of policy issues that are related to divisions between the parties among the electorate (Aldrich and Rohde 2000, 2005).

Like partisan theories, informational theory does not attempt to explain why legislatures have committees. Instead, informational theory presumes "that an institutionalized legislature has emerged" (Gilligan and Krehbiel 1990, 539). Committees are portrayed as valuable sources of expertise about the effects of policy proposals. However, the principal explanation for why committee members invest in issue-area expertise is arguably at odds with the theory's majoritarian assumption about policy making. The puzzle is why committee members invest in expertise if policies ultimately reflect the preferences of the median lawmaker. According to Krehbiel, committee members anticipate a restrictive rule: "In the end, the committee is made better off because its ability to make a 'take-it-or-leave-it' offer effectively guarantees it a distributional commission of sorts" (Krehbiel 1991, 91–2). As Hall notes, Krehbiel's "informational, majoritarian account of legislative organization, it seems, rests directly on distributive, non-majoritarian foundations" (1995, 285).

Equally important, while these theories emphasize committees as the primary source of expertise and partisan agenda pursuits, committees are just one of many possible venues for these activities. Nothing inherent in the theories requires committees to assume these roles. For instance, John Aldrich and David Rohde draw attention to extralegislative lawmaking institutions – collections of party insiders and leadership-crafted "task forces" – as means by which Republicans propelled forward their policy agenda after the Gingrich-led revolution (Aldrich and Rohde 2005). With respect to expertise, scholars have highlighted other entities such as caucuses (Ainsworth and Akins 1997), staff (Bimber 1996), and interest groups (Esterling 2004; Wright 1996) as alternative sources of information about the likely effects of policies. Thus, only one of the "big three" theories (distributive) provides a truly essential role for committees, and unfortunately one that offers little reason to expect committees to make significant contributions to the policy-making process.

LEGISLATIVE INSTITUTIONS AND PROBLEM-SOLVING CONSTRAINTS

A problem-solving perspective on legislative organization begins with the assumption that lawmakers share common concerns on many policy issues. The committee system enables lawmakers to address collective problem-solving challenges more efficiently and effectively (Rohde 2005a). Committee systems increase problem-solving capacity. By dividing the labor, they effectively expand available plenary time. As Joe Cooper, a close observer of committees in Congress noted, "The Legislature must not only define and oversee effective policies, it must do so in a large number of areas to maintain its overall position as basic policy maker. Deficiencies in output capacity inevitably lead to the cessation of authority and discretion to the executive implicitly or explicitly. Thus the sheer quantity of the legislature's output is a variable of importance" (Cooper 1970, 95).

Through the creation of stable and coordinated issue responsibilities and by rewarding seniority, committee arrangements lower information-gathering costs. The committee system reduces shirking by delineating lines of accountability for policy. Lawmakers support the maintenance of committee systems because they anticipate that whether Congress addresses pressing public problems (such as education, transportation, and defense) matters for their own individual reelection prospects.

Agenda Scarcity and Committee Division of Labor

During the earliest congresses, legislative deliberations in the House of Representatives began in the Committee of the Whole. If legislation was desired, the House would then typically appoint an ad hoc select committee to draft a bill reflecting the general principles decided on in the Committee of the Whole (Cooper 1970; Stewart 2001, 284). After the issue was addressed, the committee was typically disbanded. By the 3rd Congress (1793–4), this process was viewed as increasingly unwieldy with so many committees formed to consider different issues and legislative proposals (Haynes 1938, 272). Starting with the Ways and Means Committee in the 4th Congress (1795–6), the House gradually developed a permanent standing-committee system. The Senate committee system developed later but more quickly. By 1816, both chambers were operating under permanent standing-committee systems. By 1820, "almost all original oversight over legislation in the House had been given to standing committees" (Stewart 2001, 286).

Research finds that policy-making capacity was a central motivation for the establishment of permanent congressional committees (Schickler 2011, 713–18). "Most probably," conclude Gerald Gamm and Kenneth Shepsle, "the coinciding developments in the House and Senate reflected similar institutional solutions to similar organizational problems" (1989, 59). In the early 1800s, Congress was deemed to be ill equipped to oversee the executive branch or to respond to its legislative initiatives (Cooper 1970; Gamm and Shepsle 1989; Monroe and Hammond 2006). The shift from "serial" issue processing in the committee of the whole, to "parallel" processing in standing committees enabled Congress to accomplish more with its limited manpower (Workman, Jones, and Jochim 2009). Rohde observes,

> Congress's committee system was established to accomplish certain ends for the membership: to gather information and to shape legislation for the committees' parent chambers. Committees served these interests well because they stretched the capacity of each chamber through division of labor (so only part of the membership had to work on each issue) and fostered the development of expertise (which would happen naturally if members focused disproportionate time and attention on the subjects of their committees jurisdictions). (2005a, 207)

Congress was not the first legislative body to recognize the advantages of a division of labor: "By the 1700s committees in these and other colonial legislatures were appointed for entire legislative sessions, had fixed memberships, and had well-defined jurisdictions" (Jameson 1894, 264–5). The benefits of division of labor systems were also documented at least as far back as Adam Smith's *The Wealth of Nations*, published in 1776.

More recently, division of labor figures prominently in industrial organization research (Alchian and Demsetz 1972; Coase 1937; Holmström and Roberts 1998; March and Simon 1993; Williamson 1975). This research has been utilized to explain centralized authority and transaction costs in legislatures (Baughman 2006; Cox and McCubbins 1993; Weingast and Marshall 1988). However, the capacity-building benefits of division of labor in legislative bodies have received markedly less theoretical attention, despite widespread empirical research recognizing these benefits. In the modern era, committees "provide the division of labor and specialization that Congress needs to handle roughly ten thousand measures introduced biennially and to review the administration of scores of federal programs" (Oleszek 2007, 8; see also Benda 1997; Kiewiet and McCubbins 1991, 4–5; Quirk 2006, 331; Shepsle and Weingast 1987).

Specialization and Committee Jurisdictions

Maass argues that another consideration leading to the development of the standing committee system was that legislators "began to lose faith in the capacity of individual members to determine and order the facts without first referring subjects to specialized committees" (1983, 36). What make permanent committees valuable from the broader legislature's perspective are their jurisdictions. Lawmakers view particular committees as possessing exceptional knowledge that stems from experience dealing with the same or similar issues over time. Each chamber codifies committee issue control in its rules. Further, these jurisdictions do not simply delegate issue responsibilities in random fashion; they generally assign responsibility for closely related issues to the same committee. Parliamentarians in the House and Senate then refer bills to committees based on jurisdiction, or refer bills to the committee responsible for the most closely related issues in cases where jurisdiction is ambiguous. As a result, the vast majority of bills (about 85%) are referred to just one committee. This nearly exclusive issue control, along with norms that reward seniority and property rights in assigning committee seats and leadership positions, encourage lawmakers to invest their own limited time and attention to committee-related issues.

Although "issue monopolies" of this kind create the potential for committees to extract distributive rents, it is important to recognize that these potential costs are offset by substantial problem-solving benefits for the general membership. One of the most important is to raise the level of policy discussions. Committee deliberations hold the promise of altering how lawmakers understand issues. They hold hearings to gather information about problems in society; they compel executive agencies to be responsive to the concerns of lawmakers and their constituents; they discover what is and is not working with respect to particular programs; and as a result of this process they propose policy improvements. These efforts lead to different policy choices than would occur in the absence of such investigative activities. Moreover, as noted earlier, systematic research offers little evidence to indicate that committee members on allegedly distributive panels, such as the House Transportation and Infrastructure Committee, disproportionately benefit from the policies their committees propose (Evans 2004; Lee 2003; Stein and Bickers 1995).

Whether statutory jurisdictions imply issue control has also been questioned. Scholars have shown that there is substantial jurisdictional overlap when issue control is measured in terms of committee hearings activity. This has led scholars to portray jurisdictions as up for grabs (Jones, Baumgartner, and Talbert 1993; King 1997). Research examining the rise of multiple referrals (bills referred to multiple committees) also raises questions about whether statutory jurisdictional boundaries remain meaningful (Baughman 2006). In Chapter 6 we systematically investigate the consequences for issue control of jurisdictional change by examining the largest set of committee reforms of the postwar period. Our findings indicate that statutory jurisdictions are important mechanisms of determining influence over policy arenas. In addition, problem-solving goals, not distributive or partisan goals, offer the best explanation for the reforms enacted. The main effects of committee jurisdictional reforms instituted in the mid-1970s were to resolve jurisdictional ambiguities stemming from the rise of new issues for the purpose of promoting information sharing and reduced policy conflicts.

Individual Shirking and Committee Hierarchies

The same industrial organization literature that illuminates the efficiency benefits of a division of labor also highlights the potential benefits of hierarchical arrangements for reducing shirking (Coase 1937; Moe 1984; Williamson 1975). Small group arrangements make it easier to monitor actor contributions (Alchian and Demsetz 1972) while creating clearer lines of accountability for firm output (Holstrom and Milgrom 1991; 1994). In the legislative context, delegating responsibilities to committees and to members within committees makes it easier to credit legislators for their contributions to problem solving. Assigning leadership responsibilities and conferring resources to accomplish committee goals further promotes accountability. Thus we should not be surprised to discover that certain committee members play more active roles in legislative deliberation and adoption for particular issue areas, and that committee and subcommittee leaders play more central roles.

However, the comparison of legislatures and firms applies only to a point. Leaders of legislatures do not possess the same ability to sanction nonperformers as leaders of firms. Lawmakers are ultimately accountable to a different set of stakeholders – the constituents in their district or state. Seniority rules and majoritarian procedures further limit the ability of legislative leaders to hire and fire. Hierarchical committee arrangements alone will therefore have a limited impact on committee members' decisions about whether to invest in committee work.

Researchers examining committee participation have found that it is highly variable – on any given issue only a few lawmakers will be closely involved (Evans 1991; Hall 1996). That participation is induced in several ways. Issue interest is a central explanation for policy involvement, whether originating in constituency characteristics or personal experience. Additionally, opportunities to claim credit for successful legislation are rare in Congress and for many of the reasons elaborated above credit-claiming opportunities largely revolve around committee participation: the vast majority of successful bills are sponsored by committee of referral members. We contend that this pattern is evidence of a rewards system where committee members who oversee the development of legislation receive the lion's share of the credit. Although legislatures cannot force members to invest in issues under threat of being fired, they do have the ability to offer members who make such investments extraordinary credit-claiming opportunities in the form of successful bill sponsorship.

Problem-Solving Priorities: Compulsory versus Discretionary Issue Agendas

Committee structures expand legislative capacity, promote information sharing, and begin to address important problems of collective action. Additional procedural developments, such as special rules in the House and the cloture procedure in the Senate can also be viewed as mechanisms for shaping how scarce agenda space in legislatures is allocated (Bach and Smith 1988). Yet, these features represent general responses to the problem of agenda scarcity. In contrast, legislators frequently share a common interest in seeing particular problems addressed efficiently and effectively. Legislatures are constantly making decisions about which issues deserve attention first. Existing legislative research can be criticized for a general lack of attention to this important question.

A central argument of this book is that legislatures prioritize what we term "compulsory" issues. Exogenous developments (e.g., a crisis) effectively force certain issues onto the agenda. In addition, existing policies and programs must be maintained. To the extent that each type of problem is viewed as having potential electoral consequences for a broad swath of lawmakers, the legislative body will direct scarce collective and individual attention toward them. As a result, limited time and resources remain to address other "discretionary" issues reflecting the agendas of individual lawmakers or parties. Although it is easy to appreciate why congressional leaders would find space on a crowded agenda to respond to a salient crisis, it is less obvious why those leaders would want to make room for policy-updating activities if it means less time to address other issues. Deferred policy maintenance raises the possibility of a deficient policy that provokes a voter backlash, but there is always next year.

In the next chapter, we argue that an important yet understudied feature of lawmaking – temporary authorizations – plays an important role in promoting policy maintenance activities in Congress. Individual committee members have limited reasons to invest in problem-solving activities such as program oversight and policy updating, particularly if the legislature is unlikely to take up the issue. A legislature that passes a short-term authorization is effectively committing itself to revisit the issue in the near future. This alters members' calculations about whether and when to invest in issues. Temporary authorizations give committee members added incentives to make sustained issue investments. We show that, because legislative agenda space is scarce, such "compulsory" events are important policy focal points that help to explain the ebb and flow of attention to issues. In addition, as focal points, they are also central to appreciating the dynamics of policy change more generally.

SUMMARY

How Congress allocates its time and resources has important consequences for legislative output and – by extension – for incumbent lawmakers' electoral prospects. The purpose of this chapter has been to highlight important features of congressional organization and committee systems that relate to these goals. Lawmakers face more policy demands than they can satisfy and share a collective interest in the quality and timeliness of the policies Congress produces. Yet each incumbent has limited incentives to invest in issues where the benefits are broadly distributed.

Through a division of labor, committee systems increase the legislature's capacity to address policy problems. By grouping responsibility for closely related issues, congressional committee jurisdictions promote specialization of production that can result in higher-quality policy responses at lower cost. By rewarding seniority and through nearly exclusive bill referral practices, the congressional committee system enhances credit-claiming opportunities and thereby encourages individual investments in problem-solving activities. Authorizing laws on a temporary basis further enhances Congress's ability to steer collective and individual attention toward particular problems. Lawmakers support the maintenance of this system because it benefits their own electoral prospects.

The theoretical argument of this chapter and the next generate a number of novel predictions about congressional committees, agenda setting, and policy change that are the focus of the succeeding chapter. Before turning to those empirical investigations, however, we delve more deeply into the understudied subject of temporary laws.

5

Agenda Scarcity, Problem Solving, and Temporary Legislation

> Nothing ... could justify [a perpetual law] but the necessity, simplicity, and the immutability of the object, and the immutability of the circumstances which related to it [–] circumstances which would render a law equally necessary now, and on all future occasions.
>
> Rep. Thomas Tudor Tucker, 1789 (cited in Bickford, Bowling, and Veit 1992)

Enacting a law to address a problem in society is just the first step in an ongoing governing process. Problems are often difficult to understand; changing societal conditions warrant occasional reviews and adjustments. The preceding quote comes from the debate over the Impost Act, the very first substantive law enacted by the Congress (in 1789), which imposed duties on imports.[1] Instead of making it "perpetual," Congress specified a temporary law that would expire in 1796. Temporary laws have been enacted throughout Congress's history and have become increasingly common in recent decades. Why do lawmakers often choose to enact laws on a temporary basis when nothing prohibits them from amending a permanent law at a future point in time?

This is the question explored in this chapter. We begin by examining the scope and history of temporary legislation and then review a range of explanations offered for their use. We then argue that a central explanation for why short-term expirations have been used with increasing frequency since the 1960s is to promote more regular reviews of policy effectiveness as a means of addressing problems before they become crises.

---

[1] The first law enacted established procedures for administering the oath of office.

A short-term authorization steers limited congressional (and executive) attention and resources toward particular policies. For a permanent law, the reversion point if no action is taken is the policy status quo. For a temporary law, it is no policy at all. Expiring programs receive priority consideration, which in turn influences how lawmakers invest their own limited time and resources. Walker argues that such recurring issues represent a substantial proportion of the Senate's agenda. We conclude by examining lawmaking activity in the House of Representatives at three different stages – bill introductions, passed bills, and roll call votes – and find that such recurring issues make up a substantial proportion of the House agenda.

SCOPE AND HISTORY OF TEMPORARY LEGISLATION

The term *temporary legislation* can refer to many different types of laws (Gersen 2007). The common denominator is that inaction by the legislature leads to the termination of a program, regulation, or funding. Temporary or short-term authorizations are the most common form of temporary legislation. Authorizations are the "basic substantive legislation enacted by Congress, which sets up or continues the legal operation of a federal program or agency either indefinitely or for a specific period of time" (Schick 1980, 581). In a very broad range of policy areas, such as defense, education, transportation, taxation, law enforcement, and civil rights, important federal programs are authorized for limited time periods often ranging from just a few weeks to possibly as long as ten years or more. Temporary authorizations are meaningful because of long-held prohibitions against unauthorized appropriations ("expenditures not previously authorized by law") in the rules of the House and Senate (Hall 2004, 11–15).[2] To the extent that such prohibitions are enforced (we return to this subject later in the chapter), not acting means no program or the discontinuation of the program's funding.

Appropriations, which provide the legal authority for outlays, are another important example of legislation with a finite life. Normally, an appropriations act and its substantive provisions expire at the end of the fiscal year (Schick 2007, 215). Congress has resisted pressure to move to multiyear appropriations, "preferring the short-term control that comes from annual action to the longer-term perspective that might be gained from biennial decisions" (ibid.). Other statutes also create a predictable

---

[2] See House Rule XXI, clause 2, k and Senate Rule XVI.

urgency of action but on a more sporadic basis. For example, Title 31 section 3101 of the U.S. Code limits the borrowing authority of the federal government. As became very evident in 2011, a failure to increase this debt limit risks serious consequences for the economy and federal programs – as a result the debt limit has always been increased despite lawmakers' reluctance to vote in favor of more public debt (Evans 1997; Shuman 1988).

At the state level, so-called sunset laws became increasingly popular in the mid-1970s. Whereas temporary authorizations at the federal level vary in duration and can apply to specific programs within larger laws, state sunset clauses typically provide that the entire law is repealed after ten years (Gersen 2007, 260). The first statutes providing for automatic termination of state government programs were enacted in Colorado in 1976 (Blickle 1985; Hamm and Robertson 1981; Kearney 1990). By 1982, thirty-six states had sunset laws on the books. However, by 2010, Kearney and Bayoumi (2010) could only find sunset statutes in thirteen of fifty states.

History of Temporary Legislation

A voluminous literature on sunsets pegs the conceptual beginnings of temporary legislation to a suggestion by Franklin Roosevelt's Chairman of the Securities and Exchange Commission, William O. Douglas, that all federal agencies be subject to renewal after ten years (Behn 1977). However, termination clauses have been a regular part of federal policy making throughout U.S. history. Gersen traces the concept of temporary laws to the founders and possibly further back (2007, 256–7). Thomas Jefferson exhibited support for legislative expirations in letters to James Madison (Kysar 2006, 350), and advocated that constitutions and laws be sunsetted every nineteen years to ease the transition to changes in governance (Calabresi 1982, note 2). Article I (§ 8, clause 12) of the Constitution contains a two-year limit on military appropriations. The Sedition Act, passed in July 1798, expired at the end of John Adams's presidency in 1801 (Gersen 2007, 250–3; Kysar 2006, 350–1). The War Revenue Act of 1899, enacted to fund the Spanish-American War, expired in 1902. In the early twentieth century, the Reciprocal Trade Agreements Act of 1934 (P.L. 73-316) authorized the president to enter into trade agreements for renewable three-year time periods (Cox 2004; Young 2009). The Reorganization Act of 1939 (P.L. 76-19) restricted the president's ability to reorganize agencies to a two-year time period (Arnold 1998).

Temporary legislation became much more common after World War II and can now be found in nearly every area of federal law. Scholars trace this sea change to a 1961 amendment to the Military Construction Authorization Act (P.L. 87-57) that established the now familiar practice of annual defense authorizations (Hall 2004, 16–17). Other defense-related programs were placed on annual authorizations in 1964, 1966, 1967, 1969, 1970, 1982, and 1983 (Maass 1983, 121–2). By the 1970s, it was estimated that more than 25 percent of all enacted laws were reauthorizations (Schick 1987). The most important programs in education, transportation, civil rights, financial regulation, and national security are all on temporary authorizations. Not all important programs are on temporary authorizations – immigration, telecommunications, and energy are some of the more prominent examples. But even these policy areas often include statutes on short-term authorizations. For instance, although major immigration laws are not on temporary authorizations, the E-Verify program that employers use to determine work eligibility is. This controversial federal program ran into political difficulty when its five-year authorization expired in 2009. Congress eventually renewed it for three more years as part of the Homeland Security Appropriations in 2009 (P.L. 111-83).

EXPLANATIONS FOR TEMPORARY LEGISLATION

Scholars have offered several explanations for the rise in temporary legislation since World War II. These include increasing the influence of authorizing committees vis-à-vis appropriations, extracting rents from groups affected by policies, fostering greater agency accountability, and promoting programmatic reviews and updating. All of these explanations have merit and some element of truth. After assessing the details of each argument we focus on the last – program review and updating – as a primary explanation, particularly for its problem-solving features.

Leverage over Appropriations

Congress has tried to separate decisions about policy and outlays since its earliest years. The Budget and Accounting Act of 1921 (P.L. 67-13) permanently separated the two processes (authorizations and appropriations) in response to lawmakers' repeated attempts to insert policy changes into "must pass" funding bills (Stewart 1989). Today, committees such as the

House Armed Services Committee or the Education and the Workforce Committee are charged with authorizing expenditures for programs under their jurisdictions (pending approval by both chambers, like all statutes), while the Appropriations committees are charged with making annual decisions about actual outlays (again, subject to the approval of Congress as a whole).

One criticism of this process has been that executive attention shifts to the Appropriations committees, where decisions about outlays continue to be made annually, when programs are permanently authorized. Authorizing programs on a temporary basis, in contrast, gives the Appropriations committees, executive agencies, and other affected interests more reason to be attentive to the authorizing committee's spending preferences (Dodd and Schott 1979; Fenno 1966, 71; Hall 2004; Schick 2007, 199; Wildavsky 1984). Interestingly, however, turf wars between the Appropriations committees and authorizing committees do not seem to explain the early rise in temporary authorizations after World War II. James Cox notes that much of the early impetus for temporary authorizations in the authorizing committees came from senators who also served on Appropriations (2004, 76). Why would Appropriations members push for reforms designed to limit the autonomy of Appropriations?

Rent-Extraction

Another, rather cynical, political rationale for the increasing frequency of short-term authorizations is that lawmakers have more opportunities to extract rents in the form of campaign contributions when laws or programs are not permanently authorized. That is, legislators limit the life of laws to keep lobbyists and interest groups guessing about the future of favored policies. Many corporate tax breaks require annual renewal ("extenders"). Internal Revenue Service Commissioner Don Alexander argued, "If there's an extender that has tremendous public interest in it, then it means two things: It means work for lobbyists who are pushing for it, and it means campaign contributions for members [of Congress]" (Davis 2002, 293). Rebecca Kysar, for example, reports that a pending expiration of an estate tax deferment benefiting the wine-making Gallo family inspired considerable campaign contributions by family members (2006, 364–5; see also Viswanathan 2007 for an account of expirations associated with the research and development tax credit in the Reagan tax cut of 1981 [P.L. 97-34], 678–81).

However, the evidence for the rent-seeking explanation is thin in general. According to Ronald A. Pearlman, a Reagan administration assistant Treasury secretary for tax policy (and a professor of tax law at Georgetown University), "It's suggested that lawmakers can sort of say, 'Yes, we'd love to do this thing permanently, but we can't,' and ... it means the interest groups that support a specific provision then have to continue to support them through campaign contributions. I've seen no evidence of that. It's pure speculation" (Davis 2002, 294).

Moreover, Jacob Gersen questions whether temporary measures are superior mechanisms for extracting rents. The immediate rent extraction benefits of a statute with a limited life span are considerably less than those of a permanent statute: "... if private interests are willing to pay only for the anticipated benefits of legislation, then the 'price' of temporary legislation should be lower than the price of permanent legislation" (Gersen 2007, 262). Why would lawmakers with inherently uncertain political futures put off the lion's share of rent-extracted benefits to periods in the distant future (Gersen 2007, 281)? This is not to say that expiring laws will not impact campaign contributions. They should. But it is another matter to suggest that the prospect of campaign contributions motivates the existence and perpetuation of temporary laws.[3]

Promoting Agency Accountability

Temporary authorizations have also been portrayed as means for ensuring agency compliance with previously enacted directives (Cox 2004; Schick 2007). Cox argues that agencies are less likely to take continued funding for granted when a program is temporarily authorized (Cox 2004, 50–1). Regular reauthorizations encourage lawmakers, particularly those on the relevant committees, to develop expertise about agency practices and related policies. As a result, Congress is less reliant on bureaucrats for programmatic information (Maass 1983, 120–3).

The evidence Cox marshals in favor of this enhanced oversight argument comes from several case studies of federal agencies whose authorizations were switched from permanent to temporary. The impetus for change in those cases usually came from the authorizing committees, "largely because committee members perceived that it had become harder

---

[3] An appropriate test of this perspective would not just ask whether expirations correlate with contributions, but instead would need to compare net rents for similar programs that are temporarily and permanently authorized.

to control agencies' implementation of policy created by Congress" (Cox 2004, 81). Louis Fisher attributes the shift of the State Department from a permanent to an annual authorization in the early 1970s to "[a] series of executive-legislative clashes, particularly the withholding of information from Congress" (1983, 35). Similarly, Maass ascribes the move to an annual Federal Bureau of Investigation authorization to congressional-executive animosities in the mid-1970s (1983, 123–4).

However, Thad Hall finds little evidence to indicate that expirations spur oversight activity. Examining oversight hearings in ten federal program areas over fifteen years, Hall observes that such hearings' activities are not tied to the schedule of reauthorizations – they occur with equal frequency throughout the authorization cycle. In addition, oversight hearings happen regardless of reauthorization status – oversight hearings continue at approximately the same pace whether or not a program authorization is active or has previously expired (Hall 2004, Ch. 5).

Policy Updating

Whereas the agency accountability perspective emphasizes policy conflict between the executive and Congress as a central motivation for temporary authorizations, short-term authorizations may have more to do with problem solving and less to do with controlling rogue agencies. The policy that can pass at any given time is not likely to be the best not only because compromise is an inevitable part of the process but also because a policy's effects are not always easy to predict. Cox reports that issue "complexity" was a significant predictor of the presence of a sunset provision in laws passed during the 101st (1989–90) and 102nd (1991–2) Congresses. Temporary authorizations "provide an opportunity for Congress to watch and guide new programs in their developmental and experimental years" (Maass 1983, 124). They encourage lawmakers to regularly reevaluate and clarify legislative intent in light of new information and changing conditions (Cox 2004, 50). "Even successful legislation needs periodic updating to close loopholes, address unanticipated shortcomings, and keep up with changing circumstances" (Waxman 2010, 72). Fisher argues that lawmakers prefer "the flexibility of annual authorizations for foreign assistance" because it allows them "to adjust funding levels from year to year in response to changing conditions" (1983, 31). Similarly, Hall finds that much of the policy guidance ("steering") Congress provides to agencies occurs during program reauthorizations (2004, Ch. 6).

In a problem-solving legislature, outcomes, not policies, are what ultimately matter (Gilligan and Krehbiel 1989, 1990; Krehbiel 1991). Gersen discusses the benefits of temporary authorizations in a similar light:

When initial uncertainty is high, staged procedures [periodic expirations and renewals] allow new information to be integrated into the policy process. In such contexts, temporary legislation will generally be superior to permanent legislation along the informational dimension. When cognitive bias is present, temporary legislation provides a compensation mechanism to allow certain forms of bias to diminish. And when the information environment is dominated by information asymmetries and the interaction between legislators and private interests would otherwise be discrete, temporary legislation creates stronger incentives for the accurate revelation of information than otherwise equivalent permanent legislation. (2007, 2780)

For example, the Terrorism Risk Insurance Act of 2002 (TRIA; P.L. 107-297) – a policy created to temporarily bolster the insurance industry after the terrorist attacks of 9/11 – was originally authorized for a three-year time period. "Against the backdrop of significant uncertainty about the need for legislation, the level of background terrorism risk, and the ability of private markets to effectively manage such risk ... temporary legislation seems to have allowed politicians to respond to public demands for action while guarding against a potentially irrational overreaction to new information about a risk" (Gersen 2007, 293). Congress has since renewed TRIA twice – for an additional two years in 2005 (P.L. 109-144) and again in 2007 (P.L. 110-160).

The constitutional provision imposing a limit on military appropriations of two years was justified by the founders in similar problem-solving terms (Article I, section 8). In *Federalist No. 26*, Alexander Hamilton wrote that "The legislature of the United States will be *obliged* by this provision, once at least in every two years, to deliberate upon the propriety of keeping a military force on foot; to come to a new resolution on the point; and to declare their sense of the matter, by a formal vote in the face of their constituents" (emphasis in original). Importantly, "a Congress that happened to favor standing armies could not use the power of inertia to impose its decision on the future" (Nelson 2003, 541).

Having to renew programs is costly. However, limiting a law's duration can also lower transaction costs by lowering the political or economic stakes of a decision and by deflecting demands to other points in time. The former is one of the reasons tax legislation (typically tax breaks) is often authorized on a temporary basis (Gale and Orszag 2003), and short-term authorizations have long been used to win key support for legislation by limiting its scope of impact. With respect to lowering trans- action costs by deflecting policy demands, Hall argues that "short-term authorizations induce stability by serving as a gate-keeping mechanism, insulating committees from the pressure to revise public policy constantly for stakeholders who lost in the last legislative battle and providing a fixed point at which the status quo will be revised" (2004, 3–4, see also 24). In the words of a former staff member, the House Transportation and Infrastructure Committee "does not move between authorizations because there is no 'have to' without a funding expiration or something similar" (Hall 2004, 4).

In sum, the notion that temporary authorizations are means for pro- moting policy reviews and updating is certainly as valid as other, more cynical, interpretations. This notion was articulated by members in the first Congress, who argued (successfully) in favor of a temporary rather than permanent law, and it continues to be a central justification for short-term expirations. When a Congress controlled by the Democrats passed the Assault Weapons Ban with considerable fanfare as part of the 1994 Crime Control Act (P.L. 103-322) it included a ten-year sunset provision. Neither the House nor Senate voted to renew the ban in 2004 (the Senate added the ban to a bill immunizing gun manufacturers from liability before rejecting both; the House did not bring up the issue at all). But why did a democratically controlled Congress and a Democratic president pass a temporary ban in the first place? A permanent law would have made it much more difficult politically for a future Congress to reverse such a hard-fought policy gain because it would have required an active effort to pass a controversial repeal (when most Americans sup- ported the ban). Moreover, why did Republicans not try to repeal the law in 2001 when they gained control of the presidency and Congress for the first time in fifty years?

We have no doubt that the ten-year limit made it easier for some law- makers to initially support the original act. However, the ban made sup- port easier because it was justified in problem-solving terms. In 1994 (and much earlier), conservative lawmakers questioned whether banning assault weapons would actually reduce violent crime. Along with the sunset, the act required that the government study its impact over the next ten years. In 2004, a Department of Justice–commissioned report by scholars at the University of Pennsylvania concluded that "[s]hould it be renewed, the ban's effects on gun violence are likely to be small at best and perhaps too small for reliable measurement" (Koper, Woods, and

Roth 2004, 3; see also Sontag 2005). Given the salience of the issue, it was probably unrealistic to think that the findings of the report had much impact on the outcome. Most of the time, however, short-term authorizations do not end in the failure of a program. In the more common circumstance where it is clear that a program will be renewed, we contend that lawmakers will value information about a program's effectiveness.

PROBLEM SOLVING, AGENDA SCARCITY, AND TEMPORARY LEGISLATION

As discussed in the previous chapter, an issue-based committee system has important benefits for problem solving. Dividing responsibilities, grouping control over related issues, and assigning nearly exclusive jurisdictions hold the potential for increasing legislative capacity and achieving better policy outcomes at lower cost. At the same time, the committee system depends on the cooperation of individual legislators who are ultimately accountable to their own constituents. Longstanding research emphasizes that lawmakers have limited incentives to invest in collectively beneficial "workhorse" activities such as oversight and policy updating (Mayhew 1974).

Several explanations have been offered for why committee members make issue investments. According to Mayhew, committees "create specialized small group settings where members can make things happen and be perceived to make things happen" (1974, 92). Additional research has highlighted the motivating prospects of side payments and disproportionate policy influence (Ellwood and Patashnik 1993; Evans 2004; Hall 1996; Krehbiel 1991; Krutz 2001; Lee 2003; Maltzman 1997; Mayhew 1974). Whether committee members can reasonably expect these benefits has also been a subject of considerable theoretical and empirical controversy (Hall 1995; Krehbiel 1991).[4]

In our view, this ongoing controversy overlooks a primary concern of credit-seeking lawmakers. Hall observes that "unlike more bureaucratic organizations, the 'division of labor' visible in Congress is not authoritatively imposed. It bubbles up as it were, from individual members' day-to-day choices about which matters warrant their time, energy, and staff attention" (Hall 1996, 10). With "so many problems pressing down upon

---

[4] Because committees do not possess formal *ex post* vetoes, committee members have reason to doubt whether their so-called distributive commissions will be preserved in the legislation that is passed by the chamber.

the system," committee members can legitimately wonder whether their own legislative investments will bear fruit. How likely is it that their carefully crafted legislative proposals will be taken up by the legislature at all (Kingdon 1995)?

We contend that an important problem-solving contribution of temporary authorizations is to alter committee members' expectations in this regard. Short-term authorizations can be viewed as legislative commitments that promote policy investments by committee members. A more formal game theoretic model offered in the next section centers on a committee member's decision to invest, and a chamber leader's decision regarding floor scheduling illustrates how short-term authorizations can promote problem solving.

Agenda Scarcity and Problem Solving

The consequences of agenda scarcity for committee issue investments can be illustrated by a game between two legislative entities – the member of the committee of jurisdiction and the chamber leader. The committee member must decide whether to invest personal resources in overseeing and developing policy recommendations on a given issue. This decision depends on the electoral and policy benefits of that investment, compared to other opportunities. Different lawmakers will assign more weight to different goals (reelection, good public policy, career advancement, etc.). The model is agnostic with respect to these goals – it assumes that the legislator receives utility from different possible outcomes and chooses a strategy (invest or not) based on those utilities.

The chamber leader faces the question of how to allocate a scarce resource; in this case, the scarce resource is plenary or floor time. Debating and passing legislation takes time, and time is a limited resource in legislatures (Cox 2006; Döring 1995). A decision to allocate plenary time to an issue means that less time is available to consider other issues. As a result, scheduling decisions are explicit or implicit decisions about chamber priorities. Leaders face pressure from different directions. As party leaders they are expected to promote the party brand, but as chamber leaders they are also responsible for steering the ship of state. This includes not only advancing preferred discretionary issues, but also ensuring that salient issues are addressed in a timely manner and that Congress attends to existing policies. With respect to the latter, leaders want to encourage issue investments at the committee level.

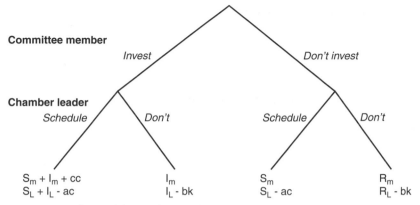

FIGURE 5.1. The Problem-Solving Dilemma.

Figure 5.1 represents this situation as a sequential game form. The committee member must make a decision about whether to invest in an issue before knowing whether the chamber leader will provide floor time for its consideration at some future date. The chamber leader decides whether to allocate scarce floor time to the issue after the committee member has made his decision to invest or not.

The game assumes that the same general considerations affect the payoffs for the two players, the committee member (M) and the chamber leader (L). These payoffs reflect policy benefits (I, S), political benefits and costs (cc, bk) and agenda opportunity costs (ac) associated with different outcomes. I_i represents the expected policy utility to player i of reviewing the existing law. S represents the policy utility of bringing a new bill addressing the issue to the floor. R (reversion point) represents the policy utility of no policy review and no new bill. If the bill is taken up, the committee member who invested in the issues is able to claim political credit (cc). For the chamber leader, scheduling a bill for consideration implies an opportunity cost in terms of reduced agenda control (ac). Addressing the issue comes at a cost to other issues. If it is not taken up, the chamber leader faces the possibility of a political backlash for having failed to address the issue (bk).

Each actor knows the other player's payoffs and acts with complete information about the alternatives and prior choices in the game. We solve the game for subgame perfect Nash equilibria (SGPNE) by first specifying when a strategy is a best response for player 2 (the chamber leader), and then "rolling back" the game to specify best response of

TABLE 5.1. *Equilibrium Conditions for the Problem-Solving Game*

SGPNE	Equilibrium Conditions	Permanent Law	Expiring Law
L: *Schedule* M: *Invest*	If $S_L + I_L - ac > I_L - bk$ and $S_M + I_M + cc > S_M$	$S_L > ac$ $I_M + cc > 0$	$S_L + bk > ac$ $I_M + cc > 0$
L: *Don't schedule* M: *Invest*	If $I_L - bk > S_L + I_L - ac$ and $I_M > R_M$	$S_L < ac$ $I_M > R_M$	$S_L + bk < ac$ $I_M > R_M$
L: *Schedule* M: *Don't invest*	If $S_L - ac > R_L - bk$ and $S_M + I_M + cc < S_M$	$R_L + ac < S_L$ $I_M < 0$	$R_L + ac < S_L + bk$ $I_M + cc < 0$
L: *Don't schedule* M: *Don't invest*	If $R_L - bk > S_L - ac$ and $R_M > I_M$	$R_L + ac > S_L$ $R_M > I_M$	$R_L + ac > S_L + bk$ $R_M > I_M$

player 1 (the committee member) given player 1's beliefs about player 2's strategy.

Table 5.1 lays out the conditions under which each of the four possible pure strategy outcomes of the game are SGPNEs. The third and fourth columns summarize the key variables affecting individual strategies under two scenarios; when the existing law is permanently authorized (column 3) and when it is temporarily authorized (column 4).

We are particularly interested in the conditions under which the committee member chooses the strategy of investing in the issue, and how making a law temporary increases the likelihood of such a strategy choice. For example, Table 5.1 indicates that for a permanent law (column 3), the chamber leader schedules the issue for floor consideration and the committee invests in the issue if and only if:

Chamber leader: the policy benefits of taking up the issue exceed the costs of reduced control over the legislative agenda (i.e., $S_L > ac$).

Committee member: the combined policy and credit claiming benefits of investing in the issue are positive (i.e., $I_m + cc > 0$).

If $S_L < ac$, the chamber leader will not schedule the bill and (based on the assumption of consistent beliefs) the decision of the committee member to invest depends on whether $I_m > R_m$. That is, he no longer expects a credit-claiming benefit for his efforts, so his decision rests solely on whether he receives positive utility from engaging in legislative oversight. Mayhew argues that, at one time, committee members invested in institutional maintenance activities such as oversight simply because doing so enhanced their reputations within the chamber (Mayhew 1974, 147). However, the erosion of such norms has meant that additional incentives are needed to encourage members to engage in such activities – external credit-claiming opportunities that depend on congressional action.

The dilemma for the committee member is that agenda scarcity means that whether the chamber leader will schedule a bill for consideration may be difficult to predict in advance. First, the policy benefits of amending the existing law will not be fully known until after the committee member has invested in oversight. The oversight investigation may ultimately reveal a need for important policy changes, or not. Second, the opportunity costs to the leader of bringing a bill to the floor will also not be known until after the committee member has decided to invest or not. The chamber leader will certainly encourage the committee member to engage in oversight and may fully expect to bring the issue to the floor. But the committee member has reason to doubt the chamber leader's commitment.

Chamber decisions to authorize laws on a temporary basis affect these calculations. By opting not to make a law permanent, the current legislature raises the costs of inaction for a future legislature. The "reversion point" is no longer continuation of the current policy (an invitation to "wait until next year" thinking in the face of competing policy demands) – inaction may now result in no policy. In the game, the chamber leader therefore faces the prospect of a political backlash (bk) that might not exist were the same law permanent. Knowing that the chamber leader has an incentive to revisit the program by a specified date gives committee members greater reason to invest in the issue because they anticipate that those investments are more likely to yield credit-claiming benefits.

Whether bk induces the chamber leader to schedule a bill (and in turn induces the committee member to invest) depends not only on bk but also on S_L and ac. If oversight reveals that major policy change is desired (i.e., S_L is large as may be the case when there is a salient crisis) then it may be brought up regardless. Similarly, when there are fewer agenda demands, the costs of scheduling it (ac) will be lower.

The policy and political implications of allowing a law to expire should also influence scheduling decisions. The political backlash (bk) of failing to act on the budget or a debt-ceiling increase will be higher than for a less salient expiring program. Thus we would expect a leader to prioritize certain issues over others. In 2011, a highly salient debt-ceiling deadline distracted lawmakers from working through what were relatively modest differences on a Federal Aviation Administration (FAA) reauthorization, leading to a temporary shutdown of certain FAA programs. Shortly after the debt-ceiling crisis was averted, the FAA reauthorization was addressed.

In addition, the credibility of the expiration threat will also affect the size of *bk*. For example, if the appropriations committee can continue to fund a program at no cost after its authorization has expired, then the fact that a law is temporarily authorized should have less impact on a committee member's investment decision (because it will have little impact on the leader's commitment to bringing up the issue).

The implications of temporary authorizations for legislative behavior are ultimately testable. Costless expirations should have no impact on the timing of policy attention or policy change. However, we have theorized that failing to address them is costly, which leads us to expect that program expirations will be important predictors of legislative attention to issues across time. In addition, we expect to see different patterns of committee involvement where temporary legislation is concerned when compared to more discretionary legislation. Committee members should play a more central role in managing programs on short-term authorizations because they have more reason to anticipate credit-claiming benefits for their efforts. Both of these expectations are examined in subsequent chapters.

INITIAL EVIDENCE OF TEMPORARY AUTHORIZATIONS AS COMMITMENTS TO PROBLEM SOLVING

It is well-known that only a few hundred of the ten thousand or so bills introduced each term make it beyond committee referral to be considered by one or both chambers. We argue that agenda scarcity, and not simply a bill's merits, helps to explain this pattern. But if not merit alone, what influences whether a bill ends up among the select few? As discussed in Chapter 1, Walker argues that the legislative agenda can be viewed as a "continuum that ranges from items with which the Senate is required to deal, either by law or political necessity, to another set of items that arises mainly from the promotional efforts of activist Senators and their allies" (1977, 424–5). On one end are issues that "flow with such predictability from past decisions" including "periodically recurring" (annual appropriations and authorizations) and "sporadically recurring" issues (other federal programs on temporary authorizations of varying durations; Walker 1977, 426). In the middle are the publicly salient issues – an oil spill, natural disaster, or other national crisis – that "burst upon the country in magnified form via the mass media ... [and] force their way onto the Senate's agenda" (Walker 1977, 426). At the other end are the discretionary problems "selected from the numerous possibilities offered up by the Senate's legislative activists" (ibid.).

Walker argues that legislative leaders "exercise little discretion over the scheduling of items for debate" because they face a raft of issues that must be addressed (Walker 1977, 424). Similarly, Barbara Sinclair observes that "[g]iven the requirement for periodic reauthorization of programs, most of any committee's agenda will consist of continuing issues" (Sinclair 1986, 37). To the extent that Walker and Sinclair are correct, a very different account of lawmaking than those offered to date is suggested – one that is driven in large part by compulsory issues such as expiring laws.

Notably, Walker does not provide systematic evidence in support of this perspective. Our goal here is to begin to assess congressional attention to such "compulsory" issues by first asking: how much congressional attention do renewals of recurring (temporary) laws consume? In later chapters we will then expand our examination of the legislative agenda to include other issues along the compulsory-discretionary continuum. Examining this question necessitates differentiating legislation that addresses recurring issues from other types of legislation. However, no simple approach currently exists. Bills proposing annual appropriations are easy to detect. Bills addressing other types of expiring laws can be much more elusive. Sometimes these bills include "reauthorization" in their titles. Often, however, that it is a reauthorization is buried in the bill's text – for example, there might be language "extending" the current authorization or language that simply authorizes a new budgetary figure for a given number of future years.

We employ a multistep keyword filtering process to first identify such likely bills, while anticipating the potential for type I (false positive) errors. We searched bill titles (generally a sentence or two in length) and bill summaries (ranging from one sentence to multiple paragraphs) available through the Library of Congress THOMAS Web site[5] for keywords and keyword combinations that experience suggested would be effective (e.g., "appropriat*,""reauthor*," "authorize appropriations for FY"). This keyword list was developed incrementally and was quite extensive. This resulted in about one thousand potential bill "hits" for each congressional term.

We next read the bill titles and summaries to eliminate the false positives. If the title and summary were inconclusive, we read the full text of the bill and/or the bill's legislative history in *Congressional Quarterly Almanac* (*CQ*) and *Lexis-Nexis Congress*. As a final step, we checked for type II (false negative) errors by searching the online *CQ* for mentions of reauthorizations that we had not already identified. The fact that we found almost no cases that our initial search method did not reveal (i.e., no false negatives) gave us added confidence in our approach.

The Recurring Agenda of the Modern Congress

We consider three indicators of progressively restrictive stages of the legislative agenda: bills introduced, bills passed by the chamber, and roll call votes. Any member of Congress can sponsor an unlimited number of bills on any subject. However, only a very small proportion of those bills see action beyond the mandate of committee referral, and an even smaller proportion are passed by the chamber (< 10%). Finally, an extremely limited number of bills are subject to roll call votes. Many bills are passed by voice vote on account of their noncontroversial nature (e.g., commemorative bills, private bills; Lynch and Madonna 2008). Where more important legislation is concerned, we assess agenda attention by examining the distribution of recorded voting decisions. What proportion of these time-consuming debate activities are devoted to recurring issues?

We examine the legislative issue agenda for the House of Representatives in the 101st through 104th Congresses (1989–96). This period was chosen because it experienced considerable electoral shifts and partisan turnover in a relatively short period of time. This would seem to suggest that the legislative agenda would be packed with new discretionary initiatives. The first two terms saw Congresses controlled by Democrats and a Republican president (George H. W. Bush); the third saw a Congress controlled by Democrats and a Democratic president (Bill Clinton); while the fourth saw a switch to a Republican-controlled Congress.

Figure 5.2 displays the proportion of the House agenda devoted to recurring issues at the three stages of deliberation. Bills addressing recurring issues make up less than 10 percent of all bills introduced. When we turn to the bills passed by the House, however, those considering

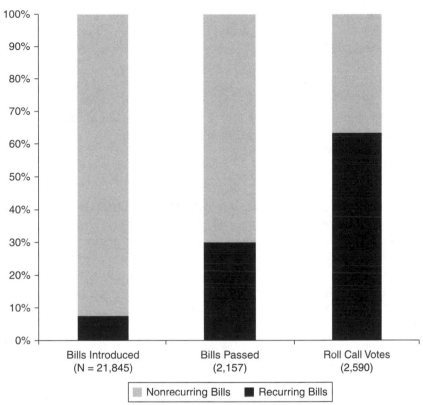

FIGURE 5.2. Attention to Recurring Legislative Matters at Different Stages of the Legislative Process, 101st–104th Congresses.

recurring issues make up about one-third of successful bills. Turning to the bills that receive the most chamber attention, nearly two-thirds of all recorded votes on the House floor occur during consideration of recurring issues.[6] These findings offer substantial support for the view that much of the legislative agenda is consumed by issues that "must" be addressed. Moreover, we have not yet even attempted to assess the proportion of the agenda that is devoted to the other type of problem solving highlighted in this book – "politically necessary" responses to salient events.

Do more recent years – those that have been characterized by what is commonly seen as partisan agendas – exhibit the same patterns? One simple metric is to consider the proportion of total enactments (excluding minor laws) that are renewals of recurring legislation. In the 104th

---

[6] There are no appreciable differences in these trends across the respective congressional terms.

Congress (1995–6) 39 percent of all nontrivial enactments[7] were prompted by a previous or current expiration. In the 110th Congress (2007–8), 43 percent of all enactments were responses to statutory expirations. At least by this metric, there is little evidence that temporary legislation has diminished in importance in recent times. One effect of increasing congressional polarization may be to focus more policy-making attention on recurring and necessary temporary legislation, thereby increasing its relevance for understanding policy change.

CONCLUSION

This chapter began with the question: why would lawmakers choose to enact laws on a temporary rather than permanent basis? We have emphasized the benefits of temporary authorizations for problem solving. Because many problems in society are not well understood and because conditions change, incumbent lawmakers have incentives to support an ongoing problem-solving process. Temporary enactments help to ensure that Congress – in particular its committees – invests in oversight and policy updating by raising the costs to the legislature of failing to revisit an issue. The rise of temporary authorizations beginning after World War II corresponds to a similar rise in policy demands and policy complexity.

If temporary authorizations are primarily programmatic trial runs – the stated intent of sunset laws that gained favor in the 1970s – then very few trials end in failure at either the state or federal levels. Programs permitted to expire are still far more the exception than the rule. Further, the typical outcome of a renewal is not a permanent law but another temporary law. Temporary laws do provide agencies with greater incentives to be attentive to the concerns of authorizing committees. However, temporary legislation also promotes congressional issue attention by moving issues up the legislative agenda and thereby providing committee members with added incentive to invest in collectively beneficial problem-solving activities. A related benefit is that the same committee is under less pressure to act when the issue is not up for reauthorization because – barring a crisis of some sort – there is little chance of congressional action. Temporary legislation thus also enhances problem-solving capacity by enabling committees to more efficiently allocate their own limited time and resources (Hall 2004).

---

[7] Those bills that were not commemorative, symbolic, or dealing with land conveyance matters.

As discussed, the presence of an expiration does not always imply that the legislature "must" act. Sometimes programs continue to be funded after they expire, and sometimes programs are simply extended with minimal revisions through continuing resolutions. Allen Schick argues that "unauthorized appropriations have become commonplace.... Since the early 1990s national defense has been the only major area whose expiring authorizations have consistently been renewed year after year" (2007, 199). Hall calculates that the number of programs that continue despite expired authorizations increased three-fold from the late 1980s to 2000 (2004, Ch. 8).

Closer inspection reveals concerns about the data on which these conclusions are based. Both studies rely on an annual report prepared by the Congressional Budget Office (CBO) titled *Unauthorized Appropriations and Expiring Authorizations* (2001). The CBO data aggregates separate expiring provisions but with no discernibly consistent methodology.[8] For example, by the CBO's accounting, the enormous farm bill passed in 1990 included fifteen expiring provisions, seven of which were scheduled to sunset in the 104th Congress (1995–6). Using our methodology, we found more than one hundred expiring provisions, sixty-six of which were set to sunset in 1995 or 1996. Later in this book we will employ a more complete accounting of expiring provisions of law across an extended time period. But even if the CBO numbers were accurate, the fact that there are more expired provisions today than in the past does not imply that a greater proportion of laws are expiring. Recall that recurring legislation as a percentage of all laws is on the rise – from 39 percent in 1995–6 to 43 percent in 2007–8.

Expiring laws are not always renewed. Often, however, these expirations are clearly intentional policy decisions that have little bearing on the question of whether expirations constitute credible commitments. Noteworthy examples include the expiration of the military draft in 1973; the general revenue-sharing expiration (a Nixon-initiated program to return power and money to state and local governments) in 1986; the independent counsel or "special prosecutor" law expiration (enacted in the wake of the Watergate scandal, and prominently featured in the investigation of the Clinton/Lewinsky affair) in 1999; and the assault weapons ban expiration in 2004. At the end of 2011, ethanol subsidies originally enacted thirty years prior to encourage the production of alternative fuels

---

[8] Private communication with the CBO official responsible for creating this report in 2003.

were allowed to expire. A spokesman for ethanol producers conceded, "The marketplace has evolved. The tax incentive is less necessary now than it was just two years ago. Ethanol is 10 percent of the nation's gasoline supply" (Pear 2012).

Although the possibilities of unauthorized appropriations and continuing resolutions certainly raise doubts about whether committee members can reasonably expect their policy investments to pay off, this is ultimately an empirical question to be explored in subsequent chapters.[9] The remainder of this book tests important empirical implications of the theoretical arguments presented in Chapters 4 and 5. In Chapter 6, we revisit a longstanding subject of legislative research, congressional reform (Adler 2011), to test alternative explanations about the effects of reform and the goals of committee organization. Because problem solving is centrally concerned with outcomes rather than policies, lawmakers turn to expert committees to set the legislative agenda. In Chapter 7, we take a closer look at the legislative agenda and legislative agenda setting. After differentiating among compulsory and discretionary agenda items, we ask whether such distinctions are helpful in terms of explaining how issues are managed in Congress.

[9] Importantly, unauthorized appropriations do not necessarily signal an absence of authorizing committee influence. To pass unauthorized appropriations, the chamber must adopt a waiver as part of the "rule" for floor consideration in the House (Tiefer 1989, 966–72). This provides an opportunity for the authorizing committee to voice its objections. In one cited case, Transportation Committee objections caused an Appropriations bill to be defeated (*CQ Almanac* 1985; see also Tiefer 1989, 965). In many cases, unauthorized appropriations stem from the fact that one of the chambers has failed to act on the authorizing legislation in time. In such cases, appropriators will sometimes rely on authorizing committee reports or the bill passed by one chamber as guidance (Tiefer 1989, 964–5 and 964n109). According to Alex Wayne and Bill Swindall, "Appropriators generally continue to allocate money for programs based on the policies in their expired authorizations, or Congress extends the expiring authorizations without altering policy" (Wayne and Swindell 2004). Cox similarly observes that even when appropriators engage in legislating through appropriations, they tread lightly on the turf of the authorizing committee.

In the late-1980s, the majority Democratic Caucus in the House adopted a rule (Rule 37) requiring the Appropriations Committee to inform the relevant authorization committee chair of any violation of House Rule XXI. Additionally, Democratic Rules Committee members "had a practice of not granting waivers to rule XXI if the authorization committee with jurisdiction protested" (Cox 2004, 48). This practice continued when the Republicans took control of the House following the 1994 elections, and was informally known as the "Armey Rule." The rule was named for the former Republican Majority Leader, Richard Armey of Texas. See debate on the Interior, Environment, and Related Agencies Appropriations Act of 2008 (*Congressional Record*, June 26, 2007, H7135–H7152; P.L. 110-161) for explicit reference to the Armey Rule.

Chapters 8 and 9 examine the same question – what drives policy change in Congress – from different angles. If legislative agenda space is scarce, then we should expect issues that "must" be addressed to drive policy attention and change. These expectations are sharply at odds with leading congressional perspectives that portray policy change as primarily driven by shifts in the preference composition of the legislature or changes in partisan control. In each chapter, the focus is on explaining attention or change within specific issue or policy areas over time. Chapter 8 examines issue "attention" across time, as measured by bill-sponsorship activity. Chapter 9 tests alternative hypotheses for when "major" laws are first reformed, both in terms of the timing and the importance of those changes. Additionally, we examine alternative hypotheses for cumulative changes in policy across time, given that policies can be products of multiple laws. These chapters provide consistent support for the problem-solving perspective presented in these pages. Established indicators of preferences and partisanship are much less robust predictors of issue attention, statutory change, and cumulative policy change than are program expirations and indicators of issue salience.

PART III

6

Rethinking Committee Reform

> It would be terribly unfortunate if the House had to continue working
> under its outmoded and obsolete system of jurisdictions.... Congress must
> organize itself so that it can unify its programs and policies in these impor-
> tant areas rather than continue to work on these problems in an uncoordi-
> nated and often counterproductive way.
>
> Rep. Bill Frenzel (R-MN) speaking in favor of the Bolling Committee
> reform recommendations in 1974.[1]

Committee structures enhance legislative capacity and lower information
costs through a division of labor and clearly defined issue responsibilities. A problem-solving account of committee organization implies that
committee jurisdictional reforms are a response to Congress's diminished
problem-solving capacity. As new issues arise and old ones get redefined,
existing jurisdictional arrangements no longer align with contemporary
policy challenges – as Frenzel argues in the preceding text. We anticipate that reforms unify programs and policies in important areas with
the goals of promoting improved policy coordination and information
sharing.

   In this chapter, we examine the Bolling-Hansen reforms of 1975,
which included the largest set of jurisdictional changes (58 in total) since
the Legislative Reorganization Act of 1946 (P.L. 79-601). Previous studies have concluded that the Bolling-Hansen reforms had little impact
on the overall organization of the committee system (King 1997, 58;
Wolfensberger 2004, 2). However, no previous study has investigated

---

[1] *Congressional Record*, September 30, 1974, 33004.

their effects on where bills are being referred – the "best" indicator of a committee's jurisdiction (Evans 1999). We ask three related questions: Did the reforms substantially alter existing bill-referral practices? If so, what objectives best explain the changes adopted? Finally, did the reforms produce a measurably improved committee system for problem solving?

PRIOR PERSPECTIVES ON COMMITTEE JURISDICTIONAL REFORM

When the U.S. Department of Homeland Security was created in 2003, many lawmakers expressed the view that a rearrangement of jurisdictions in Congress was critical to fighting terrorism. Dozens of congressional committees and subcommittees possessed jurisdiction over aspects of the new agency's functions and programs (Cohen, Gorman, and Freedberg 2003). Jurisdictional reform was also one of the primary recommendations of the 9/11 Commission (National Commission on Terrorist Attacks upon the United States 2004). Nevertheless, the subject was contentious. Speaking of committee jurisdictions, one lawmaker stated, "The 'war on terrorism' has just expanded to the war on turf" (Nather and Foerstel 2002).

Extant research highlights such distributive or "turf" concerns as the central barrier to committee jurisdictional reform (Adler 2002). Yet, collective objectives are often at the center of jurisdictional debates. The Homeland Security reform debates revolved not around turf but around whether the reforms would enhance or harm Congress's problem-solving capacity:

Supporters of reform charge those who opposed the measure with putting turf protection above national security. But those concerned about the changes say they risk discarding the expertise of lawmakers and their staff, painstakingly built up over the years. Supporters of Rep. John Mica, R-FL., chairman of the Aviation Subcommittee, for instance, argue the subcommittee's expertise with aviation security would be lost in the proposed structure, just as the well of experience is running dry at the department itself, with more than half its senior leadership departing. (Waterman 2005)

It is tempting to discount justifications of reform opposition as self-serving, and they may be. But there were legitimate reasons to consider whether transferring jurisdiction to a newly formed committee would be detrimental to aviation security as well as other objectives beyond national security. The Federal Emergency Management Agency and the Coast Guard, for example, also serve other important domestic functions such as natural disaster relief and environmental protection. Turf-centered explanations deserve consideration, but we see little reason to accept them at face value, just as it would be inappropriate to accept collectively centered explanations at face value.

Prior research in this area has focused primarily on reform decisions (e.g., vote outcomes) rather than reform effects (Adler 2002; Binder 1997; Schickler 2001; Schickler and Rich 1997). Current understandings of committee jurisdictional reforms come from a limited number of studies that conclude that formal reforms have little impact on issue control in Congress, albeit for differing reasons (Baumgartner and Jones 1991, 1993; Baumgartner, Jones, and MacLeod 2000; Hardin 1998; Jones, Baumgartner, and Talbert 1993; King 1994, 1997). David King argues that "[t]urf is gained through common law advances, *not through formal rules changes* (like the 'reforms' passed by the House in 1946, 1974, and 1980)" (King 1994, 48; emphasis added, see also 1997). Committee members (motivated by distributive concerns) sponsor bills and hold hearings on newly emerging issues. These activities influence initial referral decisions, creating precedents that influence future referrals. Thus, jurisdiction develops through a path-dependent process motivated by turf considerations. Subsequent formal changes (such as the 1974 Bolling-Hansen reforms) "codify" preexisting referral practices that develop informally.

Baumgartner and Jones argue that committees "are *constantly changing* their jurisdictions, both through attempts to grab parts of larger issues as they become more important and through unavoidable redefinitions as new policy problems rise on the governmental agenda" (1993, 660; emphasis added). This perspective suggests that formal jurisdictions are porous – they have a limited impact on whether other committees choose to become active in a particular issue area.

A problem-solving perspective, in contrast, portrays formal jurisdictions as meaningful and organized to promote collective policy objectives. Thus, jurisdictions should predict issue control, and jurisdictional reforms should do more than codify established practices. They should promote organizational capacity and informational efficiency by separating issue responsibilities while grouping responsibility for related issues. This perspective does not preclude the possibility that particular committees will pursue new jurisdictional opportunities. However, it does emphasize the collective purposes of jurisdictions, and the broader considerations that may lead legislatures to act to counterbalance such centrifugal forces.

House and Senate rules define committee jurisdictions for the purpose of guiding bill referrals by the parliamentarian. For example, House Rule X specifies that bills addressing more than twenty different subjects, including "agriculture generally," as well as "entomology and plant quarantine" and "rural electrification" are to be referred to the Agriculture Committee. Rule X also seems to provide little leeway regarding referrals: "All bills, resolutions, and other matters relating to subjects within the jurisdiction of the standing committees listed in this clause shall be referred to those committees."

The bills committees report "largely determine what each chamber will debate" (Davidson and Oleszek 2004, 226). The vast majority of bills (80%–85%, depending on the Congress) are referred to just one committee, and many multiple referrals also confer exclusive committee responsibility for particular sections within complex bills (King 1997, 101–4; Young and Cooper 1993). However, these observations provide little insight into how jurisdictions are created or the extent to which committees share jurisdiction over similar issues. Prior research also offers little insight into these questions because nearly all existing research on committee jurisdictions focuses on hearings' activity rather than on the "best" indicator of jurisdiction – bill referrals by the parliamentarian (Evans 1999).

THE BOLLING-HANSEN COMMITTEE REFORMS

To explore the question of jurisdictional arrangements, we study the impact of the largest set of jurisdictional reforms (58) of the postwar period on bill-referral practices in Congress. At the beginning of the 93rd Congress (1973–4), the House of Representatives established a temporary select committee to consider and recommend changes to its committee structure (Davidson and Oleszek 1977). The committee's chairman, Richard Bolling (D-MO), described a committee system in "disarray" (Bolling 1974, 3):

When Rule XI [later Rule X] is silent or unclear, the [parliamentarian's] office is guided by precedent, logic or political advantage. Over a period of time such a process inevitably leads to confusion and inconsistency. House committees acquire jurisdiction by accretion. Different committees receive similar subject matter. Procedural uncertainty frequently results. Public policy often suffers. (Bolling 1974, 6)

The Bolling committee proposed a comprehensive set of reforms "designed to make the House and its committees, more deliberative, responsive and efficient" (ibid). Its recommendations generated immediate and heated opposition, especially among committee chairs (Davidson and Oleszek 1977). After several months of consideration, opponents within the majority Democratic Party succeeded in referring the matter to a caucus committee chaired by Rep. Julia Butler Hansen (D-WA). The Hansen committee then proposed a less ambitious reform package that passed the House by a vote of 203–165.

The watering down of the ambitious Bolling committee proposal is often interpreted as evidence that the reform effort "failed" (Adler 2002). Donald Wolfensberger describes the Bolling-Hansen reforms as leaving "existing turf arrangements virtually intact" (2004, 2). King concludes that the "1974 'reforms,' whether expanding or subtracting from a committee's statutory jurisdiction, reflected the incremental common law changes that had been in force, in some cases, for decades" (1997, 58). However, these conclusions are not based on systematic analyses of the reforms' effects, but instead are based on cursory comparisons between what was originally proposed and what ultimately passed. Aside from King's examination of the reform's effects on hearings activity related to a single committee (the Energy and Commerce Committee), there has been no systematic examination of the actual effects of the Bolling-Hansen reforms.

Our analysis investigates the impact of a sample of seventeen of the fifty-eight jurisdictional reforms adopted in 1975. In addition, we explore bill-referral patterns across the same time period for ten additional randomly selected jurisdictions left untouched by the reforms (see Tables 6.1 and 6.2).

Reforms can establish a committee's jurisdiction over new issues, or transfer jurisdiction over existing issues from one committee to another. About two-thirds of the fifty-eight jurisdictional changes in the Bolling-Hansen reforms were transfers of existing jurisdictions, while the other third created new jurisdictions. Our stratified sample of these changes includes a similar proportion of transfers (11) and new jurisdictional authority (6). The limited jurisdictions we investigate are also consequential. They include twenty-five of Mayhew's "most important" postwar enactments (Mayhew 1991).[2] In addition, they encompass highly desired

---

[2] These important laws include the creation and reauthorization of the Food For Peace Program (in 1954 and 1966), all major highway bills (1956, 1965, 1966, 1970, 1973, 1991, and 1998), all major urban mass transit bills (1964, 1970, 1974, 1982, and 1987), all campaign finance reforms acts (1972, 1974, and 2002), the creation of the Martin Luther King national holiday (1983), and the authorization of General Revenue Sharing (1972).

TABLE 6.1. *List of House Committee Jurisdictional Changes Examined*

Jurisdictional Change	Gaining Committee	Losing Committee	No. of Bill Referrals (preform)
Agricultural Commodities (including Comm. Credit Corp.)	Agriculture	Banking, Currency, and Housing	414
Biomedical R&D	Interstate and Foreign Commerce	–	45
Consumer Affairs and Consumer Protection	Interstate and Foreign Commerce	Banking, Currency, and Housing	626
Export Controls	Foreign Affairs	Banking, Currency, and Housing	103
Food Programs for School Children (beyond lunch programs)	Education and Labor	–	75
General Revenue Sharing	Government Operations	Ways and Means	172
Hatch Act	Post Office and Civil Service	House Admin.	37
Holidays and Celebrations	Post Office and Civil Service	Judiciary	295
International Commodity Agreements (not sugar)	Foreign Affairs	Agriculture	73
International Finance and Monetary Organizations	Banking, Currency, and Housing	Foreign Affairs	32
International Fishing Agreements	Merchant Marine and Fisheries	Foreign Affairs	48
Raising and Reporting of Campaign Contributions	House Administration	Standards of Official Conduct	61
Roads and Safety thereof	Public Works and Transportation	–	429
Rural Development	Agriculture	–	166
Travel and Tourism	Interstate and Foreign Commerce	–	60
Urban Mass Transportation	Public Works and Transportation	Banking, Currency, and Housing	182
Weather Bureau/National Weather Service	Science and Technology	Interstate and Foreign Commerce	48

Note: "Gaining committees" are those committees that formally acquire a jurisdiction either through transfer from another panel or assignment of a newly created jurisdiction. "Losing committees" are those giving up a jurisdiction in a transfer. Dashes represent instances of newly created jurisdictions.

TABLE 6.2. *List of Control Cases (Stable House Committee Jurisdictions)*

Jurisdiction	Committee of Jurisdiction	No. of Relevant Bill Referrals (prereform)
Adulteration of Seeds, Insect Pests, and Protection of Birds and Animals in Forest Reserves	Agriculture	8
Human Nutrition and Home Economics	Agriculture	29
Regulation of Common Carriers by Water (except matters subject to the jurisdiction of the Interstate Commerce Commission) and Inspection of Merchant Marine Vessels, Lights and Signals, Lifesaving Equipment, and Fire Protection or Such Vessels	Merchant Marine and Fisheries	99
Municipal Code and Amendments to the Criminal and Corporation Laws in D.C.	District of Columbia	89
Municipal and Juvenile Courts in D.C.	District of Columbia	9
National Science Foundation	Science	108
Preservation of Prehistoric Ruins and Objects of Interest on the Public Domain	Interior and Insular Affairs	242
Rural Electrification	Agriculture	53
Status of Officers and Employees of the United States, Including Their Compensation, Classification, and Retirement	Post Office and Civil Service	1,701
Wages and Hours of Labor	Education and Labor	115

Notes: Stable jurisdictions were those that were not changed at all during the Bolling-Hansen reforms.
Cells in column 2 represent proportion of total "closely related" bills to each jurisdiction.

committees (Ways and Means and Commerce), constituency-oriented committees (Agriculture and Public Works), policy-oriented committees (Judiciary and Foreign Affairs), and even the least desired committees (Post Office and Standards of Official Conduct).

The central reason for adopting a sampling approach is that bills are not labeled for jurisdiction. This meant that, for each of our twenty-seven jurisdictions, we had to sift through one hundred thousand bills over seven congresses of our study period to identify the ones that were related. This was accomplished through a multistage process. We began with the Congressional Bills Project.[3] Each bill title in the Congressional Bills Project has been labeled for primary policy topic (19 topics in all) and subtopic (226 subtopics) using the policy classification system of the Policy Agendas Project. To isolate jurisdictionally relevant bills from the initial one hundred thousand, we first compared each of the twenty-seven jurisdictions as described in the postreform House rules to identify potentially relevant (and typically more encompassing) Policy Agendas Project subtopic descriptions. We next read each bill's title within the relevant subtopics (as well as those in a "general" subtopic that could include additional jurisdictionally relevant bills).[4]

Committee referral decisions about these bills, before and after the reforms, constitute the primary dependent variable of our analysis. Our list of jurisdictionally relevant bills is not perfect – even the House parliamentarian must occasionally exercise discretion in judging which committee possesses jurisdiction over a bill. The strength of our analysis is its large N approach. The final data set contains about eight thousand bill referral decisions across a fourteen-year time span.

THE CONSEQUENCES OF REFORM FOR ISSUE CONTROL IN THE HOUSE OF REPRESENTATIVES

We begin with a basic question: did the Bolling-Hansen reforms alter bill referral patterns in the House? Prior studies suggest that the answer is no. According to King, "jurisdictional arbitration was intentionally taken out of the hands of floor majorities and out of the hands of party leaders" because turf-minded lawmakers could not be trusted to enact reforms that promoted collective policy goals (1997, 21). Thus, evidence that the

---

[3] www.congressionalbills.org.
[4] Every major topic area has a "general" subtopic that includes cases that are truly general to all the associated subtopics, in addition to cases where more than one distinct subtopic is discussed.

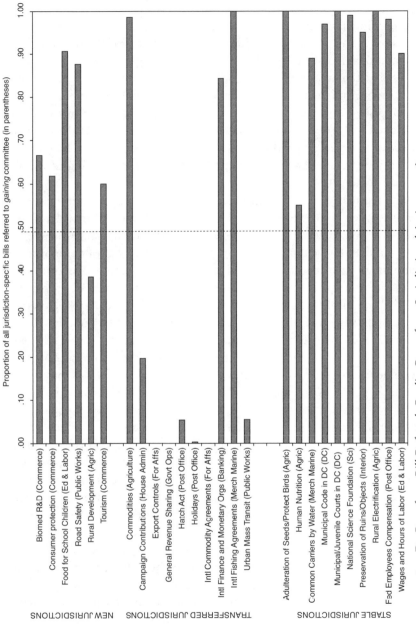

Proportion of all jurisdiction-specific bills referred to *gaining* committee (in parentheses)

NEW JURISDICTIONS

Biomed R&D (Commerce)
Consumer protection (Commerce)
Food for School Children (Ed & Labor)
Road Safety (Public Works)
Rural Development (Agric)
Tourism (Commerce)

TRANSFERRED JURISDICTIONS

Commodities (Agriculture)
Campaign Contributions (House Admin)
Export Controls (For Affs)
General Revenue Sharing (Govt Ops)
Hatch Act (Post Office)
Holidays (Post Office)
Intl Commodity Agreements (For Affs)
Intl Finance and Monetary Orgs (Banking)
Intl Fishing Agreements (Merch Marine)
Urban Mass Transit (Public Works)

STABLE JURISDICTIONS

Adulteration of Seeds/Protect Birds (Agric)
Human Nutrition (Agric)
Common Carriers by Water (Merch Marine)
Municipal Code in DC (DC)
Municipal/Juvenile Courts in DC (DC)
National Science Foundation (Sci)
Preservation of Ruins/Objects (Interior)
Rural Electrification (Agric)
Fed Employees Compensation (Post Office)
Wages and Hours of Labor (Ed & Labor)

FIGURE 6.1. Do Prereform Bill Referrals Predict Postreform Jurisdictional Assignments?

reforms did not modify preexisting referral patterns would confirm King's path-dependent account. Evidence of altered referral patterns would justify additional investigation of their effects.

As a starting point, we consider referral patterns for the ten "control" jurisdictions that were not affected by the Bolling-Hansen reforms. Our focus is on the preponderance of bill referrals (recall that we had to make a subjective judgment about whether a bill fell within the jurisdiction of interest or not based solely on its title). The bottom ten jurisdictions displayed in Figure 6.1 confirm that the committee of jurisdiction was receiving the greatest proportion of bill referrals we judged to be relevant to the jurisdiction. This is the expected pattern for meaningful formal jurisdictions.

The top-most section of Figure 6.1 examines prereform referral patterns for the six newly created jurisdictions in our sample (newly created jurisdictions represented about one-third of the fifty-eight total changes). Here we also find that the committee receiving the greatest number of prereform bill referrals was awarded the newly designated jurisdiction in five of the six cases. For example, the House Commerce committee received 67 percent of all Biomedical Research and Development (R&D) referrals before the jurisdiction was established. After it was awarded jurisdiction, the House Commerce Committee received 100 percent of all Biomedical R&D relevant referrals (not shown). These findings are consistent with what a path-dependent account would predict. Committees gain jurisdiction informally, and those practices are later codified through formal reforms.

However, the pattern for the more common cases of jurisdictional transfers is strikingly different (and these represent about two-thirds of the fifty-eight total changes adopted). In eight of the eleven transferred jurisdictions in our sample, the committee with the strongest precedent-based claim (based on prior referral patterns) was not awarded the transferred jurisdiction. Most of the time, the committee that gained the jurisdiction was receiving only a small proportion of relevant referrals prereform (typically less than 20%). For example, the Government Operations Committee did not receive any of the 172 General Revenue Sharing bills referred prior to 1973. When statutory control of Revenue Sharing was transferred from Ways and Means to Government Operations in 1975, its share of these bills increased from 0 percent to 100 percent (not shown).

Thus, for the more common cases of transfers, and unlike newly established and control jurisdictions, prereform referrals are a poor predictor of which committees benefited from transferred jurisdictions. These findings suggest that the effects of the Bolling-Hanson reforms did more than confirm existing referral practices. In many jurisdictions, there is compelling evidence to indicate that reform produced substantive changes in committee issue control. But what motivated these changes?

TESTING ALTERNATIVE MOTIVATIONS FOR REFORM

Several potential motivations for jurisdictional reforms can be gleaned from existing research, though none of them has been specifically applied to our question of interest. We consider four hypotheses: policy coordination, committee competition, constituency interest, and lawmaker interest. The first sees reforms as motivated by collective problem-solving objectives, while the latter three portray reforms as motivated by narrower concerns.

Policy Coordination

As discussed, proponents of reform claim to be promoting collectively beneficial problem-solving goals. This perspective predicts that the reforms will produce a better organized jurisdictional structure in order to "give coherent consideration to a number of pressing problems whose handling has been fragmented" (House Select Committee on Committees 1974, 1). We interpret the goal of improved policy coordination as implying that the reforms will unify responsibility for closely related jurisdictions in order to increase capacity, enhance information sharing, and reduce potential policy conflicts. This should apply not only to decisions about transfers but also to decisions about conferring newly created jurisdictions.

Committee Competition

Jones and colleagues (1993) argue that committee "issue monopolies" persist only to the extent that other committees choose to defer. The rise of new issues often draws attention to the fact that a given committee is out of step with the times, leading other committees to become active in the issue area (e.g., by holding nonlegislative hearings). This perspective suggests that evidence of jurisdictional poaching will precede jurisdictional transfers. More specifically, as more committees hold hearings in an issue area, a jurisdictional transfer becomes more likely.

Constituency Interest

Another possibility is that the objective or effect of jurisdictional reforms is to consolidate issue control in the hands of the members with the most to gain electorally (Shepsle 1978; Shepsle and Weingast 1987; Weingast and Marshall 1988). For example, King argues that formal reforms "institutionalize logrolls and make it easier to distribute benefits back home" (1994, 48). This perspective predicts that the committee that is ultimately awarded formal jurisdiction (newly established or transferred) will have a greater than expected constituency interest in the issue area.

Lawmaker Interest

A related possibility is that jurisdiction is awarded to the committee that demonstrates exceptional policy "interest" in the subject, regardless of motivation. King argues that committee members sponsor bills and hold hearings with the goal of expanding their jurisdictional turf. For example, Larry Evans (1999) argues that legislators value issue control because it increases their access to interest-group benefits. Perhaps indicators of issue interest can explain transfers as well as the awarding of new jurisdictions.

DATA AND FINDINGS

Our primary hypothesis is that the committee with control over closely related issues will be the beneficiary of jurisdictional transfers and newly created jurisdictions. Such a pattern would be indicative of an effort to consolidate issue responsibility in ways that promote problem solving. Testing this hypothesis requires a definition of "closely related" issues. Earlier we noted that we began to separate our eight thousand jurisdictionally relevant bills from more than one hundred thousand bills by first identifying the Policy Agendas Project subtopics that were likely to contain those bills. We then read the titles of all of these bills in order to identify those that fit the jurisdiction's description.

In the current analysis, we designate the committee most responsible for "closely related" jurisdictions as the one that was receiving most of the referrals of all other bills within these relevant subtopics. For example, the "Intergovernmental Relations" Policy Agendas Project subtopic contained every bill we determined to be within the General Revenue Sharing jurisdiction. However, the subtopic also included many other bills that we excluded as not relevant to General Revenue Sharing, such as those creating intergovernmental advisory commissions and proposing intergovernmental grants. These are the bills deemed "closely related" to the jurisdiction of interest.

The policy coordination hypothesis predicts that newly created and transferred jurisdictions will be awarded to the committee that received most closely related bill referrals prereform (i.e., bills within the same subtopic but not in the jurisdiction). In addition, this committee will also receive most postreform referrals of jurisdiction-specific bills.

Table 6.3 and Table 6.4 offer solid support for the policy coordination hypothesis.[5] The Bolling-Hansen reforms awarded every newly created jurisdiction and eight of the ten transferred jurisdictions to the committee most responsible for closely related issues. For instance, the Agriculture Committee picked up the Commodities jurisdiction in 1975. Prior to the reforms, 89 percent of the bills closely related to the Commodities jurisdiction – bills ranging from improvements to rice inspection to bills providing for small farm participation in the feed grain program – were being referred to Agriculture. When comparing this evidence to that in Figure 6.1 these findings do not support a path-dependent account. Prereform referrals of *closely related* bills are better predictors of jurisdictional reforms than prereform referrals of *jurisdiction-specific* bills. And as we would expect, the same patterns hold for the control jurisdictions (Table 6.4). In eight of these eleven cases, the committee of jurisdiction was also primarily responsible for closely related referrals.[6]

Can another theoretical perspective, specifically a turf-centered account, explain the same patterns as well as a problem-solving account? Jones and colleagues (1993) and others measure committee issue competition using the Herfindahl concentration score. Herfindahl scores have a theoretical range between 0 and 1, where lower values indicate that a wider array of committees are holding hearings on a given issue and thus evidence of competition among committees for issue control. We ask whether jurisdictions that were subsequently transferred experienced greater issue competition, prereform, compared to those that were not.

The ten unaltered jurisdictions constitute the baseline on the assumption that their stability reflects an absence of significant competition (Table 6.5). The Herfindahl scores average .74 for these jurisdictions, indicating highly concentrated prereform hearings activity. For transferred

---

[5] Three jurisdictions (Holidays, Rural Development, and Tourism) were deemed to have no closely related subtopics and thus were not included in this analysis.

[6] According to the routines of the Policy Agendas Project and Congressional Bills Project, tax- and tariff-related bills are coded into the substantive subtopics (rather than the taxation subtopic) whenever possible. Therefore, by our measure of closely related bills, the Ways and Means Committee ranks highly on the expertise scale for several jurisdictions because, consequently, tax and tariff bills are excluded from the analysis.

TABLE 6.3. *The Comparative "Expertise" of Committees Gaining Transferred and New Jurisdictions, 1965–1972*

Jurisdiction (Gaining Committee)	Closely Related Bills Referred to Gaining Committee	Closely Related Bills Referred to Losing Committee	Next Most Expert Committee	Closely Related Bills Referred to Next Most Expert Committee	Number of Bills "Closely Related" to Jurisdiction
Transferred Jurisdictions					
Commodities (Agriculture)	.89	.05	Judiciary	.06	483
Campaign Contributions (House Administration)	.51	.01	Judiciary	.26	339
Export Controls (Foreign Affairs)	.36	.01	Ways and Means	.27	136
General Revenue Sharing (Government Operations)	.30	.15	Judiciary	.19	346
Hatch Act (Post Office)	.66	.07	Ways and Means	.07	2,270
Holidays (Post Office)	–	–	–	–	–
International Commodity Agreements (Foreign Affairs)	.00	.96	Commerce	.03	224
International Finance and Monetary Organizations (Banking)	.83	.02	Ways and Means	.09	545
International Fishing Agreements (Merchant Marine)	.80	.00	Public Works	.07	1,020
Urban Mass Transit (Public Works)	.00	.29	Banking	.71	38
Weather (Science)	.69	.09	Merchant Marine	.13	159
Mean	.50	.17		.19	
New Jurisdictions					
Biomed R&D (Commerce)	.65	–	Ways and Means	.12	696
Consumer Protection (Commerce)	.50	–	Ways and Means	.29	66
Food for School Children (Education and Labor)	.56	–	Ways and Means	.20	578
Road Safety (Public Works)	.60	–	Ways and Means	.12	197
Rural Development (Agriculture)	–	–	–	–	–
Tourism (Commerce)	–	–	–	–	–
Mean	.58			.18	

Note: Cells in columns 2, 3, and 5 represent proportion of total "closely related" bills to each jurisdiction prior to the reforms. It is therefore a measure of the committee's prior expertise in closely related issue areas.

TABLE 6.4. *Committee of Jurisdiction "Expertise" for Stable Jurisdictions, 1965–1972*

Jurisdiction (Committee)	Closely Related Bills Referred to Committee	Number of Bills Closely Related to Jurisdiction
Adulteration of Seeds (Agriculture)	.74	199
Human Nutrition (Agriculture)	.50	156
Common Carriers (Merchant Marine)	.83	978
Municipal Code in D.C. (D.C.)	.84	1,061
Municipal/Juvenile Courts in D.C. (D.C.)	.85	1,144
National Science Foundation (Science)	.21	29
Preservation of Ruins (Interior)	.78	914
Collisions at Sea (Merchant Marine)	–	–
Rural Electrification (Agriculture)	.00	140
Federal Employee Compen. (Post Office)	.68	1,992
Wages and House of Labor (Education and Labor)	.90	80
Mean	.63	

jurisdictions, the average Herfindahls are essentially the same (.69). For newly created jurisdictions, prereform hearings activity is even more highly concentrated (.80). Thus, above average issue competition among committees does not appear to distinguish the jurisdictions that were transferred.

A related possibility is that reforms bring similar issues under the same committee umbrella, not to promote problem solving, but to place them in the hands of the most interested lawmakers. To investigate this possibility, we first ask whether the gaining committee was an "interest-outlier" relative to the chamber. Specifically, is there evidence to indicate an exceptionally high level of constituency interest in the jurisdiction compared to other committees?

Several of the jurisdictions do not have obviously measurable indicators of constituent's interests (e.g., Consumer Protection). Our measures of interest for nine of the seventeen jurisdictions come primarily from the *Congressional District Data Set* (Adler 2000; Adler and Lapinski 1997).[7] For example, for the Commodities jurisdiction we ask whether Agriculture Committee members have a greater district interest in the issue – measured as the median percentage of the district population living in rural farm areas – than the average committee.

---

[7] http://socsci.colorado.edu/~esadler/Congressional_District_Data.html.

TABLE 6.5. *Does Prereform Committee Competition (Herfindahl Scores) Motivate Jurisdictional Transfers?* 1965–1972

	Herfindahl Scores for Bill Referrals	Herfindahl Score for Days of Hearings	Total Days of Hearings
Stable Jurisdictions			
Adulterate Seeds/Protect Bird	1.00	.76	22
Municipal/Juvenile Courts in D.C.	1.00	1.00	26
Rural Electrification	1.00	.68	21
National Science Foundation	.98	.94	60
Federal Employees Compen.	.96	.67	360
Municipal Code in D.C.	.94	.65	171
Preservation of Ruins/Objects	.89	.52	19
Common Carriers by Water	.79	1.00	19
Wages and Hours of Labor	.79	.68	66
Human Nutrition	.39	.51	27
Mean	.87	.74	
Transferred Jurisdictions			
International Fishing Agreements	1.00	.86	13
General Revenue Sharing	.99	.67	19
Holidays and Celebrations	.98	1.00	4
Agricultural Commodities	.97	.91	87
Hatch Act	.90	–	0
Export Controls	.82	1.00	24
Weather Service	.75	.63	4
International Finance/Monetary Organizations	.72	.37	55
Urban Mass Transportation	.72	.51	22

International Commodity Agreements	.70	.40	34
Raising Campaign Contributions	.52	.51	9
Mean	**.82**	**.69**	
New Jurisdictions			
Roads and Safety	.82	1.00	46
Food Programs for Children	.77	.53	13
Biomedical R&D	.50	1.00	29
Travel and Tourism	.50	1.00	6
Consumer Protection	.42	.42	123
Rural Development	.41	.85	42
Mean	**.57**	**.80**	
F-test Stable vs. Transferred	.455 (p = 0.835)	.421 (p = 0.837)	
F-test New vs. Transferred	122.4 (p = 0.068)	7.90 (p = 0.114)	

Note: The Herfindahl index is the sum of the squared proportions of each jurisdiction's hearings or bill referrals by committee [Herfindahl index = $(S_1)^2 + (S_2)^2 + (S_3)^2 + \ldots + (S_n)^2$]. Herfindahl scores approaching o indicate that activity is more dispersed across committees (more competition), while Herfindahl scores approaching 1 indicate less dispersed activity (less competition).

TABLE 6.6. *Are Transferred Jurisdictions Awarded to Committees with Disproportionate Constituency Interests?*

Jurisdictional Change (measure of interest)	Chamber Median	Gaining Committee Median	P-value	Losing Committee Median	P-value
New Jurisdictions					
Rural Development (% of district living in rural farm areas)	1.72	9.47 (Agriculture)	.00	—	—
Roads and Safety (% of district employed in construction)	5.71	6.33 (Public Works)	.01	—	—
Food Programs for School Children (median family income)	$9,566.75	$10,130.00 (Education and Labor)	.92	—	—
Transferred Jurisdictions					
Agricultural Commodities (% of district employed in farming)	1.51	8.02 (Agriculture)	.00	0.35 (Banking)	.99
Export Controls (% of district employed in manufacturing)	9.50	10.43 (Foreign Affairs)	.17	(Banking)	.24
General Revenue Sharing (total revenue sharing to state)	$450 million	$570 million (Government Operations)	.40	$610 million (Ways and Means)	.26
Hatch Act (% of district employed by federal government)	1.24	1.00 (Post Office)	.50	1.00 (House Administration)	.84
International Commodity Agreements (% of district employed in farming)	1.51	1.17 (Foreign Affairs)	.72	8.02 (Agriculture)	.00
Urban Mass Transportation (% of district using public transport for work)	1.16	0.92 (Public Works)	.84	4.02 (Banking)	.00

Note: All analyses are Monte Carlo difference-in-medians test (see Adler and Lapinski 1997; Groseclose 1994), except General Revenue Sharing. General Revenue Sharing is a Wilcoxon rank sum test because of the use of state-level data.

TABLE 6.7. *Are Transferred Jurisdictions Awarded to Committees Expressing Disproportionate Interest?*

	Mean Bills Sponsored by Entire Chamber	Marginal Effect of Membership on Gaining Committee	P-value
New Jurisdictions			
Consumer Protection	1.06	2.50	0.00
Food Programs for Children	0.13	0.60	0.00
Roads and Safety	0.57	1.53	0.00
Rural Development	0.34	1.15	0.00
Biomedical R&D	0.07	0.21	0.04
Travel and Tourism	0.10	0.22	0.09
Transferred Jurisdictions			
Agricultural Commodities	0.54	1.84	0.00
International Finance/Monetary Organizations	0.05	0.51	0.00
Urban Mass Transportation	0.28	−0.08	0.00
International Fishing Agreements	0.07	0.25	0.01
Hatch Act	0.05	0.15	0.16
International Commodity Agreements	0.07	0.15	0.16
Holidays and Celebrations	0.43	0.64	0.17
Raising Campaign Contributions	0.10	0.20	0.21
Export Controls	0.13	0.20	0.34
Weather Service	0.07	0.13	0.35
General Revenue Sharing	0.23	0.18	0.52

Note: "Mean bills sponsored" is the average number of bills sponsored per member of the 93rd Congress in each jurisdiction for the eight years prior to the reforms. The "marginal effect" coefficient is generated by regressing (using a Poisson distribution) the number of jurisdiction-specific bills that every legislator sponsored in the same period on whether or not she or he was a member of the committee that subsequently gained the jurisdiction.

Instead of simply comparing the reformed and control cases, or the gaining committee to the losing one in cases of transfers, we ask whether the gaining committee's interest level was significantly greater than the average committee. This approach raises the bar in terms of making rejection of the constituency interest hypothesis less likely (Adler and Lapinski 1997; Groseclose 1994).

Nevertheless, the evidence presented in Table 6.6 indicates that in only three of the nine jurisdictions was the gaining committee a clear interest outlier. Moreover, in two of the remaining six cases (International Commodities and Urban Mass Transit), the most interested committee actually lost the jurisdiction. Taken together, these findings suggest that constituency-based motivations may explain why reform efforts fail (Adler 2002), but they do not appear to explain why jurisdictional reforms succeed.

A final possibility is that reforms reward member interest that is not necessarily constituency driven. We measure this kind of committee interest in terms of prereform bill-sponsor activity. Specifically, we regress the number of jurisdictionally relevant bills a given member sponsors during the prereform period against whether he or she was a member of the committee that later gained the jurisdiction.[8] A positive coefficient indicates that members of the gaining committee demonstrated above average interest in the issue area.

Table 6.7 indicates that committee member interest helps to predict the assignment of newly created jurisdictions, but not the more common cases of transfers. In only three of the transfer cases did the gaining committee's members sponsor significantly more jurisdictionally relevant bills. In one case (Mass Transit), the gaining committee was significantly less interested in the issue area prior to the reforms than other legislators.

MULTIVARIATE REGRESSION ANALYSIS

The previous analyses focused on a relatively small number of statutory jurisdictional reforms. In this section, we turn our attention to predicting a standing committee's share of postreform bill referrals within a given jurisdiction – its de facto jurisdictional control. This provides an opportunity to test the same hypotheses head-to-head. The dependent variable is the proportion of postreform bill referrals to each of twenty House

---

[8] We employ a Poisson distribution because the dependent variable is a count of bills.

TABLE 6.8. *Testing Alternative Explanations for Postreform Bill Referrals*

	Coefficient	S. E.
Prereform Bill Referrals	0.114	0.109
Prereform Bill Sponsorship	0.116	0.097
Prereform Hearings Activity	0.263*	0.113
Prereform Referral of "Close By" Bills	0.615*	0.123
Constant	0.015	0.037
Number of Observations	540	
R-squared	0.733	

Note: * = $p < .05$.

committees for all twenty-seven jurisdictions in our sample (n = 540).[9] The independent variables predicting the proportion of referrals a committee receives are drawn from those used to test most of the alternative hypotheses considered in the previous section: prereform bill referrals (path dependence), prereform referrals of closely related bills (problem solving), prereform hearings activity (committee interest), and prereform bill-sponsor activity (member interest). We are not able to test the constituency interest hypothesis against the other hypotheses for reasons noted earlier.

Table 6.8 reports results for an OLS multivariate regression model with robust standard errors.[10] Only two coefficients for independent variables are significant and in the correct direction – prereform referrals of closely related bills (problem solving) and prereform hearings activity (committee interest) within the jurisdiction. Prereform bill referrals (path dependence) and bill-sponsor activity (member interest) do not consistently predict postreform bill referrals (after controlling for the other independent variables). These findings suggest that policy coordination and (one form of) committee interest best explain bill-referral patterns after jurisdictional reforms.

However, the fact that some of the independent variables are colinear suggests the need for additional robustness tests.[11] We conduct two follow-up tests. An extreme-bounds analysis assesses the fragility of each independent variable to the inclusion of other variables into the model

[9] Budget and Rules are excluded because these panels have narrow jurisdictions and do not normally consider regular legislation.
[10] Robust standard errors are used to address issues of normality or homogeneity of residual variance. We also include fixed-effects indicators for both committees and jurisdictions.
[11] Although the variance inflation factors are in the moderate range, none goes above 7.

TABLE 6.9. *Extreme-Bounds Analysis of Alternative Explanations for Postreform Bill Referrals*

Variable	Minimum Value (S. E.)	Maximum Value (S. E.)	Average Value	Proportion Significant ($p < .05$)
Prereform Bill Referrals	0.114 (0.109)	0.637 (0.080)	0.291	0.50
Prereform Bill Sponsorship	0.116 (0.097)	1.181 (0.120)	0.411	0.63
Prereform Hearings Activity	0.263 (0.113)	0.710 (0.078)	0.432	1.00
Prereform Referral of "Close By" Bills	0.615 (0.1240	1.027 0.076	0.741	1.00

(Leamer 1983; Levine and Renelt 1992). Table 6.9 confirms that the same two variables (prereform closely related bill referrals and prereform hearings activity) are robust predictors of postreform referrals. Finally, the J-test of variance encompassing (sometimes referred to as the Cox test) tests whether a rival variable retains explanatory power in a model when a variable of interest is included (Granato and Suzuki 1996; Greene 2007). When the independent variables are paired against one another (analysis not shown), only prereform referrals of closely related bills (the problem-solving hypothesis) encompassed all of the other explanations. That is, after controlling for the explanatory power of this indicator of problem-solving motivations for reform, the inclusion of the other independent variables provides no additional explanatory power.

THE BROADER CONSEQUENCES OF THE BOLLING-HANSEN REFORMS

Finally, the broader question: did the reforms produce a better organized committee system overall? Specifically, did they produce a less confused and scattered committee structure that reformers envisioned? Or did the restructuring have no detectable consequences of congressional issue control as others have suggested? Entropy is a widely used measure in the physical sciences of disorganization in a system (Chaffee and Wilson 1977; McCombs and Zhu 1995; Shannon, Weaver, and Shannon 1998). It has also been used to study political organization as well (Jones and Baumgartner 2005; Talbert and Potoski 2002). Entropy is similar to the Herfindahl measure, except that lower (not higher) entropy values indicate better organization. Formally, entropy (H) is defined as:

$$H = \Sigma \ [p(x)\log(p(x))] \equiv - \Sigma \ [p(x)\log(p(x))].$$

Where x represents an object, $p(x)$ is the probability that the object falls within a particular category, summed across all categories.[12] Thus, if every object of the same type (e.g., closely related bills) is found in the same category (e.g., referred to the same committee), then the system is perfectly organized and entropy is zero. A system is less organized if the objects of the same type (closely related bills) are found in different categories (referred to different committees) and entropy is higher.

The question of interest is whether jurisdictional entropy declined as a result of the Bolling-Hansen reforms. A decline in average entropy (i.e., referrals of bills within each of 226 subtopics capturing closely related bills) between the prereform 94th Congress (1975–6) and the postreform 95th Congress (1977–8) would indicate that the reforms helped to promote a measurably improved committee structure for problem solving. Figure 6.2 displays this average jurisdictional entropy for the period from the 80th to the 105th Congress (1947–98). There is a very evident decline in entropy from the 94th to the 95th Congresses (1975–8), just as the reforms took effect. Average entropy declines by one-third, confirming that the Bolling-Hansen reforms produced a committee structure where control over similar issues became much less "scattered." Importantly, the figure indicates a second (though less dramatic) decline in jurisdictional entropy in the 104th Congress (1995–6). This corresponds to the adoption of another set of jurisdictional reforms by the newly elected Republican majority.

Figure 6.2 also displays entropy including and excluding bills that were referred to more than one committee postreform (multiple referrals).[13] Not surprisingly, jurisdictional fragmentation (entropy) is lower when these bills are excluded. This raises the question of why reformers who sought to consolidate control over related issues would also pass a reform that permitted the Speaker to refer a bill to multiple committees for the first time. We believe that the two reforms are closely linked. Consolidating issue control reduces flexibility where it is sometimes

[12] Because logarithms are undefined at 0, and many categories will have 0 entries, we added a very small fraction (.000001) to the actual proportions (estimates for $p(x)$).

[13] The Bolling-Hansen reforms also permitted bills to be referred to multiple committees rather than just one for the first time in the House.

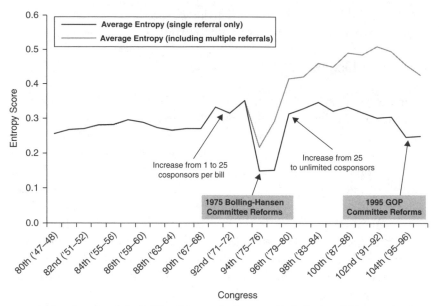

FIGURE 6.2. Impact of the Bolling-Hansen Reforms on Jurisdictional Disorganization (Entropy).

needed. The multiple referral option provides an alternative outlet – a safety valve – for less common complex issues that cut across tightened jurisdictional boundaries (Davidson, Oleszek, and Kephart 1988, 5).

Figure 6.2 also contains an unexpected puzzle. Entropy increases dramatically just a couple of congresses after the reforms (the 97th Congress: 1981–2). Does this indicate that the benefits of the reform were short-lived? Not likely. There are two such spikes – one in the 97th and one in the 91st Congress (1969–70). These spikes correspond to two other procedural changes. The 91st Congress saw cosponsorship of bills permitted for the first time (to a maximum of 25 per bill). The twenty-five-cosponsor limit was then eliminated in the 96th Congress (1979–80) (Wilson and Young 1997). Both of these reforms reduced the number of duplicate bills introduced.[14] If fewer bills are introduced and the reductions are not proportionate across subtopics, then entropy may increase without any corresponding change in bill referral patterns. The 97th Congress experienced the sharpest reduction in bill introductions – a 50 percent decrease and a correspondingly larger increase in entropy compared to the 91st Congress.

[14] A graphic can be found at http://congressionalbills.org/identicals.htm (accessed January 31, 2012).

CONCLUSION

This chapter argues that a problem-solving perspective provides a more compelling explanation for why Congress has reformed its committee system in the past. Prior studies have focused on the controversy surrounding reform efforts, without systematically examining their effects (Adler 2002; Davidson and Oleszek 1977; Evans and Oleszek 1997; Rieselbach 1994; Sheppard 1985; Wolfensberger 2004). Although the most ambitious plans are typically swept aside (perhaps appropriately so), scholars have been too quick to conclude that controversy implies that little was accomplished. We carefully examined the most significant set of committee jurisdictional reforms enacted during the twentieth century and found that the greatest measured improvements in House jurisdictional organization over the past sixty years coincide with two sets of formal reforms adopted in the 95th (1977–8) and 104th Congresses (1995–6).

The findings of this chapter do not imply that reform efforts always succeed, or that jurisdictions always end up in the hands of the most qualified committees. They also support much of what King (1994, 1997) discovered in his careful examination of House Commerce Committee politics. However, they do challenge the conventional view that committee reform efforts are ineffectual at best and counterproductive to the pursuit of collective goals at worst. Rather than reinforcing the status quo, the Bolling-Hanson reforms produced measurable changes that correspond to the stated goals of the reformers of the time. Congress directly addressed problems of jurisdictional drift that are an inevitable part of a changing society and the "turf wars" King and others describe.

The failure of a reform effort may also reflect valid problem-solving considerations. In the beginning of this chapter, we noted that opponents of reform during the more recent debate over Homeland Security jurisdiction argued that preserving existing jurisdictional arrangements was the best way to preserve institutional expertise. Whereas prior studies of legislative reform have highlighted the political considerations that discourage change and promote institutional decay, our findings demonstrate that legislators recognize the downside of such dynamics for legislative problem solving and are willing to act in a collective fashion to counteract them.

7

Agenda Setting in a Problem-Solving Legislature

> Most bills that become law do so after a fight for space in the calendar
> rather than a fight with an opposition of a more direct kind.
>
> Arthur Bentley (1908, 493)

Why do some lawmakers sponsor more successful bills than others? In
this chapter, we argue that a bill's issue content is crucial to appreciating its progress. Certain issues must be addressed. Expiring programs
must be renewed and Congress must respond to external events. Scarce
agenda space means that attention to these "compulsory" issues sup-
plants opportunities to take up other matters (Walker 1977). More often
than is generally appreciated, successful bill sponsorship is less suggestive of a sponsor's entrepreneurial skills, and more indicative of a policy
caretaking process.

For nearly fifty years, the common metric political scientists have
used to assess legislative effectiveness has been the progress of the bills
a lawmaker sponsors. Most of these studies assume that a bill's progress
is indicative of the ability of individual lawmakers to advance their policy priorities. William Anderson and colleagues nicely capture this line
of thought when they ask: "What 'remarkable skills' allow some legislators to guide their bills successfully out of committee, and perhaps out
of the House, while others are routinely met with legislative defeat?"
(2003, 357).

The prospect of sponsoring a successful bill is central to appreciating why committee members invest in such collectively beneficial policy-
making activities. Most lawmakers will fail to sponsor even a single
successful bill in a given Congress, much less one of profound policy

significance. When committees address high-priority issues, the reward for the lawmaker who takes primary responsibility for managing an issue is often sponsorship of the bill that is the vehicle for the committee markup process. These vehicles are exceptionally attractive opportunities for lawmakers to tout their effectiveness at home because they are far more likely to pass than a typical bill.

This problem-solving explanation for bill-sponsor success highlights collective governing responsibilities rather than individual preferences and entrepreneurship. To test the evidence for these alternative perspectives, we first classify more than twenty thousand bills introduced over four congresses according to the type of issue addressed (building on the issue typology first developed in Chapter 5). The substance of bills has not been a central variable of interest in prior studies. We next examine the issue agenda at different stages of the legislative process (bill introductions, bills reported out of committee, roll call voting) before turning our attention to systematically testing alternative explanations of bill success. Our findings clearly demonstrate important patterns of success for different types of bills. "Compulsory" issues make up a large proportion of the bills passed by the House. For bills addressing such issues, the only significant predictor of success is whether the sponsor is a member of the committee of jurisdiction. This finding provides important support for the theoretical arguments presented in Chapters 4 and 5. Committee members who invest in core committee issues are rewarded with truly distinctive credit-claiming opportunities.

For less pressing (i e , "discretionary" issues), other sponsor characteristics (such as majority party membership or specialization) are significant predictors of bill success, but discretionary bills also make up a smaller proportion of overall legislative output. In addition, our typology further differentiates bills addressing minor issues as a third category. The progress of these bills is governed by yet another set of dynamics. Overall, this chapter provides a more holistic view of the issue agenda-setting process – one that draws renewed attention to lawmaking as a committee-centered problem-solving process.

EXISTING RESEARCH ON BILL SUCCESS

To appreciate why this chapter is important, it is necessary to first appreciate how bill progress in Congress is currently portrayed. This is a subject with a remarkably long history in legislative scholarship. Interestingly, the first systematic study argued that bill success offered insights into broader institutional processes. In his study of Senate folkways, Donald Matthews concluded that senators who played by the rules (i.e., adhered to institutional norms) were more legislatively successful (1960, 114–17, 278–9). In a follow-up study, David Olson and Cynthia Nonidez (1972) reported that adherence to institutional norms did not appear to affect bill-sponsor success in the House. Subsequent studies then began to test whether a wide variety of sponsor characteristics were related to bill success, including (but not limited to) legislative activism, ideological moderation, experience, gender, specialization, majority party membership, and leadership position (Anderson, Box-Steffensmeier, and Sinclair-Chapman 2003; Baughman 2003; Cox and Terry 2008; Frantzich 1979; Hasecke and Mycoff 2007; Koger and Fowler 2006; Krutz 2005; Volden and Wiseman 2009). A smaller set of studies have tested theories of legislative organization (Baughman 2003; Cox and Terry 2008; Hasecke and Mycoff 2007; Koger and Fowler 2006; Krutz 2005), but with the same underlying assumption that a bill's progress is indicative of a lawmaker's ability to advance personal policy goals.

A focus on the success of individual sponsors fits the popular narrative about "how a bill becomes a law." Yet the progress of many bills obviously transcends the sponsor's entrepreneurial skills (Wawro 2000). Congress passes appropriations bills every year because failing to do so would lead to a politically unacceptable government shutdown. That some issues, such as appropriations, are different is not novel. In *Unorthodox Lawmaking*, Sinclair finds that bills addressing important issues sometimes follow a different path to the floor (Krutz 2001; Sinclair 2007). However, the extent to which the paths of bills vary by issue has received limited attention. As a result, the conventional wisdom seems to be that "must pass" legislation is relatively rare and therefore not central to understanding why bills progress more broadly.

PROBLEM SOLVING, POLICY CARETAKING, AND THE LEGISLATIVE ISSUE AGENDA

When lawmakers return to their districts "they describe, interpret, and justify their pursuit of power and their pursuit of policy in Washington. Explanations concerning their power pursuits focus on their legislative effectiveness" (Fenno 1978, 137; see also Lipinski 2004; Yiannakis 1982). Voters cite effectiveness as a central reason for liking or disliking the incumbent (Jacobson 2009), and in Chapter 2 we found that lawmakers are aware of the importance of their accomplishments in constituent evaluations.

But, when lawmakers claim to be effective, what is the source of their effectiveness? During five terms in office, Rep. Dennis Eckart (D-OH) sponsored forty-three bills on subjects ranging from trucking safety to the regulation of professional sports teams. However, his legislative successes were limited to just three bills, each of which addressed the topic of hazardous waste. How did Eckart become interested in hazardous waste and why was he so much more successful here than for other issues? According to Eckart, House Energy and Commerce Chair John Dingell (D-MI) encouraged him to focus on the Superfund reauthorization. As chair, Dingell would find "some eager beaver who is looking to make a name for himself ... and who is willing to really work on a bill.... He had the role of convener and sometimes he was the shotgun behind the door" (Stanfield 1988, 792). Given a choice between promoting a personal policy goal that (statistically speaking) has a small chance of success and working toward a collective policy objective where success is almost assured, many lawmakers will opt for the latter. When a policy caretaker like Eckart sponsors a committee bill such as the Superfund reauthorization, he or she can credibly claim, "I put that bill through committee" (Mayhew 1974, 92).

A problem-solving account portrays bill-sponsor success as a valuable credit-claiming opportunity that motivates committee members to promote collective policy objectives. Bill-sponsor success is more a reflection of an institutionalized problem-solving process than it is of a lawmaker's entrepreneurial skills. Consider these three examples of successful lawmakers. The most noteworthy accomplishment of Rep. Romano Mazzoli's (D-KY) legislative career was the 1986 Simpson-Mazzoli Act (P.L. 99-603), which granted amnesty to certain illegal immigrants who entered the United States before 1982 and was the first law to require employers to attest to their employees' immigration status. Senator Slade Gorton's (R-WA) signal legislative accomplishment, the Shipping Act of 1984 (P.L. 98-237), has been described as one of the most important commercial shipping industry reforms of the twentieth century. During his long tenure in Congress, Rep. Bud Shuster (R-PA) took the lead on numerous air transportation issues. Of particular importance was Shuster's sponsorship of the monumental FAA reauthorization of 2000 (P.L.106-181).

Little in these lawmakers' backgrounds or districts would have predicted these accomplishments. Rep. Mazzoli's Kentucky district included few immigrants. Sen. Gorton knew nothing about maritime issues when he was first elected to the Senate.[1] The largest airport in Rep. Shuster's central Pennsylvania district ranked a lowly 366th in the United States in 2000 for passenger traffic, and by 2009 it had declined to 429th.

What these lawmakers did share in common were institutional responsibilities. Shuster's aviation activities stemmed from the fact that the House Transportation Committee, of which he was a member and eventual chair, was charged with overseeing the renewal of important aviation laws. Mazzoli was encouraged to take a lead in crafting immigration policy by the longtime chair of the Judiciary Committee, Rep. Peter Rodino (D-NJ; Perry 2007, 28). As a freshman senator in 1981, Gorton immediately jumped into the position of subcommittee chair due to a change in Senate partisan control. Researching the responsibilities of his new committee, he learned that shipping regulations were in dire need of reform (Hughes 2011). In each of these examples, the issue came first. The legislator who played a central role in managing it received most of the credit for its progress.

DECONSTRUCTING THE LEGISLATIVE ISSUE AGENDA

To systematically investigate whether bill-sponsor success varies depending on the type of issue, we first categorize bills by issue type. Earlier we portrayed the legislative agenda as a continuum of issues ranging from "compulsory" to "discretionary" agenda items. We anticipate that agenda scarcity and compulsory issue demands leave limited opportunities for legislatures to take up such discretionary issues.

For the purposes of this book, discerning the true proportions of the agenda that are devoted to compulsory and discretionary issues is of less importance than discovering whether such a typology provides valuable insights into lawmaking. Do we observe different patterns of deliberation and success that are consistent with our theoretical expectations? Our typology differs slightly from that proposed by Walker, who was only concerned with what made it onto the agenda. Because one of our goals

[1] Personal communication with the senator, October 2010.

FIGURE 7.1. A Typology of Congressional Bills.

is to compare the bills introduced to bills that progress, our typology includes two main categories of legislation (Figure 7.1). The first, "compulsory" legislation, includes bills that address recurring and pressing issues. The second category, "discretionary" legislation, includes all other bills. In this respect it is more encompassing than Walker's "chosen" category, because it also includes (noncompulsory) bills that were not selected for consideration by the chamber. We next briefly describe how these two main categories are operationalized. Additional details can be found in Appendix B.

Compulsory Issues

This category includes bills addressing recurring issues and bills addressing salient and important issues. Legislation addressing expiring laws or provisions were discussed in detail in Chapter 5. Here we focus on the "pressing problems" that Walker and others argue create a collective sense of urgency for legislative action. The notion that visible or salient events – what Walter Lippmann (1922) termed "the pictures in our heads" – can move issues onto the political agenda is familiar to scholars (Baumgartner and Jones 1993; Iyengar and Kinder 2010; McCombs and Shaw 1972; Page and Shapiro 1992; Schattschneider 1960).

Examples of crises compelling congressional action are easy to come by. However, they need not be as visible as the Exxon Valdez oil spill in 1989 or the terrorist attacks of September 11, 2001, to induce a legislative response. For example, a sharp increase in gas prices in 2008 substantially reduced federal gas tax revenues (as demand for gas declined). This development threatened to drain the federal highway trust fund, prompting Congress to enact legislation transferring $8 billion from the general fund. Had this additional money not been made available, thousands of road construction projects would have ground to a halt. As Rep. John Lewis (D-GA) explained, "We must act. The trust fund is broke, out of money. Our state and local governments, drivers, construction workers and many others suffer when highway projects are delayed" (Abrams 2008).

How and why issues become salient is an important topic that is deserving of more attention (Birkland 1997). Our main interest is in whether salient events often create pressure for legislative action. Furthermore, finite agenda space means that legislative attention to salient issues means fewer opportunities to take up other issues. We anticipate that committees will play a more central role in managing how Congress responds to salient issues than is true for discretionary issues. Committees possess *ex ante* information that helps to ensure effective and timely responses to pressing problems.

To identify salient and important issues, we turn to the *Congressional Quarterly Almanac* (hereafter *CQ*). Others have relied on *CQ* coverage to assess the importance of laws (Anderson, Box-Steffensmeier, and Sinclair-Chapman 2003; Carson, Finocchiaro, and Rohde 2010; Edwards, Barrett, and Peake 1997; Mayhew 1991; Stimson, Mackuen, and Erikson 1995). However, *CQ* also reports on issues as well as enactments. According to its editors, *CQ* provides "[a]n unbiased look at the issues that *mattered most* in a given year."[2] Thus, coverage in *CQ* is a valuable proxy for the importance of an issue in the legislative domain (in the judgment of elite observers). A bill is considered to be important if it (or a related bill) is discussed in *CQ* regardless of whether it came to a vote or not.[3] We anticipate that legislative responses to issues covered in *CQ* are more likely to be committee centered than is the case for other issues.

Discretionary Issues

Bills that do not address expiring laws or one of the issues covered in *CQ* are included in this category. Because they do not address high-priority matters from the perspective of the legislature as a whole we anticipate that success will be less committee centered. We further distinguish discretionary bills into two groups, "ordinary" and "minor," to test the possibility that success where minor bills (such as commemorative legislation, building designations, and land transfers) are concerned is

---

[2] Description from online archive of *CQ Almanac*, emphasis added. Carson et al. 2010 cite similar observations from a variety of scholars who have employed *CQ* for the same enterprise.

[3] Any other bill that was considered "related" to the bills mentioned in *CQ*, according to the Congressional Research Service on its THOMAS Web site was included to ensure that all tangential and "unsuccessful" versions of the bills are deemed important.

shaped by different considerations than is the case for more important discretionary bills. Specifically, we anticipate that minor issues do not require the same level of scrutiny, or incur the same level of controversy, as other discretionary bills. As a result, success for minor bills will tend to be more frequent and widespread than is true for more significant discretionary bills.

THE LEGISLATIVE ISSUE AGENDA

Figure 7.2 applies this issue typology to all public bills sponsored in the House of Representatives across four congressional terms (101st–104th Congresses, 1989–96). As with the more limited analysis of Chapter 5 (Figure 5.3), the figure summarizes the agenda at three different stages of deliberation. The first bar reports the breakdown of bills that the legislature might have addressed (i.e., all introduced bills). Of these, only 14 percent addressed compulsory issues while the vast majority (86%) treated discretionary issues. However, the patterns change as we observe later stages in legislative deliberation. For the bills that pass the chamber, compulsory issues make up the majority (55%) of such legislative proposals. Finally, turning to a measure of floor activity to assess chamber allocation of attention, about 90 percent of all roll call votes occur during consideration of compulsory issues, compared to just 10 percent for discretionary issues (and as expected, the success rate for minor discretionary bills is more than twice as high as that for other discretionary bills).

Although we will never be able to precisely estimate the proportion of the agenda devoted to compulsory issues because the categories are imprecise, Figure 7.2 confirms our broader expectations. The same patterns emerge for the indisputably exogenous indicator of compulsory issues (expiring laws) as for the more endogenous and less ideal *CQ* indicator of pressing or important issues. In contrast, only a small proportion of (nonminor) discretionary bills advance. On average, legislators who sponsor bills addressing compulsory issues are 900 percent more likely to see their bills succeed than those who sponsor bills addressing discretionary issues.

RECURRING LEGISLATION AND COMMITTEE RESPONSIBILITY

We anticipate that there will be a strong correspondence between committee role and issue type. Compulsory issues appear to make up a large

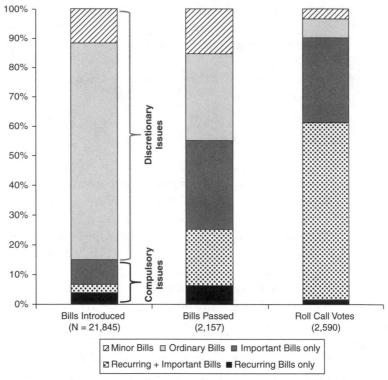

FIGURE 7.2. The Composition of the House Agenda at Different Stages of the Legislative Process.

Note: 101st–104th Congresses. The two categories of compulsory bills – recurring and important – overlap because recurring issues are often considered important enough to be covered in *CQ Almanac* as described in Appendix B.

proportion of the legislative agenda. Is it also the case that these issues are managed differently – in line with our problem-solving account? As a first cut at this question, we consider the views of congressional insiders: congressional staff. In 2004 the Annenberg Public Policy Center surveyed more than 250 House and Senate staff members. They were asked to name a specific bill they or their members worked on that made it to the floor in the 108th Congress (2003–4). They were then asked, "What role did the majority party leadership play in developing the bill that came to the floor? Did they make the main decisions, just give the committee guidelines, or leave the decisions to the committee?" This questionnaire provides an opportunity to compare the roles of party leaders and committees for different types of issues. Specifically, we anticipate that for

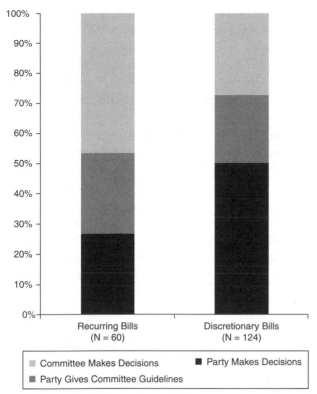

FIGURE 7.3. Staff Perceptions of Committee versus Party Influence for Different Types of Legislation.
Note: The figure is based on the staffer's assessment of a particular bill with which she or he was closely involved.
Source: 2004 Annenberg Survey of Congressional Staff, authors.

recurring issues staff will report that the party leadership played a less important role, and the committee of jurisdiction played a more important role in developing the legislation. This would be reflective of our "committees as policy caretakers" argument.

We were able to identify a specific bill for 184 of the 250 responses.[4] Figure 7.3 compares the reported influence of party and committee for bills addressing recurring issues (first bar) and discretionary issues

---

[4] The remaining respondents either did not offer a bill, gave a response that was too vague to pinpoint a specific bill for coding ("education," e.g.), or answered "don't know" to the party versus committee question.

(second bar). Fully half of the respondents said that the party had made the main decisions when the issue was discretionary, while the party left decisions to the committee about 25 percent of the time. As expected, this pattern reverses when the referenced bill addresses an expiring law. Nearly half said the party left the committee to its own devices, while one-quarter said that the party leadership made the main decisions. Thus, congressional staff make the same distinctions in terms of how recurring/ discretionary issues are managed that we hypothesize will emerge from a statistical analysis of bill-sponsor success. In the next section we turn our attention to that analysis.

REASONS FOR BILL-SPONSOR SUCCESS

To reiterate, where compulsory issues are concerned, committee of juris-diction membership should be the central predictor of sponsor success due to the fact that committee membership offers opportunities for individ-ual lawmakers to secure much of the credit for collective outputs. As a result, committee members are more willing to make sustained invest-ments in policy-making activities that have significant positive externalities. Committee leaders will reap a larger share of these credit-claiming oppor-tunities for similar reasons. Committee leaders possess disproportionate resources and agenda authority, are highly experienced in the affairs of the committee, and are the ones who are ultimately accountable to the chamber for panel performance and output (Evans 1991; Fenno 1973; Hall 1996, 86). The collective benefits of policy caretaking should be less important where bills addressing discretionary issues are concerned. As a result, other sponsor characteristics, such as those previously associated with greater legislative effectiveness, should contribute to whether a bill progresses.

Dependent Variable – Bill Passage

Prior studies of legislative effectiveness measure success in different ways. One approach has been to focus on the batting averages or "hit rates" of individual lawmakers (Jeydel and Taylor 2003; Matthews 1960; Moore and Thomas 1991) or more simply counts of bills reported or passed (Anderson, Box-Steffensmeier, and Sinclair-Chapman 2003; Cox and Terry 2008; Frantzich 1979; Hasecke and Mycoff 2007). A second general approach has been to examine the progress of individual bills, with the goal of identifying the common attributes of the sponsors of the successful bills (Baughman 2003; Koger and Fowler 2006; Krutz 2005;

Sinclair 2001; Volden and Wiseman 2009). The latter approach is more conducive to answering the questions posed here. Tracking the progress of individual bills allows us to simultaneously distinguish the effects of sponsor and bill characteristics. Were we to focus on sponsor hit rates, it would be much more difficult to control for the issue type. The dependent variable is therefore a dichotomous indicator of whether or not a House bill introduced during the 101st–104th Congresses was passed by the chamber.

Independent Variables

Policy Caretaking Hypothesis
Committee of Jurisdiction Membership. The primary indicator of whether policy caretaking is being rewarded is whether the sponsors of successful bills addressing compulsory issues are members of the committee of jurisdiction.[5] Being a leader of such a committee should be even more important. Less clear is the impact of party status in committee. Given the demands facing the legislature and the fact that lawmakers often share a collective interest in addressing compulsory issues, problem solving would seem to suggest a less partisan process. We therefore also distinguish committee members for majority or minority party leadership and majority or minority committee rank and file.

Legislative Effectiveness Hypotheses
As discussed, extant research finds a large number of sponsor characteristics to be related to greater legislative effectiveness as measured by the progress of bills. We include the most important of these in our analyses.

Party Affiliation. To the extent that parties behave as cartels to control the legislative agenda, bills sponsored by majority party members should not only be more successful, minority party members should have no successes. Majority party status is commonly found to be the most important predictor of legislative effectiveness. We distinguish noncommittee majority party members in addition to our previous distinction between majority and minority committee members. The omitted category, therefore, is a minority party member who is not on the committee of jurisdiction.

---

[5] When a bill is referred to multiple committees ("multiple referrals"), the sponsor is deemed to be a committee member if she or he serves on any referral committee.

Ideology. Existing studies also commonly incorporate a measure of sponsor ideology (Anderson, Box-Steffensmeier, and Sinclair-Chapman 2003; Cox and Terry 2008; Frantzich 1979; Hasecke and Mycoff 2007; Jeydel and Taylor 2003; Krutz 2005). The assumption is that bills sponsored by moderate lawmakers – those closer to the chamber median – are more likely to succeed because they are more moderate in substance. Partisan theories, in contrast, would seem to predict greater success when a majority party sponsor possesses preferences that lie closer to the majority party (as opposed to chamber) median. We measure ideological distance as the absolute difference between the first dimension DW-NOMINATE scores of the sponsor and the chamber (or party) median (*Distance from Chamber Median, Distance from Majority Party Median*).[6]

Seniority. Lawmakers who possess greater legislative experience and broader networks of support may be able to translate those advantages into greater legislative success (Cox and Terry 2008; Frantzich 1979; Hasecke and Mycoff 2007; Jeydel and Taylor 2003; Krutz 2005; Volden and Wiseman 2009). Seniority is measured by terms served (*Tenure*). An additional dichotomous indicator (*Freshman*) is used to distinguish the special cases of freshman legislators (who should be particularly ineffective).

Legislative Activism. Prior studies offer mixed findings regarding the benefits of activism. However, some have reported that lawmakers who adopt a "shotgun approach" of sponsoring many bills tend to be more successful (Anderson, Box-Steffensmeier, and Sinclair-Chapman 2003; Cox and Terry 2008; Frantzich 1979; Hasecke and Mycoff 2007). Activism is gauged by total bills introduced by each lawmaker per Congress (*Legislative Activity*).

Specialization. A lawmaker who knows his subject should be more effective. Because our Congressional Bills Project classifies each bill into nineteen major topics of the Policy Agendas Project, a lawmaker is considered a specialist on the issue if the bill falls within the top two major topics of his legislative activity over the previous three congressional terms

---

[6] Per the predictions of partisan theories, which discounts the input of minority party lawmakers very heavily, the measure of majority median distance codes all minority party bill sponsors at the value of the majority party member furthest from the majority median on the minority party side of the ideological continuum.

(*Specialist*). We also include an interaction of specialist and ideological distance to capture the possibility that specialization matters less when the sponsor is an ideological outlier (*Specialist* × *Distance from the Chamber Median*).

Bill Characteristics

Although our problem-solving approach emphasizes that policy topic is consequential for a bill's treatment in Congress, prior research notes that other specifics about a bill may be related to its prospects of success. Two in particular stand out as necessary controls.

Cosponsorship. The number of cosponsors a bill attracts may signal something about its merits that sponsor-related information fails to capture (Krutz 2005). Bills that attract more cosponsors may be more likely to pass the chamber.

Committee of Jurisdiction. The progress of a bill may be influenced by how committees do their business. Different committees have different procedures, norms, and workloads (Fenno 1973). For example, some committees tend to bundle many different proposals into a single omnibus bill (e.g., the Ways and Means Committee). This makes it less likely that the average Ways and Means bill will make it to the floor compared to a bill referred to a different committee that does not have a practice of bundling proposals (e.g., the Energy and Commerce Committee). We therefore control for committee of jurisdiction.

FINDINGS

Our central argument is that bill-sponsor success is affected by different factors depending on the type of issue addressed. To analyze this argument we test whether the same variables predict the progress of bills addressing two different types of issues – compulsory and discretionary. We further break out bills addressing ordinary and minor discretionary issues because we anticipate that minor issues do not require the same level of scrutiny or generate the same level of controversy as other discretionary bills.

Figure 7.4 begins to demonstrate the value of distinguishing bills according to the issues they address. Members not serving on the committee of jurisdiction sponsor just 6 percent of all successful compulsory bills, compared to one-third of all ordinary discretionary bills and more

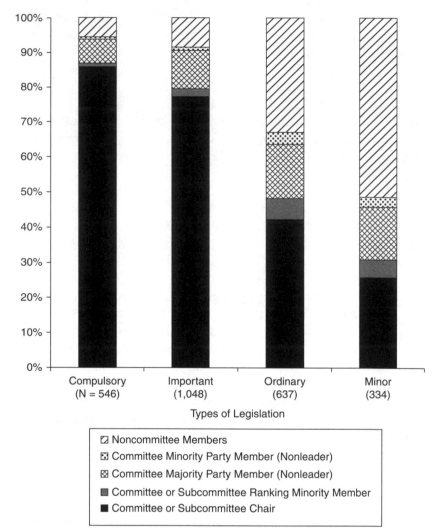

FIGURE 7.4. Characteristics of Successful Sponsors by Type of Legislation.

than half of all successful minor discretionary bills. Success is more widespread within the committee of referral where discretionary bills are concerned. Rank-and-file committee members sponsor between 19 and 25 percent of all successful discretionary legislation, compared to fewer than 10 percent of all successful compulsory bills.

This very basic finding – that bill-sponsor success varies dramatically depending on the type of issue a bill addresses – has gone largely unnoticed in the extensive political science literature that examines variations in bill-sponsor success. A central reason is that prior quantitative studies do not include variables indicating whether the sponsor is a member or leader of the committee to which a bill was referred (Anderson, Box-Steffensmeier, and Sinclair-Chapman 2003; Cox and Terry 2008; Volden and Wiseman 2009).[7] In our analyses, these variables have the largest effects! Furthermore, their effects differ dramatically depending on whether the issue addressed is a compulsory, discretionary, or minor one.

Multivariate Analysis

The results reported in Figure 7.4 provide considerable support for our contention that the opportunity to sponsor a successful bill helps to explain why committee members invest in policy caretaking. However, it is possible that such aggregate patterns mask alternative explanations. Perhaps committee leaders are so much more successful because they also possess other attributes related to effective entrepreneurship. For example, they may be more likely to possess moderate ideological views or they may be more legislatively active. To test such alternative explanations for bills addressing compulsory, discretionary, and minor issues, we construct three multivariate probit regressions (using robust standard errors) with fixed effects for committee of jurisdiction (Table 7.1). The dependent variable in each model is a dichotomous [0,1] indicator of whether a particular bill passed the House of Representatives. For each model, we also report each (significant) variable's estimated effect on a bill's probability of passage.[8]

Model 1 confirms that where compulsory issues are concerned, bill-sponsor success is committee centered. Other things equal, a bill sponsored by a committee of referral chair or subcommittee chair is 45 percent more likely to pass than other bills addressing compulsory issues. Compulsory bills sponsored by rank-and-file committee members are also significantly more likely to pass, including those sponsored by minority party committee members. Bills sponsored by majority party members not on the committee of referral, in contrast, are no more likely to pass than bills sponsored by noncommittee members of the minority party.

---

[7] The one study that does control for committee of referral (Baughman 2003) finds no consistent effects.
[8] Probabilities are calculated by holding all other variables at their mean/mode and shifting the variable of interest from its minimum to its maximum.

TABLE 7.1. *Predictors of Bill Success by Type of Legislation*

	Compulsory Bills		Discretionary Bills		Minor Bills	
	Coefficient Estimate (S. E.)	Probability Change	Coefficient Estimate (S. E.)	Probability Change	Coefficient Estimate (S. E.)	Probability Change
Policy Caretaking						
Committee/Subcommittee Chair	1.316* (0.152)	.445	1.121* (0.106)	.112	1.103* (0.217)	.189
Committee/Subcommittee Ranking Minority Member	0.138 (0.152)		0.362* (0.104)	.022	−0.057 (0.195)	
Committee Nonleader (Majority Party)	0.618* (0.165)	.232	0.484* (0.112)	.030	0.355 (0.214)	
Committee Nonleader (Minority Party)	0.509* (0.205)	.194	0.375* (0.122)	.023	−0.191 (0.223)	
Sponsor Effectiveness						
Majority Party, not Committee Member	0.242 (0.162)		0.307* (0.107)	.015	0.069 (0.193)	
Distance from Majority Median	−0.373 (0.235)		−0.111 (0.186)		−0.247 (0.333)	
Distance from Chamber Median	−0.007 (0.214)		−0.340* (0.155)	.012	0.051 (0.316)	
Specialist	0.154 (0.225)		−0.111 (0.168)		0.303 (0.295)	
Specialist × Distance	−0.145 (0.307)		0.198 (0.230)		−0.410 (0.410)	
Tenure	0.005 (0.003)		0.011* (0.003)	.035	0.007 (0.006)	

Freshman	0.092		0.062		0.143	
	(0.132)		(0.085)		(0.138)	
Legislative Activity	−0.007*	−.208	−0.011*	−.027	−0.011*	−.050
	(0.002)		(0.002)		(0.004)	
Bill Characteristics						
Cosponsors	0.002*	.266	0.002		0.005*	.373
	(0.001)		(0.001)		(0.001)	
Constant	−3.414		−0.491		−4.367	
	(2.489)		(2.217)		(4.011)	
N	3,255		15,699		2,529	
Log Pseudo-likelihood	−1701.322		−2035.979		−605.911	
Pseudo R^2	0.201		0.219		.373	

Note: 101st–104th Houses combined. Cell entries are probit coefficients and robust standard errors. Fixed effects for committee of jurisdiction not shown.
*$p < .05$.

These findings, combined with the staff survey results reported earlier, suggest that sponsor success on compulsory issues is not just a proxy for partisan agenda control. Staff report that party leaders play a much less central role in shaping legislation addressing compulsory issues. In addition, no partisan theory that we are aware of predicts that majority party leaders will extend credit-claiming opportunities to members of the minority party, particularly where high-profile bills are concerned.

After controlling for committee membership and cosponsorship, none of the other sponsor characteristics – ideological disposition, specialization, or seniority – are significant predictors of whether a compulsory bill will pass the chamber. Table 7.1 additionally indicates that sponsors who have more focused legislative agendas (i.e., sponsor fewer bills) tend to be more successful, and that bills with more cosponsors are more likely to pass (across all types of issues).

Sponsor success for discretionary issues is examined in models 2 and 3. The first thing to recall is that these findings apply to less than half of all bills passed by the House for the period examined. The more general story is that of model 1 (accounting for 55% of all passed bills). With respect to models 2 and 3 (bills addressing discretionary issues), the patterns support prior research that argues that multiple sponsor characteristics affect bill-sponsor success. Majority party membership is now significantly related to bill success. In addition to party and committee membership, the sponsor's ideology, experience, and legislative activism are significantly related to success. Thus, the conventional legislative effectiveness narrative does capture legislative success where nonminor discretionary issues are concerned. However these bills make up only about one-third of all passed bills.

The final category – bills addressing minor discretionary issues – yields another set of results (model 3). In contrast to other discretionary bills, majority party membership and ideology do not predict success for these bills. This is consistent with our argument that such bills invite much less scrutiny and are almost three times more likely to pass than other discretionary bills. Thus, the standard effectiveness variables are poor predictors of success in this case because success tends to be widespread.

Taken together, the three models of Table 7.1 offer a more holistic view of bill-sponsor success. The issue a bill addresses is central to appreciating its progress. In addition, the factors influencing its progress also vary depending on the type of issue involved. When the House takes up compulsory issues, the debate almost always centers on a bill sponsored by a member of the committee of jurisdiction (typically a committee leader). This reflects the high-priority nature of these bills and the policy caretaking role that committees often assume. For ordinary discretionary issues, the promotional efforts and institutional advantages (e.g., majority party membership) of the sponsor play a larger role in shaping which limited bills progress because action is less urgent. Here, factors that impact a sponsor's ability to successfully negotiate the "legislative labyrinth" come into play (Franzitch 1979). Ideologically moderate sponsors, for example, are more likely to experience success with discretionary bills, consistent with theories emphasizing the pivotal role of the median voter in deciding policy outcomes (Black 1948; Krehbiel 1998). On minor issues, where the stakes are low and multiple demands are more easily accommodated, success is more likely and politics and ability appear to be less important filters. Finally, some variables also seem to have different meanings in different contexts. Cosponsorship, for example, is a significant predictor of the progress of both compulsory and minor bills (but not nonminor discretionary bills). Where compulsory bills are concerned, cosponsorship is probably an indicator of wealth sharing. Lawmakers who anticipate that a bill's passage is inevitable hope to claim some of the credit through cosponsorship. Where minor bills are concerned, cosponsorship probably operates in the other direction. More cosponsors improve a bill's prospects by signaling to leaders that it is noncontroversial.

Policy Caretaking and Committee Influence

The previous analysis supports our theoretical contention in Chapters 4 and 5 that successful bill sponsorship is an important inducement for committee work. However, another potential incentive to engage in problem-solving activities is policy influence. When committees take the lead in overseeing and updating policies, they acquire specialized knowledge that should lead to greater influence as the chamber debates the policy. Committees should not exercise the same level of influence over discretionary issues as compulsory issues because they are less likely to possess a significant informational advantage. This final section briefly explores the question of whether the committee of jurisdiction's recommendations carry more weight when Congress takes up compulsory issues.

Cox and McCubbins (2005) reason that the less often a party is rolled on the floor, the greater its influence over the agenda. They define a roll as occurring when a majority of a party's voting members in a chamber oppose a bill that ends up passing. The finding that the majority party is rolled less often than the minority party constitutes the central evidence in favor of party cartel theory.[9]

We employ a similar metric to begin to assess committee (as opposed to party) influence. Specifically, we assume that lower committee roll rates are suggestive of greater committee influence. Ultimately we are not able to prove committee influence – there is always the possibility that committees get rolled less often because they successfully anticipate chamber preferences.[10] But lower committee roll rates are consistent with a problem-solving account. They are what we would expect if the chamber responds positively to the committee's recommendations.

To construct committee-specific roll rates we group lawmakers by House committee membership and then derive the majority position (yea or nay) of each committee for each roll call vote across the period examined (see Appendix C for additional details). We then compare the position of the committee to the chamber position on each roll call involving a bill referred to that committee. A committee roll occurs when the committee of jurisdiction's position is the losing one on the floor. We then calculate committee roll rates for different types of motions (all votes, amendments, final passage votes).

Table 7.2 reports these aggregate roll rates for three entities (the committee of jurisdiction, the majority party, and the minority party).[11] It indicates that the committee of jurisdiction is rolled significantly less often. On final passage votes, committees and the majority party experience similar roll rates (more on this shortly). Table 7.3 further distills the focus to just those roll call votes where the majority party and committee positions were in opposition. In these instances, by a 3 to 1 margin (148–54), the committee of jurisdiction's position prevailed over the majority party's position.[12]

Cox and McCubbins (2005) propose that final passage votes are the clearest indicators of party influence because they indicate that the

---

[9] However, Krehbiel (2007) notes that the minority party will also be rolled more frequently in a majoritarian legislature.

[10] Cartel theory is subject to the same critique. The majority party may be rolled less often because it anticipates the preferences of the median legislator (also a member of the majority party), not because it exercises negative agenda control to advance only those policies preferred by the majority party median.

[11] We also computed committee roll rates for multiple referrals by averaging majority positions across all referral committees. The patterns mirror those reported for single referral bills.

[12] Roll rates calculated individually for each of the terms between the 101st and 104th Congresses show almost identical results.

TABLE 7.2. *Roll Rates on the House Floor*

	Roll Rate		
	All Votes	Amendment Votes	Final Votes
Minority Party	39.3%	44.3%	28.0%
	(839)	(658)	(181)
Majority Party	11.2%	15.3%	2.0%
	(240)	(227)	(13)
Committee of Referral	6.8%*	8.9%*	2.0%
	(147)	(133)	(13)
Number of Roll Calls	2,134	1,487	647

Note: 101st–104th Houses combined, single referral only. *Indicates that the committee was significantly less likely to be rolled on the floor than the majority party ($p < .05$). All Votes includes all recorded votes on bills except for rules votes.

TABLE 7.3. *Committee Positions Tend to Prevail over Majority Party Positions*

	Majority Party Prevails	Majority Party Is Rolled
Committee of Jurisdiction Prevails	83.3% (1,840)	6.9% (148)
Committee of Jurisdiction Is Rolled	2.5% (54)	5.0% (92)

Note: 101st–104th Houses combined, single referrals only. When the majority party and committee of jurisdiction positions differ, the chamber's position is more likely to correspond to the committee's position.

majority party is exercising negative agenda control to keep issues the party opposes from reaching the floor. If one subscribes to this view, the important finding in Table 7.2 is that committees of jurisdiction are not less likely to be rolled on the votes that count – final passage votes. However, we have argued that parties exercise limited control over their agendas. Certain issues "must" be addressed regardless of which party is in power. Republicans took up Medicare reform in 2001 not because it was a party priority but because doing so was essential to promoting the party's reputation in the electorate. If the majority party cannot practically keep issues off the agenda, then the key decisions are often the ones that determine the content of "must pass" policies. And these decisions (on amendments) are where committee of jurisdiction positions are more likely to prevail.

TABLE 7.4. *Factors Influencing Whether a Committee Is Rolled on the Floor*

	All Committees		Committee of Jurisdiction Only	
	Coefficient	S. E.	Coefficient	S. E.
Committee of Jurisdiction	−.069*	.028	–	
Committee Sponsor			−.272*	.101
Distance from Chamber Median	.562*	.134	1.573*	.509
Final Passage Decision	−.287*	.026	−.317*	.102
Amendment Decision	0.095*	.021	0.242*	.082
Majority Party Roll	.999*	.189	1.178*	.066
Constant	−1.541*	.023	−1.583*	.121
N	57,714		4,610	
Log Pseudo-likelihood	−16,141.547		−1,178.297	
Pseudo R^2	0.102		0.158	

Note: 101st–104th Houses combined. The first model predicts rolls for all committees. The second predicts committee of jurisdiction rolls. Cell entries are probit coefficients and robust standard errors. *$p < .05$.

It is possible, however, that lower committee roll rates merely indicate that committees are more ideologically representative of the chamber than the median party members. That is, perhaps lower committee roll rates simply validate the majoritarian perspective (Krehbiel 1991). If this were the case, the committee of jurisdiction would be no less likely to be rolled than other committees. Model 1 of Table 7.4 predicts whether a committee is rolled on a given floor vote. The independent variables capture potential explanations for why a committee might be rolled, including the ideological distance between the committee and chamber medians, the type of issue addressed, whether the majority party was also rolled, and – of particular interest – whether the committee in question was the committee of jurisdiction. Controlling for all of these factors, the committee of jurisdiction is significantly less likely to be rolled on the floor than the average committee.

A problem-solving account would seem to predict that a committee's influence is greatest when the legislation in question is committee developed. As a final cut, model 2 of Table 7.4 asks whether the committee of jurisdiction is less likely to be rolled when the bill under consideration is committee sponsored (as opposed to referred to the committee but not sponsored by a committee member). Once again, the evidence is suggestive of greater committee policy influence on such issues. The committee of jurisdiction is significantly less likely to be rolled. Taken together, these findings provide substantial (though not iron clad) evidence that the chamber values the domain expertise of the committee of jurisdiction, particularly when the issues involved originate in committee.

CONCLUSION

We began this chapter by posing the question – why do some legislators sponsor more successful bills? We argued against a common portrayal of bill-sponsor success as an indicator of a legislator's entrepreneurial skills, and in favor of an alternative perspective that portrays bill-sponsor success as a reward for collective policy-making contributions. The credit-claiming benefits associated with sponsoring an important, likely successful, bill helps to explain why committee members invest in policy caretaking activities with broadly distributed benefits.

Distinguishing bills by the type of issue addressed, we found that almost every successful compulsory bill is committee sponsored. Majority party membership and many other variables were important predictors of the progress of ordinary discretionary bills, but it conferred no advantage where compulsory issues were concerned (after controlling for committee of jurisdiction membership). Conventional effectiveness perspectives also do not do a good job of explaining the large proportion of successful bills that address minor discretionary issues. The conclusions of prior effectiveness studies that factors such as party, seniority, and ideology are the main contributors to legislative success stem from the common practice of aggregating large numbers of less important discretionary bills with smaller numbers of much more consequential compulsory bills. Overall, the picture painted in this chapter is one where attention to the substance of policy is critical to appreciating the dynamics of policy making. This theme will become even more apparent when our investigation shifts to examining legislative issue attention and policy change in Chapters 8 and 9, respectively.

We concluded this chapter by exploring whether floor voting behavior offers evidence that committee caretaking activities lead to influence in the chamber. We found that committees of jurisdiction are significantly less likely to be rolled on the floor than the party caucuses or other committees, particularly when the legislation being considered originates in committee. Such a finding does not definitively establish that committees exercise greater influence over floor outcomes, but it is consistent with greater chamber deference in contexts where committees are most likely to possess exceptional domain expertise. Overall, we hope that the findings of this and earlier chapters restore interest in the important contributions that committees make to the policy-making process – contributions that have been downplayed in more recent legislative theorizing. Congress addresses different types of issues, and legislative opportunities and incentives vary depending on which type of issue is being addressed. In particular, we would note that our findings point to the potential benefits of reconsidering long-held explanations for legislative outcomes, such as Black's (1948) median voter theorem. In the next two chapters we turn our attention to the implications of a problem-solving perspective for a different, equally important subject – policy change.

PART IV

8

Problem Solving and Policy Focal Points

> Nine out of ten times, we're occupied with expiring legislation. I know that
> doesn't sound very inspiring, but, frankly, that's the truth.
>
> A Senate committee staffer interviewed by John Kingdon (1995, 186)

Policies are a legislature's most important products. Scholars study agenda
control, committee composition, voting decisions, lobbying, and many
other topics because these factors are assumed to have important consequences for the policies legislatures produce (Baumgartner et al. 2009;
DeGregorio 1999; Krehbiel 1991; Poole and Rosenthal 2007; Shepsle
and Weingast 1987). Party polarization is a growing concern of political
observers, academics, even members of Congress, because it is believed
to contribute to "policy gridlock" (Brady, Ferejohn, and Harbridge 2008;
Hamilton 2009; Jones 2001; McCarty 2007; Theriault 2008).

Yet, systematic studies of policy change in legislatures are surprisingly
thin. Most of the studies that do exist focus on a small number of "historic"
enactments that represent just a small proportion of overall legislative
activity (Berry, Burden, and Howell 2010; Krehbiel 1998; Maltzman
and Shipan 2008; Mayhew 1991). In the next two chapters we extend
existing research on issue attention and policy change in important new
ways. We focus on legislative policy action (as opposed to the many
other domains where government policy is made, for example, by unilat-
eral presidential action or bureaucratic implementation; see Dye 2010;
Howell 2003; Ripley and Franklin 1990). In the realm of legislative policy making, existing perspectives emphasize macrolevel shifts in partisan
or ideological preferences as the key drivers of policy change in Congress.
In contrast, our problem-solving perspective highlights microlevel policy

specific factors, such as program expirations and salient events, as central to appreciating policy change.

This chapter examines legislative issue attention over time. We expect to find that policy change is in large part an opportunistic process because necessary attention to high-priority compulsory issues leaves limited opportunities for a legislature to take up discretionary issues. Previous studies portray bill sponsorships as proactive attempts to shape the legislative agenda. We hypothesize that anticipated agendas strongly influence bill-sponsorship activity. For example, an expiring law should spur lawmakers to introduce related bills as they attempt to couple their policy ideas to likely legislative priorities.

The next chapter (Chapter 9) investigates policy change (as opposed to attention) from two perspectives – statutory change and policy change. We lower the traditional threshold of "historic" enactments to consider many more significant statutory changes than prior studies. In addition, we make an important distinction between statutory change and policy change. To examine policy change, as opposed to change to individual statutes, we identify changes to a policy area that occur within broader laws or across multiple laws.

Laws are legislative vehicles that often address multiple policy issues. For example, the USA PATRIOT Improvement and Reauthorization Act of 2005 (P.L. 109-177), mainly aimed at reauthorizing provisions of the original antiterrorism act, also included the Combat Methamphetamine Epidemic Act of 2005 (CMEA) – a provision that could be fairly considered outside the realm of antiterrorism. Furthermore, policies can be viewed as products of multiple laws. The CMEA is not the only law to address methamphetamine manufacturing and trafficking (see, e.g., the Comprehensive Drug Abuse Prevention and Control Act of 1970 [P.L. 91-513], and its subsequent amendments). Federal "aviation policy," for example, is a composite of the Civil Aeronautics Act of 1938 (P.L. 75-706), Federal Airport Act of 1946 (P.L. 79-377), the Federal Aviation Act of 1948 (P.L. 80-647), the Airport and Airways Development Act of 1970 (P.L. 91-258), the Federal Aviation Act of 1958 (P.L. 85-726), the Airline Deregulation Act of 1978 (P.L. 95-504), and subsequent amendments to these laws, as well as provisions of other laws that are not primarily about aviation (Bailey 2002; Vietor 1990).

A striking feature of the analyses reported in Chapters 8 and 9 is the similarity of the findings. Indicators of microlevel problem-solving concerns are consistently more robust predictors than macropolitical conditions, regardless of whether the focus is on member bill-sponsorship activity, statutory change, or policy change. In our view, these findings paint a very different picture of the lawmaking process – one that highlights governing considerations and downplays the importance of electoral shifts for appreciating congressional agendas and policy dynamics.

A PROBLEM-SOLVING PERSPECTIVE ON ISSUE ATTENTION AND POLICY CHANGE

In late 2000, President-elect George W. Bush both announced publicly as well as directly to members of Congress that reforming and bolstering the Head Start program was one of his top policy priorities (Oppel and Schemo 2000). Shortly after taking office, he submitted a major education bill to the Republican-led Congress (what eventually became "No Child Left Behind" Act of 2001 [P.L. 107-110]). Perhaps surprisingly, the massive education proposal did not address Head Start. The omission was intentional however. It reflected awareness that Congress had its own schedule. According to *The New York Times*, "Mr. Bush's aides said this week that they would not seek to move Head Start until the program is eligible for reauthorization by Congress, in 2003" (Steinberg 2001, quoted in Hall 2004).

If plenary time and resources were infinite, the entire spectrum of legislative policy demands could be accommodated. Change would depend only on whether lawmakers were convinced that a proposed policy advanced their personal or partisan interests. Scarce time and resources force choices – which limited issues will a legislature take up? Existing legislative scholarship tends to highlight two implications of scarcity. First, legislatures will reserve their scarce floor time for the issues that can pass (Krehbiel 1998). It is not a coincidence that bills are rarely defeated on the floor. Second, political factions will strive to ensure that their preferred policies receive priority consideration (Cox 2006).

Agenda scarcity also creates incentives for legislatures to prioritize problem solving. Reelection-oriented lawmakers have reasons to address salient public concerns and to ensure the proper functioning of programs valued by voters. They also have incentives to support processes that allocate scarce time and resources to program oversight and policy updating. A financial meltdown, a quickly escalating military conflict, or a sharp increase in fuel prices are all examples of "pressing problems" that demand legislative attention. Issue attention and policy change should therefore center in large part on the policy focal points presented by problem-solving routines such as program reauthorizations and the less predictable opportunities spurred by external events (Kingdon 1995). Head Start illustrates these dynamics. In 2001–2 several other children's programs were due to expire before Head Start.[1] Said one staffer, "Everyone will be talking about Head Start before it expires, but the fact of the matter is, nothing was going to be done about it until it expires" (Hall 2004, 93–4).

ISSUE ATTENTION

A problem-solving perspective on issue attention and policy change builds on a longstanding American politics research tradition examining problem selection processes (Baumgartner and Jones 1993; Downs 1972; Kingdon 1995; Sheingate 2006; Sulkin 2005). One of the most influential books in this area, John Kingdon's *Agendas, Alternatives and Public Policies*, specifically discusses different types of "windows of opportunity" for policy change in Congress (Kingdon 1995, Ch. 8). Kingdon differentiates between "unpredictable" policy windows, such as an external event or an election, and "predictable" policy windows, such as the expiration of a program or the president's annual State of the Union address. However, Kingdon says little about the relative importance of these different types of windows, and we are not aware of any explicit efforts to systematically test whether, for example, external focusing events, election outcomes, or program expirations are better predictors of policy change in Congress.

Instead, empirical studies in the policy tradition have tended to highlight external "focusing events" as central to appreciating shifts in issue attention (Birkland 1997). Historically, these studies relied on selected case studies and thick description. For example, Baumgartner and Jones (1993) illustrate how nuclear power, once viewed by the public and lawmakers as an energy solution, came to be viewed as an environmental and public safety problem following the events of Three Mile Island. More recent research adopts a more quantitative approach to investigating the dynamics of issue attention and policy change, although the emphasis

---

[1] Including the Child Abuse Prevention and Treatment Act Amendment of 1996 (P.L. 104-235), Federal Payments for Foster Care and Adoption Assistance, HHS Adoption Opportunities Services, Missing and Exploited Children's Task Force, and Community-based Family Resource and Support Grants (Congressional Budget Office 2001).

continues to be on how external inputs (as opposed to internal routines such as reauthorizations) produce shifts in political attention (e.g., Jones and Baumgartner 2005).

Policy Change

Legislative studies of policy change, in contrast, have downplayed policy-specific factors in favor of quantitative investigations of the importance of macropolitical conditions such as changes in partisan control or ideological polarization. Each approach has its strengths, and more recent legislative research is beginning to bridge the divide (Berry, Burden, and Howell 2010; Burstein, Bauldry, and Froese 2005; Clinton and Lapinski 2006; Howell et al. 2000; Mayhew 1991; Patashnik 2008; Sheingate 2006). Much of the research on congressional policy change has focused on aggregate legislative productivity as measured by counts of laws (Binder 2003; Clinton and Lapinski 2006; Coleman 1997; Edwards, Barrett, and Peake 1997; Erikson, MacKuen, and Stimson 2006; Fiorina 1996; Grant and Kelly 2008; Heitshusen and Young 2006; Howell et al. 2000; Kelly 1993; Krehbiel 1998; Lapinski 2008; Mayhew 1991; Shipan 2006). Yet, laws vary in importance, and these studies typically treat all laws above a threshold as equally significant, and all laws below that threshold as nonexistent (for an exception see Howell et al. 2000). As a consequence, only a small part of the overall legislative agenda may be considered. For example, relying on Mayhew's "major law" threshold limits attention to just several hundred laws (less than 10%) of the thousands of laws enacted during the post–World War II era (Mayhew 1991).

More recent research seeks to explain change at the level of the individual law or program. The objectives – to explain why a given statute is reformed (Maltzman and Shipan 2008; Ragusa 2010) or why a particular government program endures (Berry, Burden, and Howell 2010; Corder 2004; Lewis 2002) – are decidedly more policy centered than studies examining legislative productivity. Statutory reform studies often seek to explain why the "historic" laws identified by Mayhew are significantly amended for the first time (Maltzman and Shipan 2008; Ragusa 2010). For example, the Elementary and Secondary Education Act of 1965 (ESEA; P.L. 89-10) has been updated multiple occasions since its enactment. In 2002, it was reauthorized as the No Child Left Behind Act of 2001 (NCLB). However, because the NCLB was not the first major amendment to the ESEA, it is not one of the policy changes considered. Thus, an even more limited set of policy changes are examined in these studies. The dominant explanations considered are almost exclusively electoral: changes in partisan control (Berry, Burden, and Howell 2010; Lewis 2002), seat losses by the majority party (Berry, Burden, and Howell 2010), ideological discord between the chambers (Maltzman and Shipan 2008), unified versus divided government (Carpenter and Lewis 2004; Lewis 2002; Ragusa 2010), and an "unfriendly" president (Lewis 2002).

POLICY FOCAL POINTS AND LEGISLATIVE ISSUE ATTENTION

We first examine changes in legislative attention to issues over time. Agenda scarcity should mean that high-priority compulsory issues become important policy focal points that attract policy entrepreneurs seeking to couple their policy proposals to issues that are already on the agenda.

Dependent Variable: Issue Attention

There are many potential indicators of changing attention to legislative issues in Congress. The most common measure has been congressional hearings activity (Baumgartner and Jones 1993). However, hearings are relatively rare events, especially when the legislative agenda is divided into narrow policy areas. We opt for member bill-sponsorship activity for a number of reasons. Bills are "a rich source of information about how legislators interact with their institutions when there appears to be few rules to limit their behavior" (Schiller 1995, 186–7). Bill introductions are also meaningful indicators of lawmaker interests (Sulkin 2011), and an "indicator of a willingness to participate in the legislative forum" (Hibbing 1991, 113; see also Burstein, Bauldry, and Froese 2005). Finally, bills provide an "opportunity to examine strategic behavior when consequences are further 'downstream'" (Woon 2009; see also Ainsworth and Hanson 1996). Because so many more bills are introduced than hearings held, they should also be more sensitive indicators of changing legislative attention (Wilkerson et al. 2002).

We investigate bill introductions within each of twenty-seven issue areas over eighteen years of lawmaking (1980–98). These issue areas will also play an important role in the next chapter, where we investigate policy changes over time. The twenty-seven issue areas come from the Policy Agendas Project, which partitions the governmental agenda into nineteen major topics and 225 subtopics. We study issue attention within twenty-seven of these subtopics that capture most of the important legislative action in Congress. The Policy Agendas Project classifies *CQ* stories in two ways – the primary topic of the law and the primary topic of the story, which might address only one part of a broader law. Using *CQ* article lines of law coverage (excluding coverage of defense, appropriations, and budgets), we selected for our analysis the most important subtopic in every major topic area. We then added a second subtopic within a major topic area if and only if it was also among the top fifty subtopics in terms of *CQ* coverage.[2] All told, laws pertaining to these twenty-seven subtopics received two-thirds (67%) of all *CQ* coverage of laws. Our dependent variable in the current analysis is therefore the number of bills introduced each year in each of the issue areas displayed in Table 8.1.

Independent Variables

The dependent variable in the current chapter is issue attention, measured by bill-sponsorship activity of lawmakers in the House of Representatives. (In the next chapter it is policy change, measured in several different ways.) In this section we introduce the independent variables that will be tested in both chapters. We anticipate that problem-solving motivations captured by expiring authorizations and salient events will serve as important policy focal points and will be significant predictors of policy change. Prior research suggests other variables, many related to shifting policy preferences through legislative replacement or (less likely) conversion, should be central to appreciating legislative attention and policy change (Asher and Weisberg 1978; Brady and Sinclair 1984; Brady and Volden 1998; Poole and Rosenthal 2007).

Problem-Solving Motivations for Issue Attention and Policy Change
Expiring Provisions. We hypothesize that expiring provisions of law in an issue area will be significant predictors of issue attention and policy change. Identifying expiring provisions was a challenging task. We first identified every law in each of the twenty-seven subtopics starting in 1975. We then examined the law summaries produced by the Congressional Research

---

[2] It is substantially more difficult to locate expiring provisions within the statutes of certain subtopic areas. As a result, a small number of subtopic areas were excluded from the analysis: tax policy (subtopic 107), employee benefits (503), foreign aid (1901), Latin America (1914), natural resources (2,103), and water resource development (2,104).

TABLE 8.1. *List of Issue Areas Examined (Policy Agendas Project Subtopics)*

Policy Subtopic	Subtopic Code	Expiring Provisions
Civil Rights, Minority Issues, and Civil Liberties, General (includes combinations of multiple subtopics)	200	6
Handicap or Disease Discrimination	205	18
Insurance Reform, Availability, and Cost	302	31
Regulation of Drug Industry, Medical Devices, and Clinical Labs	321	17
Government Subsidies to Farmers and Ranchers, Agricultural Disaster Insurance	402	255
Food Inspection and Safety (including seafood)	403	7
Immigration and Refugee Issues	530	34
Higher Education	601	212
Elementary and Secondary Education	602	164
Hazardous Waste and Toxic Chemical Regulation, Treatment, and Disposal	704	31
Air Pollution, Global Warming, and Noise Pollution	705	2
Energy Conservation	807	25
Highway Construction, Maintenance, and Safety	1002	217
Airports, Airlines, Air Traffic Control, and Safety	1003	57
Illegal Drug Production, Trafficking, and Control	1203	37
Police, Fire, and Weapons Control	1209	19
Poverty and Assistance for Low-Income Families	1302	28
Elderly Issues and Elderly Assistance Programs (including Social Security Administration)	1303	50
Housing and Community Development	1401	211
U.S. Banking System and Financial Institution Regulation	1501	34
Securities and Commodities Regulation	1502	10
Telephone and Telecommunication Regulation	1706	30
Broadcast Industry Regulation (TV, cable, radio)	1707	12
Trade Negotiations, Disputes, and Agreements	1802	32
Export Promotion and Regulation, Export-Import Bank	1803	26
Government Efficiency and Bureaucratic Oversight	2002	9
Government Employee Benefits, Civil Service Issues	2004	21

Service made available on the THOMAS Web site[3] and documented each law's expiring provisions (in particular, the future year in which the law, program, or funding expired). If the Congressional Research Service summary was ambiguous or failed to provide sufficient details, we read the entire text of the law (either on THOMAS or *Statutes at Large*).[4] We started with laws enacted in 1975 to ensure that we identified expirations during the period of our analysis (1980–98) that were provisions of laws enacted prior to 1980.[5]

A second concern was that we might overlook expiring provisions contained in laws that were labeled as primarily about a different subtopic.[6] To address this concern, we conducted additional subject searches of the online *CQ Almanac* and *Lexis-Nexis Congressional Histories*. If additional laws came up, we would then review those laws for germane expirations. Finally, we used the same resources to search for laws passed prior to 1975 that might include relevant provisions expiring in 1980 or after.

For the 1980–98 study period, we documented nearly 1,600 expiring provisions across the twenty-seven issue areas of our sample (see Table 8.1). It is evident that a recurring calendar of reauthorizations does not drive policy making in some of these issue areas (e.g., air pollution, global warming, and noise pollution). In others, such as higher education and agriculture policy, expiring provisions are much more common and potentially important factors shaping legislative issue attention and policy change. "How important compared to other factors?" is the primary question of this and the chapter that follows.

To create the expirations variable (*Expiring Provisions in Law*), we simply sum the number of expiring provisions across all laws within a given policy subtopic. Each expiration is therefore assumed to be of equal importance. For a massive farm bill, the number of expiring provisions (upward of 100) does a good job of capturing the potential importance of this variable. The key to the continued effectiveness of the federal program authorizing hazardous and toxic waste cleanups (the 1980 Comprehensive Environmental Response, Compensation, and Liability

---

[3] www.thomas.gov.
[4] As noted in Chapter 5, prior studies of expirations have relied on a compilation of the CBO (MacDonald 2007). The CBO aggregates expiring provisions with no discernibly consistent methodology and thus were not employed in this analysis.
[5] The vast majority of short-term authorizations expire within five years or less.
[6] Laws labeled as primarily about a particular subtopic sometimes contained expiring provisions addressing other subtopics.

Act, or CERCLA; P.L. 96-510) is a single expiring provision – the "Superfund" tax on the petroleum and chemical industry. Thus, relying on counts avoids the thorny issue of trying to measure the importance of an expiring provision, but it also stacks the deck against finding confirmatory statistical support in cases where a single expiring provision is key.

Issue Salience and Policy Mood. Lawmakers and policy advocates should also mobilize around and respond to issues that have the public's attention. We test several indicators of the importance of issue salience: elite salience, the public's sentiment as to the most important problems, and the public's general policy mood. Each captures a different aspect of salience. Interestingly, the three measures are also not very highly correlated (the highest bivariate Pearson's r amongst them is 0.21).

With respect to elite salience, Binder employs newspaper editorials (specifically *The New York Times*) as a "proxy for the public or political salience of the issue" (Binder 2003, 37). Editorial writers see themselves as capturing issues on the rise and putting them "on people's radar screen" (Binder 2003, 37). We classify Binder's brief (less than one sentence) editorial descriptions by Policy Agendas Project subtopic and use counts of editorials per term as our proxy for changing elite salience of an issue (*Elite Salience*).

The "most important problem" question offers a more direct indicator of public sentiment regarding major political issues of the day (*Most Important Problem*). The Policy Agendas Project includes a most important problem series based on responses in Gallup public opinion polls. However, the series is limited to major topics (Jones, Larsen-Price, and Wilkerson 2009). An additional limitation of the most important problem series as a measure of policy concern is that it only measures the percentage of the public that considers a particular problem (e.g., the economy or crime) to be "the" most important problem facing the nation (for use of opinion poll questions as measures of policy salience, see Baumgartner and Jones 1993; Price 1978; Wlezien 1995).

Finally, we employ Stimson's aggregation of survey responses to capture public's general "mood" or enthusiasm for greater policy activism (Stimson 1999; see also Kingdon 1995, 146–9). This variable (*Mood*) gauges public preferences for more or less government action in the domestic arena as a whole, and has been shown to be an important predictor of law productivity across time (Epstein and Segal 2000; Erikson, MacKuen, and Stimson 2006).

Alternative Explanations for Issue Attention and Policy Change

Existing legislative research tends to highlight a different set of factors as central to appreciating policy change. Most of these factors are variations of the same theme – lawmakers' preferences. Accordingly, we test a comprehensive list of preference indicators grouped into five categories: policy preference coalitions, majority party coalitions, committee effects, interbranch influences, and policy-specific factors. Table 8.2 provides a list of these variables and their origins. Whenever possible, we use the same (or very similar) measure to the ones employed in prior studies.

Policy Preference Coalitions. Gridlock models predict that conditions will be more conducive to policy change when the ideological distance between pivotal legislative actors is smaller (Brady and Volden 1998; Krehbiel 1998). Forrest Maltzman and Charles Shipan hypothesize that "laws are less likely to be amended when partisan control of government is divided and when the House and Senate have distinct policy preferences" (2008, 259–60; divided government is addressed in the following text). John Lapinski (2008) proposes a one-chamber polarization score as a shortcut to capturing the dynamics of the gridlock interval (*House Polarization*). Binder (2003) finds that the ideological distance between the two chambers (*Chamber Preference Distance*) is related to the likelihood of policy change.

Majority Party Coalitions. The notion that partisan control impacts policy change is also well established in the congressional literature (Aldrich and Rohde 2001; Cox and McCubbins 1993, 2005; Hurley, Brady, and Cooper 1977; Rohde 1991). Parties exercise discipline to advance policies that promote the party's reputation in elections. Unfortunately, parties rarely publish their policy priorities (the 1994 Republican Party *Contract with America* being a notable exception). We construct a start-of-the-term majority agenda (*House Majority Party Agenda*) from two sources: the speech given by the Speaker of the House immediately following his or her election at the beginning of each congressional term and the topics of the first ten bills introduced in the House of Representatives (traditionally reserved for the Speaker).[7] Table 8.3 displays the results of this

---

[7] These two sources were suggested by Prof. Larry Evans (personal communication, May 2009), who has considerable experience in the offices of party leaders in the House of Representatives.

TABLE 8.2. *List of Independent Variables Used in Issue Attention and Policy Change Analyses*

	Data Source	Expected Effect	Mean	Standard Deviation	Minimum	Maximum
Governing Theory						
Expiring Provisions in Law	(Authors)	+	6.564	15.329	0	117
Salient Events and Mood						
Elite Salience	Binder's data on editorials from *The New York Times*, coded by Policy Agendas Project subtopics	+	17.403	17.924	0	105
"Most Important Problem"	Size of change in the proportion who state that *major* topic is the "most important problem facing nation" in Gallup polls (only when change is positive from the previous period)	+	.010	.026	0	.211
Mood	Stimson's measure of public mood	+	59.56	2.623	54.96	63.41
Policy Preference Coalitions						
Chamber Preference Distance	Absolute difference in chamber preferences using Poole and Rosenthal's DW-NOMINATE scores	−	0.029	0.025	0.007	0.084
House Polarization	Absolute difference in House Democratic and Republican mean preferences using Poole and Rosenthal's DW-NOMINATE scores	−	0.713	0.091	0.603	0.856
Majority Party Coalitions						
House Majority Party Size	Percent of House seats controlled by the majority party	+	0.571	0.038	0.51	0.61
Senate Majority Party Size	Percent of Senate seats controlled by the majority party	+	0.547	0.012	0.53	0.57

			Mean	Std. Dev.	Min.	Max.
Gain of Majority Party Seats	Net gain of seats for the majority party in both chambers, 0 if no gain or loss	+	9.667	19.391	0	63
Majority Party Issue	House and Senate controlled by same party, and that subtopic is determined by Petrocik (1989) to be "owned" by the majority party = 1, otherwise = 0	+	0.374	0.485	0	1
House Majority Party Agenda	Subtopic included in first 10 majority party–sponsored bills for term or in Speaker's election speech	+	0.123	.330	0	1
Committee Effects						
Turnover in House Committee Chair	If the term of a new chair of the primary committee of jurisdiction = 1, otherwise = 0	+	0.222	0.417	0	1
Turnover in Senate Committee Chair	(same)	+	0.366	0.483	0	1
Change in Committee Preferences	Absolute difference in the preferences of the primary committee of jurisdiction from previous term using Poole and Rosenthal's COMMON SPACE scores	+	0.166	0.206	0	0.964
Interbranch Influences						
Unified	Both chambers and presidency controlled by same party = 1, otherwise = 0	+	0.111	0.315	0	1
Presidential Attention	Aggregation of presidential message by subtopic from Rudalevige's data on presidential messages	+	0.401	0.354	0	1
Supreme Court Cases	Number of unique case citations by subtopic for the three years prior to the beginning of the congressional term	+	2.074	2.696	0	14
Policy-Specific Conflict						
Policy Conflict	Percent of roll call votes in subtopic for previous term that were party unity according to Rohde's data	+/−	0.009	0.013	0	0.086

TABLE 8.3. *Example of House Majority Party Agenda, Using Speaker Statements and First Ten Bills, 106th Congress (1999–2000)*

Subject Matter	Subtopic Code	Source
Government spending	105	Speaker
Tax relief/reduce income tax/eliminate marriage penalty and estate tax	107	Speaker/Bills
Funds to classrooms/safe schools/use Individual Retirement Account funds for elementary and secondary education	602	Speaker/Bills
Reform social security/eliminate earnings test	1303	Speaker/Bills
Reform regulation of financial services industry (repeal Glass-Steagall Act)	1500	Bills
Deploy a national missile defense	1600	Bills
Better equip and train military	1604	Speaker
Improve quality of life for military families	1608	Bills
More efficient/smaller government	2002	Speaker

approach for one congressional term (the 106th Republican-controlled Congress; 1999–2000).

Another way to infer majority party priorities is to rely on the public's views of a party's competencies or "issue ownership" on the assumption that parties will focus on their strengths (Petrocik 1989). For example, Republicans may be more likely to focus on crime because the public views them as more competent on the issue. We create a binary variable (*Majority Party Issue*) to signify when the public thinks that the majority party in the House is better able to "handle" the issue/policy than the minority party (Petrocik 1989; Pope and Woon 2008; Woon and Pope 2007).

Finally, we also consider the size of the legislative majority. Lapinski (2008) has argued that the majority party's ability to make changes in law is related to majority party advantage in terms of seats in the legislature. Christopher Berry and colleagues (2010) report that changes in partisan composition or partisan strength of the enacting majority help to explain the durability of federal programs. Accordingly, we also test an aggregate measure of majority party seat gain across both chambers.

Committee Composition Effects. Some prior studies argue that committees possess independent authority to move issues onto the legislative agenda (Sinclair 1986). Committees and their chairs control the pace and direction of policy change within their jurisdictions – they are not simply tools of the parties or beholden to the chamber median (Deering and Smith 1997; Fenno 1973; Weingast and Marshall 1988). This suggests that changes in committee composition may lead to shifts in legislative issue attention and policy change. *Turnover in House/Senate Committee Chair* is a binary variable indicating whether the chair of the committee of jurisdiction has changed since the last term. We assume that the committee of jurisdiction is the one that receives the majority of bill referrals within a subtopic for the study period. *Change in Committee Preferences* indicates whether the composition of the committee has changed – based on the absolute differences between the current and previous median committee member's "Common Space" ideology scores (Poole and Rosenthal 2007). A single score is produced by summing the absolute differences across the two chambers.

Interbranch Influences. Partisan agreement or discord between the president and Congress is one of the most frequently investigated questions related to policy change (Brady and Volden 1998; Fiorina 1996; Krehbiel 1998; Mayhew 1991). Prior research has drawn differing conclusions about the impact of divided government on legislative productivity. Some studies conclude that it has a significant dampening effect on productivity, while others argue that it shifts the zone of possible policy changes but without necessarily diminishing overall productivity. We test for any affect with a simple binary variable that connotes periods of unified versus divided government (*Unified Government*).

Presidents may also be able to focus congressional attention through their formal powers, including the veto, and through their informal powers, such as their willingness to "go public" in order to build public support for policy changes (Canes-Wrone 2005; Edwards 2003; Edwards, Barrett, and Peake 1997; Jones 1994; Kernell 2006). Rudalevige (2002) has compiled presidential messages on legislation and potential legislation. We code these messages for subtopic to produce a presidential attention score (number of messages per year) for each of our twenty-seven issue areas (*Presidential Attention*). Although we do not explicitly consider this to be a problem-solving variable, we would note that standard portrayals of presidential power in Congress emphasize that this influence often stems from efforts to sway voters in lawmakers' districts (Canes-Wrone 2005; Kernell 2006). In this respect, presidential attention has effects similar to that of media coverage of issues.

Following the work of Maltzman and Shipan (2008), we also ask whether federal court decisions provoke congressional attention within specific policy areas (Barnes 2004; Eskridge 1991). The logic behind this variable is that Congress is sometimes compelled to respond to court interpretations. For example, one of the first laws passed by the 111th Congress was a direct response to a Supreme Court decision that (in the Democratic Congress's view) interpreted an existing employment discrimination statute too narrowly.[8] As do Maltzman and Shipan, we focus on the amount of Supreme Court activity (*Supreme Court Cases*) within each subtopic for the three years prior to each congressional term. The Policy Agendas Project has prelabeled the Spaeth Supreme Court decision database[9] by Policy Agendas Project subtopic.

Policy-Specific Conflict. Finally, a number of studies hypothesize that the contentiousness or divisiveness of a policy area affects possibilities for policy change but in different ways. Some predict that policy divisiveness inhibits legislative action (MacDonald 2007); others predict that "divisive laws are less likely to be protected against future laws" (Maltzman and Shipan 2008, 257), while still others conclude that the effects of divisiveness vary by chamber (Binder 2003). Following Binder, we measure policy-specific partisan polarization (*Policy Conflict*) by the percentage of roll calls within a subtopic during the preceding congressional term that are party unity votes.[10]

ANALYSIS OF ISSUE ATTENTION

To recap, the dependent variable (*Legislative Issue Attention*) is the number of bills members introduced in the House of Representatives in each of twenty-seven issue areas, from 1980 to 1998. We therefore considered two modeling approaches. The first was a conventional robust OLS model with clustered standard errors by policy area (De Boef and Keele 2008; Keele and Kelly 2006). The second was an OLS specification with panel-corrected standard errors (PCSE) (Beck and Katz 1995). The findings were nearly identical, so we only report the OLS models with PCSE.[11]

---

[8] The Lilly Ledbetter Fair Pay Act of 2009 (P.L. 111-2).

[9] Now located at http://scdb.wustl.edu/index.php (accessed January 31, 2012).

[10] Party unity votes are defined as roll call votes where a majority of one party votes in opposition to the majority of the other party.

[11] The models reported do not include a lagged dependent variable to address potential autocorrelation (Achen 2001; Keele and Kelly 2006). However, inclusion of a lagged dependent variable in the models was inconsequential for the primary findings. As well, we report the results for the model without fixed effects for subtopic. Even when we

A central challenge of considering so many suggested variables is potential colinearity – for example, between different specifications of legislative preferences (e.g., chamber polarization and majority party size). We therefore tested a large number of model specifications. Table 8.4 presents the findings for a selected set of these (PCSE) models. The baseline model reported in the first column includes the variables capturing problem-solving motivations along with some of the suggested explanatory variables capturing other motivations. The models reported in the other columns test additional suggested explanatory variables. Table 8.5 then summarizes the findings of a much larger set of PCSE models testing different variable combinations. Each model is a column: shaded cells are variables included in the model; ✓ = variables statistically significant at $p < .05$ and in the predicted direction; and ✗ = variable statistically significant but not in the predicted direction.

The baseline model (first column of Table 8.4) is representative of the overall findings. One set of variables stands out as important and robust predictors of issue attention (bill introductions) across all of the specifications. These are statutory expirations, elite salience, presidential attention, and Supreme Court activity. The greater the number of expiring provisions in a policy area during a congressional term induces more legislative activity in that issue arena. Similarly, elite and presidential interest in a policy area is also strongly predictive of bill-sponsorship activity by members of Congress within an issue area. These factors are quite robust; they predict legislative attention across all of the model types and variable combinations.[12]

Of equal importance, changing preference, partisan, or committee conditions have little if any impact on legislative issue attention. Most of the indicators of these variables are not significant or are significant in the opposite direction of normal expectations (i.e., chamber preference differences, Senate majority party size, and gains in majority party seats). Other factors not predictive of bill activity include unified government,

include fixed effects – which slightly changes the interpretation of our variables – there is no substantive difference in the findings.

[12] It is important to note that the number of expiring provisions is not highly colinear with other independent variables. For instance, elite salience and expirations are correlated at relatively weak Pearson's r of -0.15. That is, expirations of large programs (highways, higher education, farming, etc.) do not explain variations in the elite salience of issues as measured by *The New York Times* editorials. Similarly, presidential attention does not seem to be explained by the presence or absence of big expiring programs (Pearson's $r = 0.09$).

TABLE 8.4. *Predictors of Legislative Issue Attention (Bill Introductions)*

	Baseline	Baseline + Preferences	Baseline + Parties	Baseline + Committees
Problem Solving				
Expiring Provisions in Law	0.464*	0.452*	0.499*	0.463*
	(0.159)	(0.157)	(0.166)	(0.158)
Elite Salience	8.869*	8.365*	8.852*	8.602*
	(2.480)	(2.544)	(2.559)	(2.535)
Most Important Problem	6.577	14.99	12.21	2.664
	(50.24)	(54.46)	(57.57)	(52.75)
Mood	-0.100	-0.434	-0.515	-0.077
	(0.621)	(0.670)	(0.573)	(0.645)
Policy Preference Coalitions				
Chamber Preference Distance		-15.72		
		(82.36)		
House Polarization		-50.68*		
		(17.18)		
Majority Party Coalitions				
House Majority Party Size			116.4*	
			(27.23)	
Senate Majority Party Size			-124.2	
			(132.0)	
House Majority Party Agenda			-9.197	
			(7.994)	
Gain of Majority Party Seats			-0.058	
			(0.058)	
Majority Party Issue			2.605	
			(3.616)	

	(1)	(2)	(3)
Committee Effects			
Turnover House Committee Chair			0.819
			(5.894)
Turnover Senate Committee Chair			−0.319
			(4.121)
Change in Committee Preferences			−17.59
			(12.80)
Interbranch Influences			
Unified/Divided	−0.164	−0.218	−2.497
	(5.794)	(3.604)	(5.570)
Presidential Attention	418.4*	427.5*	439.1*
	(110.0)	(116.7)	(113.7)
Supreme Court Cases	2.668*	2.336*	2.634*
	(0.863)	(0.858)	(0.867)
Policy-Specific Conflict			
Policy Conflict	2.958	4.245	1.776
	(4.837)	(5.098)	(5.078)
Constant	16.23	42.79	19.08
	(37.47)	(63.98)	(38.28)
Observations	243	243	243
R^2	0.172	0.198	0.181

Note: OLS regression with PCSE; standard errors in parentheses; * $p < .05$.

TABLE 8.5. *Summary of Models Predicting Legislative Issue Attention (Bill Introductions)*

	Expected	B	1	2	3	4	5	6	7	8
Problem-Solving Theory										
Expiring Provisions in Law	+	✓	✓	✓	✓	✓	✓	✓	✓	✓
Salient Events and Mood										
Elite Salience	+	✓	✓	✓	✓	✓	✓	✓	✓	✓
Most Important Problem	+									
Mood	+									
Policy Preferences										
Chamber Preference Distance	−		✗							
House Polarization	−			✓						
Majority Party Coalitions										
House Majority Party Size	+				✓					
Senate Majority Party Size	+									
House Majority Party Agenda	+									
Gain of Majority Party Seats	+						✗			
Majority Party Issue	+									
Committee Effects										
Change in House Committee Chair	+									
Change in Senate Committee Chair	+									
Change in Committee Preferences	+									
Interbranch Influences										
Unified Government	+									
Presidential Attention	+	✓	✓	✓	✓	✓	✓	✓	✓	✓
Supreme Court Cases	+	✓	✓	✓	✓	✓	✓	✓	✓	✓
Policy-Specific Conflict										
Policy Conflict	+/−									

Note: OLS regression with PCSE; shaded cell = variable included in the model; ✓ = variable is statistically significant and in the predicted direction; ✗ = variable is statistically significant but not in the predicted direction.

TABLE 8.5 *(cont.)*

	Expected	9	10	11	12	13	14	15	16	17	18
Problem-Solving Theory											
Expiring Provisions in Law	+	✓	✓	✓	✓	✓	✓	✓	✓	✓	✓
Salient Events and Mood											
Elite Salience	+	✓	✓	✓	✓	✓	✓	✓	✓	✓	✓
Most Important Problem	+										
Mood	+			✓	✗						
Policy Preferences											
Chamber Preference Distance	–		✗	✗				✗			
House Polarization	–				✗	✓	✓		✓		✓
Majority Party Coalitions											
House Majority Party Size	+	✓			✓						
Senate Majority Party Size	+				✗						
House Majority Party Agenda	+										
Gain of Majority Party Seats	+			✗				✗			
Majority Party Issue	+										
Committee Effects											
Change in House Committee Chair	+										
Change in Senate Committee Chair	+										
Change in Committee Preferences	+										
Interbranch Influences											
Unified Government	+										
Presidential Attention	+	✓	✓	✓	✓	✓	✓	✓	✓	✓	✓
Supreme Court Cases	+	✓	✓	✓	✓	✓	✓	✓	✓	✓	✓
Policy-Specific Conflict											
Policy Conflict	+/–										

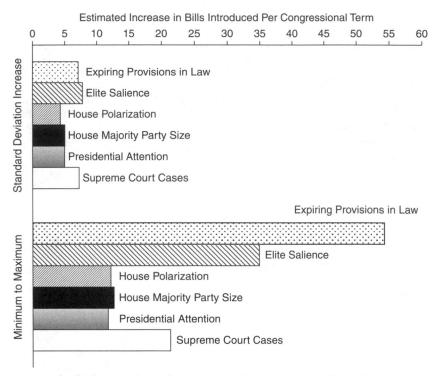

Note: Coefficients are estimated from a model that includes all the baseline variables plus the polarization variable. For the House Majority Party Size variable we use a model that includes all the baseline variables plus the Party Size variable.

FIGURE 8.1. Effects of Key Predictors of Legislative Issue Attention (Bill Introductions).

Note: Coefficients are estimated from a model that includes all the baseline variables plus the polarization variable. For the House Majority Party Size variable we use a model that includes all the baseline variables plus the Party Size variable.

conflictual/nonconflictual issues, and general public issue salience and policy mood.

The notable exceptions are House majority party size and the degree of preference difference between Democrats and Republicans in the House (*Polarization*). These indicators of political conditions are significant in the expected direction in a limited number of model specifications. However, their effects on issue attention are not always significant and sometimes in the wrong direction. In contrast, the variables capturing problem-solving considerations are robust across all of the specifications.

To gain a sense of how the meaningful covariates relate to each other and their relative impact on bill activity, we present two perspectives that demonstrate the impact of each significant factor on the predicted level of bill activity. Figure 8.1 displays the effect of each of the statistically significant variables on the predicted value of bill activity for the models presented in Table 8.4 for a one standard deviation increase from the mean (top frame), and as its value goes from its minimum to maximum (bottom frame).[13] To show the relative effect of each covariate on the predicted value of bill activity controlling for the other factors included in the model, we hold the values of the other variables at their means (or mode when a variable was dichotomous).

The top frame shows that an increase of one standard deviation for each of the variables predicts a substantial increase in legislative issue attention (about ten bills per term in a given issue area), with the largest effects coming from expiring provisions, elite salience, and Supreme Court activity. However, varying the same variables from their minimum to maximum values (bottom frame) yields much more substantial effects as well as noteworthy differences among them. A minimum–maximum shift in expiring provisions produces an estimated fifty-four additional bill introductions. Similarly, elite salience (*The New York Times* editorials) produces almost thirty-four additional introductions on average. In contrast, the best performing preference and partisan variables (polarization and majority party size) produce an estimated increase of less than a quarter of that produced by expiring provisions of law.

CONCLUSIONS

In this chapter, our goal was to systematically test different explanations for changing issue attention in the House. Public policy studies have long portrayed issue attention and policy change as often problem driven. With "so many problems pressing down upon the system" the best opportunities for policy entrepreneurs entail taking advantage of policy windows of opportunity (Kingdon 1995). These windows of opportunity can open for predictable reasons – as with program reauthorizations – or unpredictable reasons – as with external shocks or significant electoral shifts. Similarly, Walker (1977) argues that recurring and politically necessary issues leave limited opportunities for Congress to address other issues.

---

[13] The model used in the analysis of the effects of the significant covariates on the predicted values of bill activity is the baseline plus the polarization variable. The only exception is the House majority party size coefficient, which is calculated using the baseline model along with the majority party size variable. Differences in the estimated marginal effects for the other variables using the two different models are trivial.

The best predictor of changes in member bill-sponsorship activity within issue areas was the imminent expiration of an existing law. This finding affirms our broader argument that legislative agendas are to a large degree problem driven. Other variables found to be related to variations in legislative attention can also be seen as indicating legislative responsiveness to issues that have the attention of voters – such as elite salience and presidential attention. Changes in partisan control, chamber preferences, or committee composition were less important, and often unimportant, predictors of shifts in legislative issue attention. Our findings suggest that issues that Congress "must" address play a larger role in shaping legislative agendas than do shifts in the preferences of lawmakers.

This finding that legislative attention is primarily problem driven is novel and deserving of additional investigation. We have only examined one indicator – bill introductions. To what extent does such a perspective alter how we think about types of legislative activity? For example, do anticipated expirations of important programs also predict campaign contribution patterns, congressional hearings activity, or possibly even committee assignment requests?

In the next chapter we turn our attention to the critical question of what drives policy change in Congress. This is familiar territory for legislative scholars. We examine significant changes to major laws and changes within the twenty-seven policy areas that were the focus of this chapter from 1977 to 2004. In this chapter we found that indicators of problem-solving motivations predicted shifts in legislative issue attention. In Chapter 9 we expect to find that the same motivations are important predictors of legislative policy change. To the extent that this is true, we can have increased confidence in their explanatory importance.

9

Problem Solving and the Dynamics of Policy Change

with Gilad J. Wilkenfeld

In this chapter we investigate policy change – a core function of all legislatures. The previous chapter examined congressional issue attention over time through the practice of bill sponsorship. This chapter asks whether the same factors that predict issue attention also predict "macrobehavioral" outcomes (Adler and Lapinski 2006). Whereas the decision to sponsor a bill is an individual one, policy change requires collective action – both in terms of setting the issue agenda and in terms of deciding whether current policy will be reformed. Are indicators of problem-solving considerations – such as program expirations and issue salience – also better predictors of both the timing and significance of policy changes?

To date, studies of policy change in legislatures have primarily focused on statutory change – when are laws reformed or repealed? Accordingly, the first part of our analysis replicates and then extends an important approach to exploring why "major" laws are significantly amended for the first time. After first replicating that approach, we test more encompassing definitions of the dependent variable to ask whether the scope of the "significant" revisions examined impacts the findings. We then operationalize policy change in an entirely new way. Here, the dependent variable is not whether a law is amended (for the first time) but a continuous measure of the total amount of statutory change within each of twenty-seven policy areas.

Our findings portray policy change in a very different light than previous research. Policies, once enacted, require revision as more is learned about their effectiveness and as conditions change. Policies change regardless of their ideological status or existing partisan or political conditions. For example, when Congress passed the Voting Rights Act of

1965 (P.L.89-110), it enacted the most meaningful reforms of federal voting law in almost a century. Since then, the Voting Rights Act has been significantly amended on at least three occasions. In 1970 it was amended to also ban literacy requirements, in 1975 it was amended to include protections for "language minorities," and in 1982 it was amended to permanently prohibit any voting practice or procedure that had discriminatory effects (previously, proof of intent was also often needed). None of these reforms constituted policy reversals, while some occur under political conditions that would not seem conducive to an expansion of voting rights for minorities – such as in 1982 when Republicans controlled the Senate and the presidency.

As we found in the previous chapter's examination of legislative issue attention (bill-sponsorship activity), policy change is in large part an opportunistic process that centers on issues that "must" be addressed. Problem-solving considerations such as program expirations and salient events are more robust and important predictors of policy change than macrolevel preference shifts or partisan realignments. To a much larger extent than is generally appreciated, the legislative agenda in Congress is problem driven.

PART I. APPRECIATING STATUTORY CHANGE IN CONGRESS

Systematic studies of policy change initially focused on explaining the legislative productivity of a Congress as measured by counts of "major" enactments (see among others Binder 2003; Coleman 1999; Howell et al. 2000; Kelly 1993; Mayhew 1991). Efforts to explain variations in productivity in terms of changing macropolitical conditions have been far from conclusive. Contrary to expectations, Mayhew (1991) found that unified governments were not more productive than divided governments. A large number of follow-up studies have either confirmed or challenged his central findings.

Studies of aggregate productivity do not allow for the exploration of issue-specific explanations for policy change. More recent studies examining the durability or "survival" of individual laws and programs do allow for the testing of policy-specific variables. However, to date, the aim of these studies has been similar to that of prior legislative productivity research – to test the importance of macropolitical conditions. For instance, Maltzman and Shipan emphasize that statutory durability "is shaped not only by characteristics of the law, but also by initial and subsequent political conditions and by interactions across the branches of government. Ideological and partisan alignments across branches and within Congress indelibly shape the prospects for stable laws by molding both the initial configuration of the law and its subsequent chances of revision" (Maltzman and Shipan 2008, 264). Likewise Berry and colleagues find that "changes in the ideological and partisan character of Congress help explain why programs are more or less likely to survive ... a program is vulnerable to termination, spending cuts, and other changes when the Congress that inherits it is different in partisan terms from the Congress that created it" (Berry, Burden, and Howell 2010, 15; see Lewis 2002 for similar findings).

Effectively, extant research on statutory and program reform has largely explored the degree to which partisan or preference conflict, both contemporaneously and intertemporally, has defined the timing of major changes. Yet, the vast majority of policy decisions in Congress are not conflictual. Even among those that are, only a small proportion divide lawmakers along party lines (Carson, Finocchiaro, and Rohde 2010). In our view, this suggests that a meaningful exploration of factors other than political conditions might prove fruitful.

Operationalizing Statutory Change

Studies of policy change to date focus on the durability of laws or programs. A law's durability has been alternately defined as the amount of time between enactment and the first time that it is significantly amended (Maltzman and Shipan 2008), and as the amount of time between its enactment and its repeal (Ragusa 2010). Still other studies explore policy change in terms of when federal programs are modified or eliminated altogether (Berry, Burden, and Howell 2010; Corder 2004; Lewis 2002).

For practical and theoretical reasons, scholars examining statutory change have limited their attention to the universe of major or historic laws identified by Mayhew (1991). This limits the laws to be analyzed and focuses attention on the most important enactments of the modern era (by one measure). The dependent variable is a "significant" change to one of these laws occurs. Rather than devising their own definitions of a significant change – obviously difficult in the diverse world of public policy – scholars have relied on a more universally acceptable short cut. First, they identify subsequent laws that either amended historic laws using the *Statutes at Large* (Maltzman and Shipan 2008) or that repealed provisions of the original law using the "Historical and Statutory Notes" section of the *U.S. Code* (Ragusa 2010). Then these researchers define the significant changes as those amending laws that also appear on Mayhew's list of historic legislation.

This "major" amendment threshold for a significant change is a particularly high one. Consider Maltzman and Shipan's analysis of just 150 amending events over sixty years. Many other significant amending statutes fail to make the cut because they fail to make Mayhew's list. For example, the 1978 Natural Gas Policy Act (NGPA; P.L. 95-621) had wide-ranging effects on natural gas use, energy conservation, and reducing dependence on foreign oil (Mayhew refers to it as the "comprehensive energy package;" see his Table 4.1). The NGPA was amended on a number of occasions over subsequent decades. One of these reforms, the Natural Gas Wellhead Decontrol Act of 1989 (P.L. 101-60), was the culmination of thirty-five years of quarreling over price controls on natural gas, lifted wellhead price controls for natural gas for the first time since 1954 (*CQ Almanac* 1989)! However, this change, along with other important changes to the NGPA over the years did not make Mayhew's list of historic enactments. This is just one of many examples of meaningful changes to historic statutes that are not considered in current approaches to examining statutory change.

When readers think about "significant" amending laws, they probably also envision a law that significantly weakens or strengthens the core purpose of the original enactment. However, the methodology described in the preceding text only considers the duration of a law and not the effects of the amending law. Consider the Food and Agriculture Act of 1977 (P.L. 95-113), an historic law on Mayhew's list that increased commodity subsidies and revised and expanded the food stamp program. The first "significant" law to amend this act (according to *Statutes at Large* and the Mayhew threshold) was the Energy Security Act of 1980 (P.L. 96-294). The Energy Security Act did amend the Food and Agriculture Act, but it did not "seriously amend" or "significantly revise" that law's core purpose (Maltzman and Shipan 2008, 258). Its main goals – authorizing funds for synthetic fuel, renewable energy research and development, and energy conservation programs – had very little to do with the core purposes of the Food Security Act. *Statutes at Large* references the energy act as amending the agricultural act because the former includes a minor provision allowing for changes in commodity pricing and assistance for agricultural products to be used for synthetic fuels. The actual substance of the amending law was not examined. Instead, the sole criterion was whether it was on Mayhew's list.

To gain a better sense of this potential methodological concern – that significant amending laws do not significantly revise the original law – we read the online *CQ Almanac* stories for all of the amending laws examined by Maltzman and Shipan.[1] We then grouped these amending laws into five categories based on their reported effects: major contraction of the original law, contraction, technical or indeterminate change, expansion, and major expansion of the original law. An amending law was categorized as contracting the original law when the coverage emphasized "contraction," "reduction," "weakening," "repeal," and so forth. When the coverage emphasized adjectives such as "expansion," "strengthening," and "increasing," it was categorized as an expansion. A "major" expansion or contraction was deemed to have occurred when an article used language such as "dramatically" or "significantly" expanding or contracting the act. The final, middle (technical or indeterminate) category includes other amending laws that *CQ* reports as addressing a different primary purpose (such as the Energy Security Act discussed previously), as expanding some parts of the original law while contracting others, or as making largely technical changes to the law.

Perhaps surprisingly, most of these "major" amending laws (88 out of 150, or about 60%) fell into the middle category (Figure 9.1). These amending laws did not "significantly revise" the original law's core purpose – in most cases there was no *CQ* coverage of their impact on the major law in question. They were similar to the Energy and Security Act of 1980 that – though a major law in its own right – did not make noteworthy changes to the Food and Agriculture Act of 1977.

For the amending laws that did alter the purpose of the original law, there was a substantial bias in terms of effect. More than 75 percent of the time, the effect was to expand the original law. Thus, the "duration" of a typical historic law in prior studies is defined not by a policy reversal, but by a further expansion of the law's original purpose (or by changes that do not significantly alter that purpose). This discovery is consistent with the findings of Bob Erikson and colleagues (2006, Ch. 9), who report a largely "liberal" trend or expansion of governmental activities through the major statutory changes adopted during the second half of the twentieth century.[2] For the current study, it suggests the value of considering an alternative to relying solely on Mayhew's list to judge the significance of amending laws.

[1] We are grateful for Sean Freeder's research assistance in completing this analysis.
[2] Erikson et al. 2002 analyze a list of 124 statutes enacted between 1953 and 1996, also derived from Mayhew's compilation of historic acts of Congress.

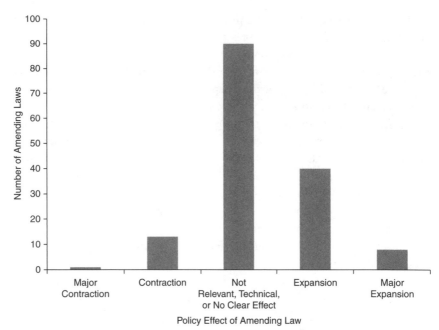

FIGURE 9.1. The Effects of "Historic" Amendments to Historic Laws.

A New Approach to Measuring "Change" in Federal Statutes

We propose an alternative approach to assessing statutory change that systematically addresses concerns about germaneness and allows the "significant" amending law threshold to vary. By altering this threshold, we are able to examine a broader set of statutory change events. In Part II of this chapter we propose an approach to studying "policy" change that goes beyond just the first significant amending law that has been the exclusive focus of prior studies.

Like prior studies, we first identify laws that amend laws on Mayhew's list of historic postwar enactments using *Statutes at Large*. To address germaneness concerns, we then turn to the Public Laws database of the Policy Agendas Project to exclude referenced amending laws that are not primarily about the same topic as the original law.[3] Thus, to make the cut, a law amending an historic surface transportation bill must also primarily be about surface transportation (i.e., it must have the same Policy Agendas Project subtopic code).[4]

---

[3] http://www.policyagendas.org/page/datasets-codebooks#public_laws (accessed April 20, 2012).

[4] Although the germaneness requirement does eliminate a portion of legislation that *Statutes at Large* identifies as amending the original enactment, the criterion offers a

Next we gauge the significance of amending laws by the amount of *CQ* coverage (number of article lines) they receive. Many other studies have relied on whether or not a law received any *CQ* coverage as an indicator of its significance (e.g., Anderson et al. 2003; Edwards, Barrett, and Peake 1997; Carson, Finocchiaro, and Rohde 2010; Mayhew 1991; Sinclair 1995; Stimson, MacKuen, and Erickson 1995). We assume that the amount of *CQ* coverage a law receives is a valid indicator of its relative significance.[5] If this is the case, then *CQ* coverage provides a valuable tool for varying the significance threshold of amending laws, as well as the scope of the statutory changes to be explained.

Validating *Congressional Quarterly* Coverage as a Measure of Significance

Although there is no "gold standard" of law or policy significance that might be used to assess the validity of *CQ* coverage, other accepted indicators provide valuable points of comparison. The most obvious is Mayhew's list of the most "innovative and consequential" laws. Does his list coincide with the statutes receiving the greatest amount of coverage in *CQ*? Before comparing the two, it is important to note that Mayhew excludes appropriations and Department of Defense authorizations from his list, and admits to a bias against reauthorizations and budget bills more generally (1991, 40). *CQ* coverage does not similarly discriminate so there is no reason to expect perfect correspondence between Mayhew's list and the top-ranking laws by *CQ* coverage. Despite this caveat, for the 1981–2000 time period, thirty-two of the fifty most significant laws in terms of *CQ* coverage are also found on Mayhew's list. Of the top ten laws in terms of *CQ* coverage, eight also appear on Mayhew's list (Table 9.1).

Another perspective is to compare amending laws that make Mayhew's list to other laws amending the same statute. Is it the case that the Mayhew amending laws receive more *CQ* coverage than the other amending laws? In Figure 9.2, each bar represents one of Mayhew's historic laws. The o's and x's dispersed vertically along each bar indicate the amount of *CQ* coverage

---

minimal standard for *relevance* of the amendment. It avoids the far more common problem discussed in the preceding text where the amending law or provision is only marginally related to the original enactment.

[5] In the rare instances where more than one germane amending law is passed in the same Congress, our indicator of importance is the sum of the *CQ* article lines devoted to all amending laws. There are only six instances of multiple amendments to an existing statute in a single year in the entire data set. Description from online archive of *CQ*, emphasis added. Carson et al. 2010 cite similar observations from a variety of scholars who have employed *CQ* for the same enterprise.

TABLE 9.1. *Top Ten Statutes by* Congressional Quarterly Almanac *Coverage in Issue Areas Examined*

Public Law	Law Title	Appears in Mayhew's List of Historic Laws
P.L. 101-549	Clean Air Act of 1990	✓
P.L. 105-178	Transportation Equity Act for the Twenty-First Century of 1998	✓
P.L. 101-624	Food, Agriculture, Conservation, and Trade Act of 1990	✓
P.L. 104-104	Telecommunications Act of 1996	✓
P.L. 101-625	Cranston-Gonzalez National Affordable Housing Act of 1990	✓
P.L. 101-012	Whistleblower Protection Act of 1989	
P.L. 99-198	Food Security Act of 1985	✓
P.L. 103-322	Violent Crime Control and Law Enforcement Act of 1994	✓
P.L. 100-690	Anti Drug Abuse Act of 1988	✓
P.L. 102-325	Higher Education Act Amendments of 1992	

each of the amending laws received. The o's are the amending laws that passed Mayhew's threshold of an historic law. The x's are the amending laws that did not (but were sufficiently significant to be covered in CQ).

Once again it is important to recall that Mayhew excludes certain types of laws from his list. Nevertheless, a Mayhew amending law received the most coverage in thirty-one of the forty-one cases. When more than one Mayhew law amended a given historic statute, both tended to rank near the top in terms of CQ coverage. On average, the Mayhew amending laws received 1,711 lines of CQ coverage, compared to just 743 lines for other amending laws covered by CQ (this difference is significant at $p < .001$).

Our last points of comparison are the "significance" scores Josh Clinton and John Lapinski generate for all public laws enacted since 1789 (2006). This score combines known information regarding congressional deliberation of statutes with assessments by twenty "raters." The product is an interval level score of significance for every law.[6] Raw article lines of CQ

---

[6] The methods of Mayhew and Clinton and Lapinski are informed by CQ coverage. Mayhew uses it as a first cut (wave) in identifying potentially historic laws. Clinton and Lapinski use it as one of their 20 indicators. This usage establishes the value of CQ in our opinion and does not raise questions about its validity. Rather, the differences reflect differences in research objectives.

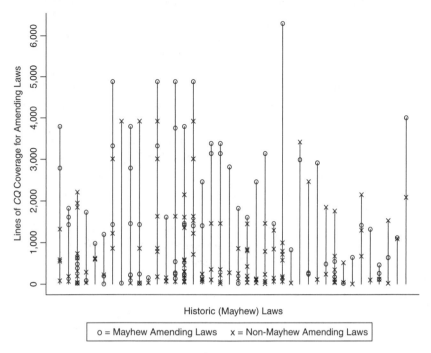

FIGURE 9.2. *Congressional Quarterly Almanac* Coverage of Amending Laws to Historic (Mayhew) Laws.

coverage correlate with the Clinton and Lapinski significance scores at a solid Pearson's $r = 0.59$ (sample n = 3,000). Why not use their scores for our study? Clinton and Lapinski produce a single score for each law. In contrast, CQ often produces multiple stories about different aspects of the same law. Each of these stories has also been coded for primary topic (by the Policy Agendas Project).[7] Thus, CQ coverage can be used to assess not only the significance of a law, but also the significance of particular provisions within those laws. In Part II of this chapter we use this noteworthy advantage to study *policy change* as distinct from *statutory change*.

A New Approach to Measuring Expiring Provisions

We anticipate that expiring provisions of law serve as a significant spur to legislative action (as discussed in Chapter 5). Existing studies acknowledge

[7] http://www.policyagendas.org/page/datasets-codebooks#congresssional_quarterly_almanac (accessed April 20, 2012).

that sunsets can play a role in the timing of policy change (Berry, Burden, and Howell, 6n10; Ragusa 2010, 1025), but only Maltzman and Shipan incorporate "a dummy variable to denote those laws that have a key provision that expires in the current session of Congress because of a sunset provision" (2008, 263).

This variable is a significant predictor of the likelihood that a major law will be amended. However, it is based on the very restrictive assumption that the only expiring provisions that matter are the ones that "sunset" entire laws. The Superfund example described earlier – where a solitary funding provision is the lynchpin for the program's continued existence – is the exception more than the rule. More often, laws contain multiple smaller expiring provisions. Additionally, those multiple provisions may not all expire in the same year. For instance, highway construction laws often have dozens of expirations that terminate three, four, or even six years after enactment. Thus, for many laws it may not be possible to pinpoint a single expiration or year that defines when Congress feels compelled to act.

We propose a different measure, discussed in Chapter 8, that is a count of expiring provisions for a given law in a given year. For the highway construction example previously mentioned, this variable would produce counts of expiring provisions for multiple years. For the current analysis of significant amendments to Mayhew laws (1977–2004), there are no expiring provisions in three-quarters of the years examined for a given law. In the other years, the number of expiring provisions for a given major law ranges from one to sixty-one (see Table 8.2).

Analyses of Statutory Changes

Because of the difficulty involved in identifying expiring provisions (see Chapter 8), and because we examine different sets of "significant" statutory changes that necessitate additional data collection, our analysis begins at the start of the 95th Congress (1977) and runs through the concluding year of the 108th Congress (2004).[8] We first confirm that Maltzman and Shipan's central findings are robust for this shorter time period. We then introduce our alternative measure of expirations before varying the first significant amendment threshold (using CQ coverage).

---

[8] The germaneness requirement in our coding procedure led us to exclude five omnibus budget and consolidated appropriations measures from our final analysis. We reran our models including the omnibus laws and found that their exclusion or inclusion has no substantive impact on our findings.

The question of interest is which variables are the most robust predictors of when major laws are significantly amended for the first time?

Maltzman and Shipan hypothesize that three sets of factors impact the durability of laws. The first set of factors capture political conditions at the time of the law's enactment, on the assumption that laws passed during periods of political division are less likely to endure. The second set captures subsequent political conditions, on the assumption that laws are more likely to be amended following substantial ideological shifts in the government or during periods of unified government. The third set of factors captures features of the law that are hypothesized to affect its duration, such as its complexity (suggesting an increased need for subsequent policy adjustments) or a sunset provision.

In the analyses reported here, the data are organized in panel form by statute and year. Because the unit of analysis is the duration or survival of a law (i.e., the amount of time between its enactment and first significant reform), a Cox model is employed to estimate the hazard rate – the relative risk that a law is amended in a given year (Box-Steffensmeier and Jones 1997). The dependent variable, therefore, has a value of 0 each year until a significant policy change ends the original law's "life." Each series ends with that first significant statutory change.

Our examination begins with two replications of Maltzman and Shipan's analysis (their Table 1, model 2) for the 1977–2004 time period.[9] The models differ in one respect only. Model 1 of Table 9.2 tests their sunset measure, while model 2 tests our alternative count-based measure of expiring provisions (model 2). The findings closely mirror those of Maltzman and Shipan's original analysis of a longer time period. Both models have good fit (the Wald χ^2 test of significance exceeds the 99% level of confidence). A positive coefficient indicates that there is an increased risk that an historic law will be significantly amended. Political conditions as well as law-specific factors are significantly associated with a law's duration. Divided government at enactment, larger chamber preference difference at enactment, smaller chamber preference difference at the time of amendment, law complexity, and the presence of a sunset (or more expiring provisions) all increase the likelihood that a law will be significantly amended. Supreme Court attention and divisiveness are not significant (these are significant in the original study), and policy mood

[9] Analysis of the Schoenfeld residuals indicates there are no violations of the global proportional hazards assumption and no individual variables have nonproportional effects on the hazard rates. Therefore no conditional variables controlling for nonproportionality in these data are necessary.

TABLE 9.2. *Replication of Maltzman and Shipan's Analysis of Historic Amendments to Historic Enactments, 1977–2004*

	Model 1	Model 2
Enactment Political Conditions		
Divided Government at Enactment	0.732**	0.716*
	(0.367)	(0.380)
Chamber Difference at Enactment	14.88*	16.10*
	(8.479)	(8.892)
Subsequent Political Conditions		
Subsequent Divided Government	0.564	0.491
	(0.460)	(0.461)
Subsequent Chamber Difference	−13.14*	−13.66*
	(7.367)	(7.315)
Policy Mood	−0.096**	−0.090**
	(0.041)	(0.042)
Court Attention	−0.088	−0.092
	(0.503)	(0.530)
Law-Specific Characteristics		
Law Complexity	0.001**	0.001**
	(0.000)	(0.000)
Divisiveness	−0.007	−0.004
	(0.007)	(0.007)
Sunset Provision (Maltzman and	0.460**	
Shipan's measure)	(0.229)	
Number of Expiring Provisions		0.0159**
(Adler and Wilkerson's measure)		(0.007)
Observations	806	806
Wald χ^2	44.95**	49.06**

Note: Cox regression, robust standard errors in parentheses; $**p < .05$, $*p < .10$. Because analysis of Schoenfeld residuals indicated violations of the nonproportionality assumption, Maltzman and Shipan included two additional variables interacting the log of time with chamber difference at enactment and subsequent chamber difference. In our models, the same test of Schoenfeld residuals did not indicate a violation of the nonproportionality assumption. We therefore do not include the same variables.

is significant but in the wrong direction (it was not significant in the original study).

We next ask whether these findings stand up to different specifications of a "significant" amending law. In Table 9.3, the covariates are the same but the dependent variable is different: a law's duration is now defined by whether an amending law was in the top one-third in terms of CQ article lines of coverage (for all years) and was germane to the original law.

TABLE 9.3. *Predictors of First Significant Amendments to Historic Enactments (Threshold of Significance = Top One-Third of All* Congressional Quarterly *Coverage)*

	Model 1	Model 2
Enactment Political Conditions		
Divided Government at Enactment	−0.213	−0.317
	(0.372)	(0.381)
Chamber Difference at Enactment	2.557	1.195
	(8.077)	(7.916)
Subsequent Political Conditions		
Subsequent Divided Government	0.411	0.331
	(0.462)	(0.451)
Subsequent Chamber Difference	3.799	4.118
	(7.534)	(7.675)
Policy Mood	0.105*	0.099*
	(0.054)	(0.054)
Court Attention	0.204	0.354
	(0.363)	(0.359)
Law-Specific Characteristics		
Law Complexity	0.002**	0.002**
	(0.001)	(0.001)
Divisiveness	−0.012	−0.011
	(0.008)	(0.008)
Sunset Provision	0.570*	
(Maltzman and Shipan's measure)	(0.327)	
Number of Expiring Provisions		0.042**
(Adler and Wilkerson's measure)		(0.008)
Observations	932	932
Wald χ^2	31.06**	60.58**

Note: Cox regression, robust standard errors in parentheses; $**p < .05$, $*p < .10$.

Using the original Mayhew threshold, many of the major laws examined are never "significantly" amended at all. Our alternative threshold is still quite restrictive but it nevertheless captures far more detailed amending activity. Specifically, the first amendments examined under this alternative threshold receive more than ninety-three thousand article lines of *CQ* coverage, compared to the thirty-eight thousand lines of coverage the Mayhew amendments receive.

This more inclusive and germane definition of a significant amendment profoundly affects the findings. Many of the indicators of political conditions that were important before are no longer predictive of when

TABLE 9.4. *Predictors of Less Significant First Amendments to Historic Enactments (Threshold of Significance* = Congressional Quarterly *Coverage or Any Amendment)*

	Model 1 (All amendments, at least some CQ coverage, and must be germane)	Model 2 (All amendments, regardless of CQ coverage or germaneness)
Enactment Political Conditions		
Divided Government at	−0.493	−0.431
Enactment	(0.378)	(0.341)
Chamber Difference at	−2.524	−0.663
Enactment	(8.216)	(7.801)
Subsequent Political Conditions		
Subsequent Divided	0.373	0.287
Government	(0.369)	(0.316)
Subsequent Chamber	5.699	−1.528
Difference	(7.686)	(6.957)
Policy Mood	0.037	0.007
	(0.043)	(0.034)
Court Attention	0.060	0.108
	(0.346)	(0.341)
Law-Specific Characteristics		
Law Complexity	0.002*	0.002*
	(0.001)	(0.001)
Divisiveness	−0.006	−0.001
	(0.007)	(0.006)
Number of Expiring	0.031*	0.057*
Provisions (Adler and	(0.012)	(0.014)
Wilkerson's measure)		
Observations	747	463
Wald χ^2	41.71*	42.58*

Note: Cox regression, robust standard errors in parentheses; *$p < .05$.

a law is significantly amended for the first time. Expirations, law complexity, and policy mood – indicative of problem-solving demands – are significant predictors. In terms of marginal effects, expiring provisions of law produce a 261 percent increase in the hazard rate as they move from their minimum to maximum values.[10] The presence of a sunset provision

[10] The marginal effects analysis conducted here examines the increase in hazard rate associated with minimum to maximum increase in the value of a variable of interest. These are estimated while holding all other variables constant.

(as defined in the original study), in contrast, increases the hazard rate by just 77 percent. Expiring provisions also compare favorably to the other significant variables. A minimum–maximum increase in policy mood elevates the risk of amendment by about 170 percent, while law complexity elevates it by 152 percent.

Table 9.4 reports two more analyses of the duration of major laws where the threshold for a "significant" first amending law is lowered even further. Model 1 defines this first significant change as the first germane amending law to receive *some CQ* coverage (recall that many laws receive no coverage at all). Model 2 defines it as the first amending law listed in the legislative histories of *Statutes at Large*, germane or otherwise, and without regard to significance. In both models, expiring provisions and law complexity continue to be significant predictors of when a major law is amended for the first time. Once again, political conditions are not robust predictors, nor is policy mood.

Across all of the specifications of the dependent variable – from Mayhew's "historic" threshold of importance to a much more permissive standard of "any amendment" – expiring provisions and law complexity were consistent predictors of when a major law was reformed for the first time. Once the significance threshold was lowered to include more than historic amending laws, thus substantially expanding the scope of the changes examined, political conditions were no longer robust predictors of statutory reform.

PART II. APPRECIATING POLICY CHANGE IN CONGRESS

In Part I of this chapter, we examined different explanations for the first significant reforms to major laws. We started with an established approach and then lowered the threshold for a significant change to examine more change events. However, a focus on the first significant statutory change leaves many other changes unexamined. In this part of the chapter, we propose a new and more comprehensive approach to studying policy change.

Our focus is on lawmaking activity in the same twenty-seven Policy Agendas Project policy subtopics introduced in Chapter 8. There we noted that these subtopics captured more than half of all of the enactment activity (based on *CQ* coverage). Here we use *CQ* coverage as a measure of the amount of policy change within each of those subtopic areas over time. By examining variations in *CQ* coverage of enactments within each subtopic from one congressional term to the next we are

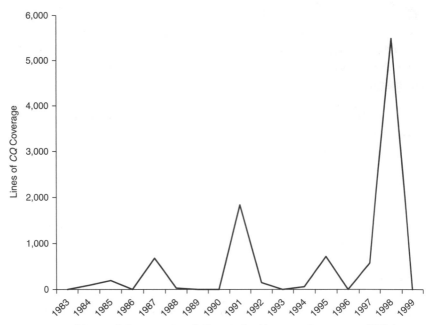

FIGURE 9.3. Lines of *Congressional Quarterly Almanac* Coverage of Highways
Enactments, 1983–1999.

effectively capturing the wax and wane of policy change. An example will
help clarify how this approach differs from the previous analysis.

The unit of analysis to measure policy changes is the policy area (by
congressional term). For the issue area of "highways," we first identify
all CQ articles addressing public laws that are primarily about Policy
Agendas Project subtopic 1002 (the highway construction, maintenance,
and safety subtopic). We then sum the number of lines of coverage (ignoring articles that covered failed legislation and any other activities other
than enacted legislation) across all of these articles for each individual
congressional term. This is our indicator of the amount of "highway"
policy change in that term. The objective is to capture the significance
of the laws passed in that congressional term. Figure 9.3 illustrates how
lines of coverage quantify policy change in this topic area. Each of the
spikes in article lines of coverage coincides with terms in which Congress
enacted significant transportation laws (in 1987, 1991, and 1998). It
should now be apparent that this is a very different dependent variable from the "first significant change" to a major law of Part I of this
chapter.

Analysis of Policy Change

In Chapter 8 we examined changing legislative issue attention (bill-sponsorship activity) within the twenty-seven issue areas over an eighteen-year time period (1980–98). Here we examine policy change within the same issue areas and time period. The independent variables are also the same as those considered in Chapter 8 (see Table 8.2) – with one addition: *House Priority Change* tests whether bill-sponsorship activity by lawmakers predicts policy change (after controlling for other factors such as expirations).

We pursue two strategies for modeling the data. In the first, we treat the dependent variable (enactment-specific *CQ* article lines within each policy area) as a *count variable* and employ a Poisson methodology that is well suited to addressing overdispersion – negative binomial. Because there are an excessive number of zero observations (often there are no enactments that meet the *CQ* threshold in a policy/term), we select a zero-inflated version of the negative binomial model (the zinb command in STATA), with the identical set of independent variables used to predict excess zeros.[11] We also expect differences in the intercepts across policy subtopics, as well as potential problems with serial correlation, so these models are estimated with clustering on the issue area (subtopic). Thus, this first modeling strategy is very conservative.

Our second modeling strategy opts for a more conventional and robust OLS approach that treats the dependent variable as continuous. In this latter specification, we log the dependent variable to control for occasional extreme outlier values. We also test a second OLS specification that employs PCSE. The findings for the two specifications are very similar. The findings reported in the following text focus on the latter (PCSE) analysis, but we also highlight any important differences in our discussion.[12]

Modeling Policy Change as a Count Variable

We first consider the negative binomial results. As in the analysis of legislative issue attention in Chapter 8, we only report a subset of the many

---

[11] In all cases, a Vuong test indicated that the zero-inflated negative binomial model was a better fit to the data than the standard negative binomial model.

[12] As with the analysis in Chapter 8, the models reported do not include a lagged dependent variable to address potential autocorrelation (Achen 2001; Keele and Kelly 2006). Inclusion of a lagged dependent variable in the models was inconsequential for the primary findings. Similarly, we report the results for the model without fixed effects for the subtopic. Even when we include fixed effects – which slightly changes the interpretation of our variables – there is no substantive difference in the findings.

TABLE 9.5. Models Predicting Policy Change (Count Variable [zinb])

	Baseline	Baseline + Preferences	Baseline + Parties	Baseline + Committees
Problem Solving				
Expiring Provisions in Law	0.025**	0.024**	0.024**	0.025**
	(0.004)	(0.004)	(0.004)	(0.004)
Elite Salience	0.260**	0.313**	0.280**	0.249**
	(0.093)	(0.089)	(0.092)	(0.089)
Most Important Problem	−1.893	−1.805	−2.396	−1.609
	(2.819)	(2.669)	(2.707)	(2.780)
Mood	0.0508*	0.0242	0.052	0.053
	(0.029)	(0.082)	(0.048)	(0.033)
Policy Preference Coalitions				
Chamber Preference Distance		−3.708		
		(9.810)		
House Polarization		1.627		
		(2.035)		
House Priority Change		−9.730		
		(9.626)		
Majority Party Coalitions				
House Majority Party Size			−5.588**	
			(2.687)	
Senate Majority Party Size			15.110	
			(16.520)	
House Majority Party Agenda			−0.012	
			(0.228)	
Gain of Majority Party Seats			−0.002	
			(0.008)	

	(1)	(2)	(3)	(4)
Majority Party Issue			−0.146	
			(0.191)	
Committee Effects				
Turnover House Committee Chair				0.040
				(0.247)
Turnover Senate Committee Chair				−0.087
				(0.196)
Change in Committee Preferences				0.314
				(0.760)
Interbranch Influences				
Unified/Divided	−0.389	−0.455	−0.737	−0.403
	(0.299)	(0.307)	(0.486)	(0.342)
Presidential Attention	30.69**	33.83**	32.13**	30.68**
	(5.361)	(7.030)	(6.289)	(5.360)
Supreme Court Cases	0.015	0.015	0.018	0.016
	(0.032)	(0.031)	(0.029)	(0.032)
Policy-Specific Conflict				
Policy Conflict	0.362*	0.384*	0.355*	0.365*
	(0.207)	(0.210)	(0.188)	(0.189)
Constant	2.170	2.586	−2.888	2.048
	(1.823)	(6.423)	(7.574)	(2.085)
Observations	243	243	243	243
Wald χ2	82.18**	78.45**	131.68**	97.21**
Alpha	1.150	1.124	1.125	1.148
	(0.143)	(0.137)	(0.141)	(0.143)
Vuong Test	2.12*	3.29**	3.13**	2.16**

Note: Robust standard errors in parentheses; $**p < .05$, $*p < .10$.

models tested. We begin with a baseline model focusing on problem-solving motivations for policy change, and then compare the findings to models that incorporate additional explanatory factors (Table 9.5). In Table 9.6, we summarize findings for a much larger set of specifications.

The baseline problem-solving model (column 1 of Table 9.5) indicates that problem-solving considerations are important predictors of policy change, while macrolevel political conditions are not. Expiring provisions of law as well as elite salience (coverage of the topic in *The New York Times* editorials) are significant and robust predictors across all of the models. One important interbranch influence variable is also persistently related to policy change – presidential issue attention. The more frequently the president communicates publicly about an issue, the more likely it is that Congress will pass policy in that issue area. One other variable – policy conflict – is also predictive of policy change in the count models reported in Table 9.5. Contentious policy areas (based on the level of consensus during roll call voting in the previous term) also experience more policy change.

Measures of public sentiment – captured by the "most important problem" variable and Stimson's gauge of the public mood for greater government activism – have mixed effects. Public mood for increased government activity is a significant predictor of policy change in about half of the models (Erikson et al. 2002), but this is often contingent on the combination of variables in the model. The proportion of the public that considers the issue to be the "most important problem facing the nation" (albeit, at the major topic level) is never related to policy change. Earlier, we noted that scholars have expressed doubts about the validity of this measure as an indicator of public priorities, so this finding is not particularly surprising (Wlezien 2005).

Substantially, none of the indicators of macrolevel political conditions consistently predicts policy change. This is the case no matter whether these variables are tested separately or in combination with other variables (Table 9.6). As well, it was almost never the case that the variables capturing preference, party, or committee factors performed as predicted. Among all the variable combinations, there was only one instance when distance between the House and Senate preferences correctly predicted policy change. Conversely, polarization was occasionally significantly associated with changes in policy, but always in the opposite direction as predicted. Similarly, measures of interbranch influence other than

TABLE 9.6. *Summary of Models Predicting Policy Change (Count Variable [zinb])*

	Expected	1	2	3	4	5	6	7	8	9	10
Problem-Solving Theory											
Expiring Provisions in Law	+	✓	✓	✓	✓	✓	✓	✓	✓	✓	✓
Salient Events and Mood											
Elite Salience	+	✓	✓	✓	✓	✓	✓	✓	✓	✓	✓
Most Important Problem	+										
Mood	+	✓		✓	✓		✓		✓		✓
Policy Preferences											
Chamber Preference Distance	–		▓								
House Polarization	–			✗							
House Priority Change	+				▓						
Majority Party Coalitions											
House Majority Party Size	+					✗					
Senate Majority Party Size	+						▓				
House Majority Party Agenda	+							▓			
Gain of Majority Party Seats	+								▓		
Majority Party Issue	+									▓	
Committee Effects											
Change in House Committee Chair	+									▓	
Change in Senate Committee Chair	+										
Change in Committee Preferences	+										▓
Interbranch Influences											
Unified Government	+	▓	▓	▓	▓	▓	▓	▓	▓	▓	▓
Presidential Attention	+	✓	✓	✓	✓	✓	✓	✓	✓	✓	✓
Supreme Court Cases	+	▓	▓	▓	▓	▓	▓	▓	▓	▓	▓
Policy-Specific Conflict											
Policy Conflict	+/–	✓		✓	✓	✓	✓	✓	✓	✓	✓

Note: Shaded cell = variable included in the model; ✓ = variable is statistically significant and in the predicted direction; ✗ = variable is statistically significant but not in the predicted direction.

TABLE 9.6 *(cont.)*

	Expected	11	12	13	14	15	16	17	18	19	20
Problem-Solving Theory											
Expiring Provisions in Law	+	✓	✓	✓	✓	✓	✓	✓	✓	✓	✓
Salient Events and Mood											
Elite Salience	+	✓	✓	✓	✓	✓	✓	✓	✓	✓	✓
Most Important Problem	+										
Mood	+					✓	✓				✓
Policy Preferences											
Chamber Preference Distance	−			✓						✓	
House Polarization	−					✗	✗				✗
House Priority Change	+										
Majority Party Coalitions											
House Majority Party Size	+								✗		
Senate Majority Party Size	+										
House Majority Party Agenda	+										
Gain of Majority Party Seats	+										
Majority Party Issue	+										
Committee Effects											
Change in House Committee Chair	+										
Change in Senate Committee Chair	+										
Change in Committee Preferences	+										
Interbranch Influences											
Unified Government	+				✗						
Presidential Attention	+	✓	✓	✓	✓	✓	✓	✓	✓	✓	✓
Supreme Court Cases	+										
Policy-Specific Conflict											
Policy Conflict	+/−	✓		✓	✓	✓	✓	✓	✓	✓	✓

presidential attention – unified/divided government and Supreme Court activity – fail to predict policy change as we conceptualize it here.

Finally, one last observation of note: the *House priority change* variable – bill-sponsorship activity – is never a statistically significant predictor of policy change in any of the models. That is, once we control for the effect of significant and important variables, such as number of expiring provisions and elite salience, bill-sponsorship activity has no influence on the degree of policy change.

Modeling Policy Change as a Continuous Variable

To explore the robustness of these findings further, we considered two more modeling approaches – robust OLS regression and OLS with PCSE – that treat the dependent variable as continuous. Table 9.7 replicates Table 9.5 (of the count model analysis) for the PCSE analysis, while Table 9.8 once again provides a graphical summary of all the PCSE models. Any differences between the OLS with PCSE results and the OLS results (not reported) are noted in the text.

The results are very similar to those reported for the count models with two notable exceptions. Expiring provisions and elite salience continue to be significant predictors of legislative policy change across the board. In addition, public mood is a significant predictor of policy change in nearly every PCSE specification, whereas it was significant about half the time in the count models. Conversely, presidential issue attention was nearly always significant before, it is now significant less than half the time (see Table 9.8). (In the standard OLS analysis, presidential issue attention is statistically significant three-quarters of the time.) However, the main conclusions of the previous analyses remain – problem-solving motivations continue to be the best explanations for policy change.

Two preference-centered variables also show signs of life in the PCSE analyses – the measure of ideological gridlock (*Polarization*) and the size of the majority caucus in the House. These are also the only preference- or partisan-oriented variables that exhibited occasional significance in our analysis of policy attention in Chapter 8. However, neither is as robust across alternative specifications as the variables capturing problem-solving motivations. The remaining political conditions variables are never significant predictors of legislative policy change.

Finally, Figure 9.4 compares the effects of the significant variables in the prior analysis. As before, we start with the baseline model and add in the polarization variable. We hold all variables at their means (or mode

TABLE 9.7. *Models Predicting Policy Change (Continuous Variable [OLS with PCSE])*

	Baseline	Baseline + Preferences	Baseline + Parties	Baseline + Committees
Problem Solving				
Expiring Provisions in Law	0.058**	0.056**	0.053**	0.058**
	(0.011)	(0.011)	(0.011)	(0.011)
Elite Salience	0.741**	0.647**	0.642**	0.741**
	(0.214)	(0.212)	(0.216)	(0.210)
Most Important Problem	−10.42	−10.78	−8.710	−10.93
	(8.111)	(8.359)	(8.270)	(8.194)
Mood	0.220**	0.247**	0.218**	0.225**
	(0.092)	(0.088)	(0.074)	(0.094)
Policy Preference Coalitions				
Chamber Preference Distance		8.658		
		(10.98)		
House Polarization		−6.097**		
		(2.236)		
House Priority Change		20.24		
		(17.38)		
Majority Party Coalitions				
House Majority Party Size			17.73**	
			(4.074)	
Senate Majority Party Size			−44.38**	
			(18.43)	
House Majority Party Agenda			0.532	
			(0.542)	
Gain of Majority Party Seats			0.003	
			(0.008)	

TABLE 9.7. (cont.)

	Baseline	Baseline + Preferences	Baseline + Parties	Baseline + Committees
Majority Party Issue			-0.017	
			(0.389)	
Committee Effects				
Turnover House Committee Chair				-0.221
				(0.510)
Turnover Senate Committee Chair				0.131
				(0.462)
Change in Committee Preferences				-0.895
				(1.470)
Interbranch Influences				
Unified/Divided	0.170	0.332	0.913*	0.0535
	(0.826)	(0.445)	(0.549)	(0.867)
Presidential Attention	27.23*	21.61	21.02	28.68*
	(16.27)	(15.35)	(15.67)	(16.12)
Supreme Court Cases	0.064	0.035	0.029	0.058
	(0.060)	(0.060)	(0.059)	(0.061)
Policy-Specific Conflict				
Policy Conflict	-0.407	-0.128	-0.120	-0.457
	(0.518)	(0.531)	(0.526)	(0.517)
Constant	-11.55**	-8.776	2.827	-11.61**
	(5.424)	(6.714)	(8.830)	(5.597)
Observations	243	243	243	243
R^2	0.194	0.248	0.250	0.200

Note: Robust standard errors in parentheses; **$p < .05$, *$p < .10$.

TABLE 9.8. *Summary of Models Predicting Policy Change (Continuous Variable [OLS with PCSE])*

	Expected	1	2	3	4	5	6	7	8	9	10	11	12	13	14	15	16	17	18	19	20
Problem-Solving Theory																					
Expiring Provisions in Law	+	✓	✓	✓	✓	✓	✓	✓	✓	✓		✓	✓	✓	✓	✓	✓	✓	✓	✓	✓
Salient Events and Mood																					
Elite Salience	+	✓	✓	✓	✓	✓	✓	✓	✓	✓		✓	✓	✓	✓	✓	✓	✓	✓	✓	✓
Most Important Problem	+	✓	✓	✓	✓	✓	✓	✓	✓	✓		✓	✓	✓	✓	✓	✓	✓	✓	✓	✓
Mood	+																				
Policy Preferences																					
Chamber Preference Distance	−		✗										✗	✗				✓			
House Polarization	−			✓													✓			✓	
House Priority Change	+															✓					
Majority Party Coalitions																					
House Majority Party Size	+					✓						✓			✗				✓		✓
Senate Majority Party Size	+					✗						✗							✗		✗
House Majority Party Agenda	+													✗							
Gain of Majority Party Seats	+																				
Majority Party Issue	+																				
Committee Effects																					
Δ in House Committee Chair	+																				
Δ in Senate Committee Chair	+																				
Change in Committee Preferences	+																				
Interbranch Influences																					
Unified Government	+	✓				✓	✓	✓	✓	✓		✓			✓				✓		
Presidential Attention	+																				
Supreme Court Cases	+																				
Policy-Specific Conflict																					
Policy Conflict	+/−																				

Note: Shaded cell = variable included in the model; ✓ = variable is statistically significant and in the predicted direction; ✗ = variable is statistically significant but not in the predicted direction.

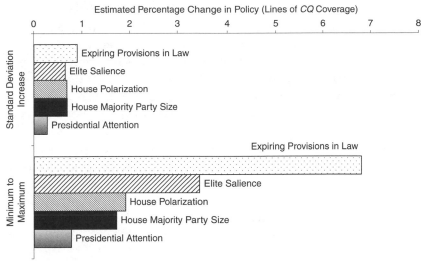

FIGURE 9.4. Effects of Key Predictors of Policy Change (OLS with PCSE).
Note: Coefficients represent the percentage increase in the log of CQ lines of coverage by policy area.

if a variable is dichotomous). The amount of policy change is estimated as each statistically significant variable is varied either one standard deviation (top frame) or from its minimum to maximum (bottom frame).[13] Because the dependent variable for these models was a log transformation of CQ article lines by policy area, the effects are read as percentage changes.

The consequences of problem-solving factors are clearly displayed here. The effect of a standard deviation change for expiring provisions is again the largest of any of the significant variables – about 20 percent larger than most of the other significant variables. However, when we look at these variables' effects across their ranges (bottom frame), the most prominent problem-solving factors explain far more policy change. The number of expiring provisions in a law is by far the most notable factor. From its minimum to maximum value, expiring provisions produce around twice as much policy change as the next most important variable (*Elite Salience*), and more than three times that of the partisan and preference factors. This is also a best-case scenario where the

---

[13] For the House majority party size measure, we utilize the baseline model plus the majority size variable. Like Chapter 8, the differences in the effects estimations between the two models are inconsequential.

preference-based variables are concerned. Unlike the issue-specific factors (expirations, presidential attention, and elite salience), their effects are not robust across the different model specifications and measures.

We conclude by considering one potential lingering question – perhaps policy changes triggered by expirations do little more than extend a program's termination date. If our measure of policy change merely captured the timing of policy changes then there would be reason for concern. However, recall that our measure of policy change was article lines of *CQ* coverage – a continuous measure that correlates with Mayhew's judgments of statute importance, and Clinton and Lapinski's continuous measure of enactment significance. A renewal that simply extends a program should not be newsworthy. A quick skim of *CQ* articles for one type of *pro forma* extensions – continuing resolutions – confirmed that the editors devote few column inches to such nonsignificant enactments.

CONCLUSION

This chapter finds that problem-solving considerations offer the best systematic explanation for when major laws are amended for the first time, as well as for fluctuations in the amount of policy change within issue areas over time. The results reported in this chapter also mirror the previous chapter's findings regarding a completely different indicator of legislative issue attention – the number of bills introduced in a policy area. These central findings were much more robust than were variables capturing macropolitical conditions. It is fair to say that across these two chapters we found little evidence to indicate that changing political conditions spur changes in legislative issue attention or legislative policy change.

How should scholars understand these striking findings? Throughout this book we have portrayed legislative attention as a scarce commodity. With so many problems and so little time, the issues that "must" be addressed – such as program reauthorizations and externally driven crises – leave limited opportunities for lawmakers (and parties) to take up discretionary issues. Whereas many perspectives emphasize the zero-sum aspects of congressional politics, we have argued that lawmakers of both parties have incentives to be responsive to problems of this kind. There is much more consensus in Congress regarding whether such problems deserve to be addressed than seems to be generally appreciated, as the consensual nature of final passage votes so aptly demonstrates. This does not mean that lawmakers will set aside their differences regarding the details of policy. But addressing recurring issues and problems that have the public's attention should also be priorities for party leaders tasked with promoting the party's "reputation" in the electorate.

To some readers it may seem unremarkable that policy change happens when statutes come up for renewal. Yet leading theories of congressional organization offer little reason to think that lawmaking activity revolves primarily around previously determined calendars and external events. Instead, the consistent theme of these theories is that electorally driven preference shifts are the central determinants of legislative policy change. Expirations and external events (other than elections) receive little if any consideration.

Nothing in congressional procedure mandates that Congress take up expiring laws or prevents Congress from making changes to those laws at other times. Yet there are good reasons to think that expirations are even more important than the results reported here indicate. For some laws (e.g., Superfund), a single expiration may be what matters and our measure (number of expiring provisions) treats such cases as less significant than others where multiple provisions expire in the same year or congressional term. In addition, Congress does not always reauthorize programs on time. An enormous highway construction bill expired in 1986 but was not renewed until the next term. Our analyses did not test for such lagged effects. Finally, we excluded recurring agenda items that come up every year (such as annual appropriations, defense, and budgetary cycles). Including these would obviously strengthen the case for a problem-driven perspective on legislative policy change.

Proponents of the conditional party government perspective, for example, note that partisan politics does not infuse every issue (Aldrich and Rohde 2000). Our findings confirm this observation. The replication of the Maltzman and Shipan analysis found that certain macropolitical conditions were significant predictors of the first instance an historic law was amending in "major" fashion (Table 9.2). However, macropolitical conditions were not robust predictors of statutory change when even slight adjustments were made to the threshold for change. Expansion of the change definition to include germane ones that made it into the top-third in terms of *CQ* coverage (Table 9.3), also quite an exclusive list (recall that most laws do not receive any *CQ* coverage), demonstrated that macropolitical factors were unrelated to periods of meaningful change. Lower thresholds further reinforced these findings. In contrast, indicators of problem-solving considerations were significant predictors of statutory change in every analysis. Thus, most of the policy change that occurs in Congress appears to be driven by dynamics that have to date received little attention in the dominant research.

Our theory predicts that broader political conditions play a limited role in shaping the legislative issue agenda. However, it is likely that political conditions play a more central role in shaping choice agendas. Congress was going to address the problem of rising prescription drug costs in 2003–4. However, the Republican response to this problem was decidedly different from what would have occurred during a democratically controlled government. As we noted earlier, existing approaches to studying policy change rarely consider such directional effects (i.e., whether an amending law moves a policy in a more liberal or conservative direction). The goal of our analyses, like nearly every study of policy change or legislative productivity to date, has been to explain the timing and amount of policy change. We anticipate that such a shift in focus will reinstate political conditions as important factors in the determination of legislative outputs.

Lawmakers' shared interests in promoting policy updating processes and addressing problems of concern to voters have an important impact on policy-making opportunities in Congress. We have shown this to be the case whether examining legislative issue attention, revisions to major laws, and policy change more generally. Although such activities may receive less media attention than a relatively small number of conflictual "high politics" issues, our findings demonstrate that the issues covered in the media (and that are often the focus of scholarly research) are not representative of congressional policy making more broadly. In the concluding chapter, we consider some additional implications of a problem-solving perspective, including the possibility that problem-solving activities promote more informed and therefore more responsible policy choices, and, possibly, that they promote bipartisan cooperation.

10

Problem Solving and American Politics

> Listen, the Founders gave us a committee of 535 people. Frankly, it was not designed to work. My job is to make it work. And it is working. Is it slow? Yes. Is it frustrating? Yes. But what I take comfort in every day is that I know members on both sides of the aisle are trying to do the right thing for the American people ....
>
> Speaker John Boehner (2011)

Congressional negotiations over the extension of the Bush tax cut in 2010 and the federal debt-ceiling increase and extension of the payroll tax holiday in 2011 confirm the very old adage about laws and sausages. Viewed from the outside, partisan or intercameral conflict appears reprehensible and irresponsible – why can't our representatives behave like adults and just work out their differences? There are reasons for these stalemates, however. Like many high-stakes negotiations, legislators who stake out extreme bargaining positions and stick to them for as long as possible are sometimes rewarded. The visible nature of contemporary congressional politics and the fact that strong partisans tend to be more attentive to politics further encourages lawmakers to engage in public posturing as a prelude to decision making.

We have argued that legislating is more often a game of chicken than a game of winner-take-all. The players in a game of chicken have incentives to act tough (or even suicidal), but they also appreciate that certain outcomes are to be avoided. Similarly for lawmakers, public pronouncements that they do not care whether they are reelected may advance their negotiating positions. For some lawmakers this may even be true. But at the end of the day, most legislators will favor compromise if the electoral costs of stalemate are too high.

Some contemporary observers suggest that party polarization has become so pronounced that bipartisan compromise no longer serves lawmakers' electoral interests. Shared societal beliefs about the responsibilities and limits of government that once encouraged members of Congress to seek common ground have given way to sharp divisions. Put another way, winner-take-all politics have replaced the traditional game of legislative chicken.

In December 2011, to the cheers of many Republican lawmakers, the House soundly rejected an extension of a payroll tax holiday that had recently passed the Senate with overwhelming bipartisan support. Evidence, it seemed, of the insurmountable differences between the parties. Yet, less than a week later, the same Republicans were in retreat, agreeing to extend the tax holiday by unanimous consent (when the objection of just one lawmaker could have killed the bill). One of the factors that apparently moved Republicans was a warning from one of their own: "Next November no incumbent is safe nor should they be," Sen. John McCain (R-AZ) said (CBS News 2011).

The fact that these lawmakers – despite considerable *ex ante* posturing – felt compelled to backtrack is a significant statement about the importance that voters continue to place on problem solving. Although it is certainly true that American politics has become more polarized in recent years, it is a very different proposition to suggest that the electoral interests of Republicans and Democrats no longer overlap. In each of the visible events just discussed, party leaders issued strong warnings about how their members were prepared to fall on their swords rather than compromise. Yet in each case, those leaders ultimately lined up the votes necessary to avoid very public instances of legislative failure. The government did not shut down, and programs valued by the public were extended.

In this concluding chapter we first review the central arguments and findings of this book. We then consider more recent political developments and their implications for Congress as a problem-solving institution. Is it the case that the mainstream American public no longer values federal government programs? Has support for such programs dramatically declined? Does partisanship now infuse every aspect of congressional policy making? In short, do lawmakers now lack incentives or the inclination to collectively address problems in society? We then conclude by considering the implications of a problem-solving perspective for policy makers and citizens.

CONGRESS AND THE POLITICS OF PROBLEM SOLVING

In his classic book, *Congress: The Electoral Connection*, David Mayhew provocatively argues that the "single minded pursuit of reelection" is antithetical to Congress's ability to address societal problems. Incumbents have incentives to focus on position-taking and credit-claiming activities that have more direct electoral payoffs than activities that promote broader institutional goals, such as oversight and policy updating. This pessimistic, realist perspective permeates congressional studies.

We have argued that reelection-minded incumbents also have reasons to be concerned about Congress's problem-solving abilities. In Chapter 2 we found that perceptions of congressional performance predict voter approval of the lawmaking body. In Chapter 3 we found that congressional approval levels had significant electoral consequences for incumbents, whether measured in terms of vote share, probability of reelection, or likelihood of returning to office (to capture strategic retirement decisions). These findings build upon other recent research linking congressional approval and lawmaking activities to incumbent approval and support. We additionally found that incumbents of both parties may be held to account under the more common condition of a divided government.

This is why government shutdowns – despite the extensive media coverage they have received in recent years – are still quite a rare occurrence. If Congress did not act to address such problems, the electoral implications of (not) problem solving would likely be much more apparent. Although the Troubled Asset Relief Program (TARP) "bailout" of 2008 and 2009 was unpopular with voters, what if Congress had allowed major banks, insurance firms, and the auto industry to fail? Lawmakers were warned that delay could have dire consequences for the economy and banking system. Economists later estimated that unemployment would have been 16 percent rather than 9 percent, and that U.S. GDP in 2010 would have been about 6.5 percent lower (Blinder 2010; Chan 2010). Although the prospect of being blamed for far worse economic conditions down the road may not have been the only reason lawmakers held their noses to support TARP, it was certainly one of them (Cillizza and Murray 2008; Hulse 2008). Rep. Paul Ryan (R-WI), a leading conservative Republican, defended his "bailout" vote as serving electoral interests: "I believed we were on the cusp of a deflationary spiral which would have created a Depression.... If we would have allowed that to happen, I think we would have had a big government agenda sweeping through this country so fast that we wouldn't have recovered from it" (Ward 2010). A problem-solving perspective highlights such costs of inaction.

Problem-solving motivations also help to explain much more routine legislative events – failing to reauthorize something as mundane as the enabling legislation for the FAA has real and profound ramifications for citizens' everyday lives. According to the *Washington Post*, when Congress allowed the FAA authorization to temporarily lapse in 2011, "4,000 FAA employees and 70,000 airport construction workers were immediately furloughed the latter due to stop-work orders issued by the FAA to construction contractors. In addition to the furloughed workers, at least 40 safety inspectors are expected to continue working without pay, even covering their own travel expenses.... It will also deny the government over $1 billion in revenue from ticket taxes, $200 million of which has been lost already" (Matthews 2011). Most lawmakers appreciate that not addressing such problems in a timely manner has consequences for real people – and quite possibly personal electoral consequences at the polls.

In Chapter 4, we built upon longstanding observations about limited capacity in legislatures to first portray the congressional committee system as enhancing Congress's problem-solving capacity, before also proposing that limited capacity has important implications for the legislative issue agenda. A division-of-labor system with largely exclusive committee jurisdictions and seniority norms expands capacity and promotes specialization, enhancing the legislature's ability to manage an overwhelming agenda of policy demands. However, not all issues are equally likely to gain access to the agenda. Drawing on earlier work by Walker (1977), we hypothesized that Congress prioritizes specific types of issues that reflect broader problem-solving concerns. In Chapter 5, we argued that temporary legislation has gained favor in more recent decades (beginning in the 1960s) as a means for prioritizing and thereby promoting policy caretaking activities in an environment of scarcity. Impending reauthorizations focus congressional attention, giving committee members an added incentive to specialize in exchange for valued credit-claiming opportunities.

In the next four chapters we applied this perspective to important areas of legislative research. Chapter 6 investigated committee jurisdictional reforms and found that the 1974 Bolling-Hansen reforms – generally regarded as quite limited in their impact – measurably improved the organization of issue control in the House of Representatives. We also found that problem-solving motivations offer the best explanation for the changes adopted. Chapter 7 examined patterns of bill-sponsorship success. One "textbook" depiction of lawmaking portrays the progress of a bill through Congress as a process akin to natural selection. Individual lawmakers sponsor bills that reflect personal or partisan priorities. Committees then "winnow" these bills based on merit or other factors such as the sponsor's institutional influence and political know-how (Krutz 2005).This portrayal is undoubtedly accurate for some laws. However, our systematic investigation revealed that it has limited applicability. Successful bill sponsorship is more often indicative of committee members engaging in the necessary work of Congress. Successful bills addressing compulsory issues were almost exclusively committee sponsored. Successful sponsors of bills addressing other discretionary issues share the characteristics associated with legislative effectiveness in prior research. However, these latter bills make up just a small proportion of those that pass the House.

With so many compulsory issues to address, median voter explanations for policy change miss a central part of the lawmaking story. Choose just about any scholarly book on congressional policy making from the library shelf and examine its table of contents. The clear impression one receives is that shifts in the preferences of lawmakers and/or partisan control are the most important predictors of legislative policy change. To a lesser extent, the priorities of the president also matter. Salient events and program expirations not only fail to make it into the table of contents, they are rarely discussed at all. Yet in Chapter 8, we found that lawmakers behave as if program expirations and salient events are more valuable "windows of opportunity" than electorally driven preference shifts. In Chapter 9 we found that variables capturing problem-solving motivations were important and robust predictors of legislative policy change over time. Macropolitical conditions (such as changes in partisan control, divided government, or the ideological distance between the House and Senate) were neither as important nor as robust. Moreover, the most important legislative accomplishments in the issue areas we examined were problem driven.

Overall, the empirical findings presented in this book challenge widely held views that lawmakers have limited incentives to cooperate and that Congress is ill-equipped to respond to problems in society. To the contrary, the institutions of Congress enhance its problem solving capacity. Members also have electoral incentives to be concerned about Congress's collective problem-solving abilities. To be sure, problem solving is not the only concern of lawmakers. The incentives pushing lawmakers in other directions are well documented. But to a much larger degree than is generally appreciated, the legislative agenda and policy change in Congress are problem driven.

PROBLEM SOLVING AND (BI)PARTISAN POLITICS

Our findings confirm that many of the issues on the agenda are not partisan issues. Aldrich and Rohde, in their conditional party government theory, argue that the "party agenda will often be small relative to the full range of House legislative activity (although it will often contain most of the issues observers would label as most important)" (2000, 3). However, neither their work nor the work of Cox and McCubbins (2005) offers an extended discussion of the issues that make up the party agenda or are deemed by party leaders to be essential to the party's reputation.

Most "major" legislation enacted since the end of World War II (Mayhew 1991) has passed with bipartisan support. That bipartisan voting coalitions on important issues have long been the norm is one of the least appreciated patterns of congressional politics. We have argued that a central reason for this longstanding pattern is that lawmakers of both parties often share common electoral interests. The notion that a broad consensus serves the public interest is inherent in the separation of the powers system that underlies the American system of government. Reflecting on his decades of lawmaking experience, Rep. Henry Waxman (D-CA) similarly touts the benefits of bipartisan cooperation:

If you can find areas of common interest and figure out how to bridge your differences, the result is usually legislation that truly works. In fact, I can think of no major law that I've had a hand in crafting that hasn't depended on bipartisan support. (Waxman 2010, 220)

Why is bipartisan cooperation so important for problem solving? One reason is that there can be a substantial difference between the intended consequences of a policy and its actual effects. Where important policies are concerned, broad support within the legislature gives lawmakers greater confidence that a policy will have the effects its advocates claim (Kessler and Krehbiel 1996). Waxman's observations about legislation that "truly works" suggest that this confidence is warranted.

Another reason is external legitimacy. On important issues, bipartisanship signals to voters that lawmakers representing diverse interests agree that a problem deserves attention and that the policy is broadly considered to be a positive step in the right direction. Given that a law's enactment is just the first step in the policy-making process, perceived legitimacy can play a critical role in a law's effective implementation. In the recent case of the Affordable Care Act (P.L. 111-148), for example, the fact that the law attracted only Democratic support in Congress undoubtedly encouraged Republicans to resist fully implementing the reforms at the state level (Sack 2010).

The value of bipartisanship as a signal of policy legitimacy was perhaps no more clearly demonstrated than in efforts by Republican leaders in the 112th Congress (2011–12) to pressure rank-and-file members to vote against Democratic initiatives, including legislation those same members might otherwise support. Said Senate Minority Leader Mitch McConnell (R-KY), "It was absolutely critical that everybody be together because if the proponents of the bill were able to say it was bipartisan, it tended to convey to the public that this is O.K., they must have figured it out" (Hulse and Nagourney 2010). Voters might conclude that policies promoted by a Democratic president (that Republicans hoped to unseat in 2012) served the public interest!

Is Partisan Polarization the "New Normal"?

In January 2011, presidential candidate Newt Gingrich proposed that the Environmental Protection Agency (EPA) be abolished (Schor 2011). Was his proposal evidence of a deep public divide over the issue of environmental protection? Apparently not. A poll conducted shortly afterward indicated that just 18 percent of respondents wanted Congress to "follow the Republican agenda and block the EPA's active role in updating pollution regulations." Among Republican identifiers, a solid majority (61%) opposed the EPA's elimination (Restuccia 2011). Almost two-thirds (63%) of those interviewed wanted the EPA to do more, not less (McGowan 2011).[1]

These are hardly new insights. Although slightly more Americans self-identify as conservative than in the past (about 5% or less), public support for most government programs remains extraordinarily high. According to a 2011 Pew Survey, staunch Conservatives and Libertarians are the only groups in which majorities say the United States has gone too far in its efforts to protect the environment. In all other groups – including Main Street Republicans and the Republican-leaning Disaffecteds – most agree "that this country should do whatever it takes to protect the

---

[1] See survey conducted by Opinion Research Corporation on behalf of the National Resources Defense Council.

environment" (Pew Research Center 2011). Surveys going back decades show steady and overwhelming support for the largest areas of federal government activity – across the political spectrum. Since its inception, the General Social Survey has asked respondents if we should spend more, about the same, or less in several very broad categories of government activity. Through 2010, problems as varied as protecting the environment, crime control, education, highways and mass transit, social security, and assistance to the poor garner support for current or increased levels of spending by 90 percent of Democrats, Independents, and even Republicans![2] Public support for core government functions has barely changed over four decades.

If incumbent lawmakers of both parties were asked to publicly declare the federal programs they would eliminate, few if any programs would be on the lists of a majority of them (with the possible exception of foreign aid). Republican congressional leaders certainly seem to appreciate that they gain little political mileage by proposing to slash specific government functions. The Republican Party's *Pledge to America*, the manifesto released with great fanfare during its all-out effort to regain a congressional majority in the 2010 elections, provided an opportunity to demonstrate a commitment to a reduced federal role in society. However, the pledge proposed to eliminate just two programs, Obama's health care reform and TARP (which was scheduled to expire automatically anyway).

Thus we see little evidence of a radical shift in public attitudes toward the role of government. Most voters support the activities of the federal government and additionally expect their elected representatives to work together to address problems of common concern. This is not true of all voters. But independent voters – the swing voters to which candidates are often seeking to appeal to – consistently prefer compromise to intransigence (Newport 2011a). And when faced with a meaningful political deadline – such as the potential economic catastrophe that was predicted

---

[2] The exact question asked on the General Social Survey is: "We are faced with many problems in this country, none of which can be solved easily or inexpensively. I'm going to name some of these problems, and for each one I'd like you to tell me whether you think we're spending too much money on it, too little money, or about the right amount" followed by the program (e.g., "mass transportation") "... are we spending too much, too little, or about the right amount on (ITEM)?" Assistance to the poor has only been asked since the mid-1980s. Partisans are aggregated in the following fashion: Democrats = Strong Democrats, Not So Strong Democrats, Independents Near Democrat; Independents; Republicans = Strong Republicans, Not So Strong Republicans, Independents Near Republicans.

if the federal government defaulted on its debt obligations in the summer of 2011– sizable majorities of Democrats, Independents, and Republicans favored compromise over inflexibility, even if the compromise plan was something with which they disagreed (Newport 2011b).

To be sure, partisan differences continue to play a role in congressional politics. However, our findings suggest that this role is often overstated. There are partisan issues in Congress but not all issues, and possibly not even most issues, are viewed in zero-sum partisan terms. The view is further supported by the survey of congressional staff conducted by the Annenberg Center in 2004 (also discussed in Chapter 7). Staff were asked to identify and answer questions about a specific bill they had worked on. In addition to questions about committee versus party influence over bill content, the survey also asked about partisanship during floor consideration.[3] For bills addressing recurring (compulsory) issues, staff reported that the process was "highly partisan" just 19 percent of the time (Figure 10.1) and "not very partisan" most of the time (52%). For discretionary bills, the process was "highly partisan" most of the time (56%) and "not very partisan" 17 percent of the time (Figure 10.1).

Thus, congressional insiders confirm that compulsory issues are managed in a largely nonpartisan manner distanced from the conflict and contentiousness that pervades the public's perception of Congress. If anything, our findings concerning the dynamics of policy change indicate that important policy changes in Congress are more likely to be enacted in response to compulsory, rather than discretionary, policy demands. A smaller set of discretionary legislative initiatives are debated in partisan fashion slightly more than half the time. Partisan controversy does not always equate with importance (e.g., the 2005 law granting the federal courts jurisdiction in the Terry Schiavo death with dignity case), just as bipartisan consensus should not be mistaken for a lack of importance (e.g., post-9/11 politics and the pattern for "major" laws mentioned previously).

IMPLICATIONS OF A PROBLEM-SOLVING PERSPECTIVE FOR POLICY MAKERS AND CITIZENS

Legislatures exist to address problems in society. When Congress takes up recurring issues (at the expense of other issues), it is supporting a policy

---

[3] Specifically, the Annenberg survey asked staffers regarding a bill they had worked on that reached floor consideration: "Was the consideration of that bill highly partisan, moderately partisan or not very partisan?"

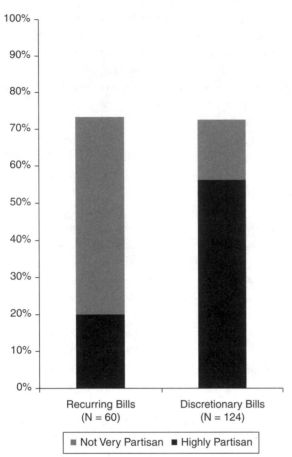

FIGURE 10.1. Floor Consideration of Recurring Issues Tends to Be Less Partisan.
Note: Based on congressional staff assessments of a bill with which they were
closely involved. Omitted category was "moderately partisan."
Source: Annenberg Survey of Congressional Staff, authors.

change process that recognizes that developing policies that work is a process. Policy making is not simply about implementing preferred policies,
and legislative oversight is not just about controlling the bureaucracy. It
is often an ongoing process of learning and adjustment. Legislative oversight activities provide opportunities for bureaucrats and other interested
parties to shed additional light on the implications of programs. Political
considerations shape how Congress responds to what it learns, but too
often public and scholarly perspectives fail to convey the challenges of
developing effective responses to problems such as education, health,
transportation, and national security.

The salience of an issue is also an important predictor of policy change. Lawmakers have incentives to be responsive to visible problems. Politics often helps to explain why issues become salient. Schattschneider theorized that the current losers in a political debate will seek to "expand the conflict" by drawing public attention to issues that the current winners are neglecting (Schattschneider 1960). Whether such attention leads to policy change depends on many things, including whether the current winners perceive that action is "politically necessary" (Walker 1977). Democratic efforts to highlight dramatic differences in the cost of drugs for insurers and individuals helped to motivate a Republican-led expansion of Medicare prescription drug benefits in 2003 (Waxman 2010). In 2011, an otherwise routine matter of raising the government debt limit ascended to the top of the agenda as a broader discussion of federal deficit spending after the Republican House revised its procedures to force a vote on the matter.[4]

But issues also become salient for reasons that have less to do with the efforts of political entrepreneurs. The Exxon Valdez oil spill and the events of September 11, 2001, did not require a partisan push to focus the public's attention or to compel a legislative response (Birkland 1997). Such issues end up on the agenda not because they alter lawmakers' policy preferences (though this can also occur), but because their visibility and potential electoral consequences alter lawmakers' policy priorities.

Considerations of partisan control or reelection sometimes encourage lawmakers to engage in behavior that is detrimental to problem solving. As Rep. Peter Welch (D-VT) noted in the wake of the 2011 failure of the House and Senate "supercommittee" to meet its mandate on deficit reduction, "We're approaching this, both sides, as though this is an ideological battle to be won, rather than a practical problem to be solved" (Welna 2011). But it is also the case that, despite increasing partisan polarization over the past three decades, there does not appear to be any consistent downward trend in legislative productivity or legislative oversight (as discussed in Chapter 1). As long as voters care about problem solving, legislators will continue to care and will continue to support institutions and processes that promote it.

It is revealing that lawmakers – even during unified governments – do not opt to "lock in" their policy gains by enacting permanent laws. The best explanation, in our view, is recognition that the goal of public

---

[4] By repealing the so-called Gephardt Rule that provided for automatic debt-ceiling increases as part of the budgeting process.

policy is to address problems in society and the future impact of a policy is always fraught with uncertainty. Policies rarely work as intended. "Staged" decision procedures facilitate experimentation by lowering the stakes of an enacted policy and enabling the integration of new information. Such focal points or policy windows for oversight and updating invite participation from a broader range of stakeholders. Widespread participation reduces information asymmetries and arguably promotes more socially optimal policies (Gersen 2007, 266–7). Short-term authorizations can also make it more difficult to conceal the long-range costs of policies (Yin 2009, 208) and can reduce the "risk of bureaucratic drift as a threat to the current majority's policies" (Gersen 2007, 279). Finally, a common argument in legislative studies is that Congress does not regularly engage in routine oversight (Bibby 1966; Dodd and Schott 1979; Fiorina 1989; Ogul 1976; Woll 1977), or when it does, the oversight is more of the "fire alarms" than the "police patrols" variety (McCubbins and Schwartz 1984). Short-term authorizations as focal points also help to explain why committee members do regularly engage in oversight activities (Aberbach 2002; Ainsworth, Harward, and Moffett 2010; Cox 2004).

Problem-solving routines such as those fostered by short-term authorizations may also promote consensus in Congress. The most contentious or partisan policy areas are frequently the ones where there are few, if any, procedures for regular review and renewal of programs and agencies. Congressional staff certainly sense less partisanship where recurring issues are concerned. In his work identifying the major legislative accomplishments for each congressional term, Mayhew also lists the noteworthy legislative failures. In recent years, these failures have included immigration reform, a comprehensive energy policy, rewriting telecommunications laws, and until recently, health care reform.[5] Significantly, none of these policy areas are subject to the strictures of periodic renewal.

The 535 lawmakers who comprise Congress represent a diverse nation with respect to priorities and preferences. Any policy that makes it through the labyrinth that is the legislative process will inevitably disappoint nearly everyone involved. Conflict and compromise are unavoidable features of effective lawmaking. Compromise does not often make for a good story, but conflict does. As one lawmaker recently noted, "The House

---

[5] The list is drawn from Mayhew's report for the 109th (2005–6) and 111th Congresses (2009–10) that catalogs the most prominent legislative failures as well as successes, and by replicating the methodology using his noted sources for the 108th (2003–4) and 110th Congresses (2007–8).

could be passing 15 things, all close to unanimously. But the one that is highly fought is the one that gets 100 percent of the [media] attention."[6] Impressions of Congress – of incessant squabbling and backbiting – are as much a reflection of the marketability of political conflict as they are a reflection of Congress at work.

FUTURE DIRECTIONS

What does this study suggest regarding future research directions in legislative politics? A focus on problem solving underscores the value of incorporating policy substance into legislative research (Clinton and Lapinski 2006; Lapinski in press; Lee 2009). It also encourages additional scholarly attention to the subject of agenda scarcity. It renews attention to the policy-making activities of committees, in particular their role in managing the large volume of programs and policies that legislatures must oversee and how institutional rules and procedures facilitate this role. Finally, a problem-solving perspective provides a new assessment of policy change that emphasizes the limited practical control that legislatures have over their agendas and the common interests that lawmakers share in ensuring that certain types of problems make it to the top of the agenda.

We appreciate that there are many opportunities to improve upon and extend the analyses presented here. Our findings ultimately leave many questions about congressional problem solving unanswered. Additional work is needed to appreciate more fully why some laws and programs are authorized on a temporary basis while others are not, even programs in the same statute; why the duration of short-term authorizations varies across programs, whether laws and programs on temporary authorizations are more likely to be updated; and how increasing partisanship has affected the updating process. We know that committee operations differ but have made little effort to explain why some committees rely more heavily on short-term authorizations than others. Similarly, our focus on the House raises questions about the applicability of our findings to the Senate and about the impact of the Senate on policy making in the House.

Chapter 3 establishes a linkage between public approval of Congress and support for congressional incumbents. However, it does not explicitly link problem-solving activities to the level of public approval of

---

[6] Rep. Jared Polis (D-CO; Dukakis 2011).

Congress. In Chapter 8 we found that bills are often introduced in anticipation of congressional action, whereas prior research typically portrays bill introductions as proactive efforts to shape the legislative agenda. Is it the case that patterns in campaign contributions or lobbying activity also predict legislative issue attention for similar anticipatory reasons? In Chapter 9, we investigated policy change and found that expiring provisions of law were the most robust predictors of change within specific policy areas. We used a blunt indicator of expiring laws that likely underestimated the true impact of important expiring provisions of law. Similarly, more fine-grained measures of policy-specific preference shifts and issue salience will improve our understanding of the factors associated with policy change.

Finally, we focused on just one side of the policy attention and change puzzle – when issues are addressed. In the context of committee activities, we suggested but did not examine whether reauthorization schedules discourage consideration of issues at other times. Whether this is the case, and the extent to which committees use short-term authorizations to manage their agendas both negatively and positively, is a matter that deserves further examination. Additionally, we (like almost every other study of policy change to date) focused on the timing and magnitude of the changes adopted. A very valuable objective of future research should be to incorporate information about the direction of policy changes, given that nearly all theorizing characterizes legislative policy change in directional terms. The challenges associated with inferring policy direction inevitably mean that fewer issues can be analyzed.

What is on the legislative agenda and why? How do committees contribute to the policy-making process? When are particular policies reformed and why? A problem-solving perspective offers new insights into these important yet understudied questions. We hope that this book will inspire attention to these and other questions related to the important problem-solving functions of legislatures as well as additional and renewed interest in the substance of congressional policy making.

Appendix A

Table A.1 presents a replication of the incumbent vote choice model presented in Table 3.2 with the addition of the incumbent approval variable. Incumbent approval is based on a 3-point scale: disapproval (−1), no opinion (0), and approval (1). Not surprisingly, the incumbent approval variable is positive and statistically significant. The first model in Table A.1 includes only the congressional approval variable without the interaction between congressional approval and majority party status. The coefficient for *Congressional Approval* is positive and close to the conventional level of statistical significance ($p = 0.11$), indicating voters are more likely to choose the incumbent regardless of party if they approve of Congress. When we include the interaction between the majority party status and congressional approval, the coefficients on *Congressional Approval* and the interaction term are statistically insignificant. This indicates that there is not a statistically significant difference between majority and minority party incumbents with respect to the effect of congressional approval.

Further, as we show in Table A.2, incumbent approval is significantly related to congressional approval for incumbents of both parties. Table A.2 presents a fixed-effects linear regression model of incumbent approval. This model contains the results estimated using all of the respondents in the ANES including those who did not cast a ballot (the results are very similar if we only analyze those who voted). We use the same independent variables as in Table 3.2, except we substitute whether the respondents can recall the incumbent (*Recall Incumbent*) as opposed to the net recall variable. Despite the fact that approval is not a continuous variable, we chose to use linear regression for a continuous dependent variable in order to retain the use of the fixed-effects specification. An estimator for

TABLE A.1. *The Impact of Congressional Approval on Incumbent Support at the Individual Voter Level (including Incumbent Approval), 1980–2004*

Independent Variable	Coefficient	S. E.	Coefficient	S. E.
Net Recall	0.84*	0.11	0.84*	0.11
Unidentified	-0.15	0.16	-0.15	0.16
Unidentified × Republican Incumbent	-0.12	0.23	-0.11	0.23
Ideology	-0.35*	0.06	-0.35*	0.06
Ideology × Republican Incumbent	0.54*	0.09	0.54*	0.09
Partisan Identification	-0.55*	0.04	-0.55*	0.04
Partisan Identification × Republican Incumbent	1.13*	0.06	1.13*	0.06
Presidential Approval	-0.46*	0.07	-0.46*	0.07
Presidential Approval × President's Party	0.74*	0.10	0.74*	0.10
Retrospective Economic Evaluation	-0.10	0.07	-0.10	0.07
Retrospective Economic Evaluation × President's Party	0.18	0.10	0.18	0.10
Congressional Approval	0.08	0.05	0.02	0.08
Congressional Approval × Majority Party			0.10	0.10
Incumbent Approval	1.68*	0.07	1.68*	0.07
Number of Observations	6,384		6,384	
Number of Groups (races)	723		723	
Pseudo R^2	0.57		0.57	

Notes: Logistic regression of vote for the incumbent (1 = vote for incumbent, 0 = vote for challenger); *$p < .05$.
Source: American National Election Studies.

TABLE A.2. *The Impact of Congressional Approval on Incumbent Approval, 1980–2004*

Independent Variable	Coefficient	S. E.
Know Incumbent	0.30*	0.01
Unidentified	−0.01	0.02
Unidentified × Republican Incumbent	0.04	0.03
Ideology	−0.04*	0.01
Ideology × Republican Incumbent	0.09*	0.01
Partisan Identification	−0.06*	0.00
Partisan Identification × Republican Incumbent	0.11*	0.01
Presidential Approval	−0.02	0.01
Presidential Approval × President's Party	0.11*	0.01
Retrospective Economic Evaluation	0.01	0.01
Retrospective Economic Evaluation × President's Party	0.01	0.01
Congressional Approval	0.07*	0.01
Congressional Approval × Majority Party	0.04*	0.01
Constant	0.22*	0.02
Number of Observations	12,673	
Number of Incumbents	1,445	
Adjusted R^2	0.05	

Notes: Fixed-effects logistic regression of incumbent job approval (−1 = disapprove of incumbent, 0 = neither approve nor disapprove, 1 = approve of incumbent); *$p < .05$.
Source: American National Election Studies.

a fixed-effects ordinal regression model is not readily available. However, if we estimate an ordered probit regression model with year fixed effects, we obtain similar results. Further, if we recode the dependent variable *Incumbent Approval* into a two-category, dichotomous variable (by either folding the "no opinion" responses into the approval or disapproval category) and estimate a fixed-effects logit model, the substantive conclusions and results mimic those derived from Table A.2.

The results in Table A.2 demonstrate that the approval ratings of both the majority and minority party incumbents are affected by citizens' evaluations of congressional job performance. The coefficients on congressional approval and the interaction between *Congressional Approval* and majority party are statistically significant ($p < .01$). The estimated effect of *Congressional Approval* on *Incumbent Approval* is approximately 57 percent larger ([0.07 + 0.04]/0.07) for majority party incumbents. These findings make it clear that both parties' incumbents are affected in the same manner by voter evaluations of congressional performance.

Appendix B

Assignment of Bills across Issue Types

Compulsory Issues

Recurring. These are policy areas where a lack of legislative action shifts the policy from the status quo to a different reversion point. These bills include appropriations as well as those that renew expiring laws or legislative provisions.

Coding: As discussed in Chapter 5, bills are identified as "recurring" in a multistep process. Using bill titles (generally a sentence or two in length) and bill summaries (ranging from one sentence to multiple paragraphs) available through the Library of Congress THOMAS Web site (www. thomas.loc.gov), a search is conducted on all bills for a list of keywords or keyword combinations (e.g., "appropriat*," "reauthor*," "authorize appropriations for FY"). The list of keywords was, in some cases, quite complicated (e.g., word combinations within the same sentence but not necessarily sequential) and was drawn from earlier case-by-case investigations of the titles and summaries of known reauthorizations and appropriations bills. Approximately one thousand bills were tagged in this way each term and were then individually inspected to eliminate false positives. In instances where a careful read of the title and summary still left uncertainty as to its appropriate coding, the full text of the bill was examined along with its legislative history found in *CQ Almanac* and *Lexis-Nexis Congress.* To reduce the chances of false negatives, we conducted a final search for mentions of (missed) reauthorizations in the online *CQ Almanac.*

Important. These are policy areas that political insiders deem to be among the most important of the term.

Coding: Bills are flagged as "important" if they receive any coverage in *CQ Almanac* during the congressional term. In addition, to ensure that we capture all tangential and "unsuccessful" versions of the bills deemed important, we include any other bills that were considered "related" to the bills mentioned in *CQ*, according to the Congressional Research Service on its THOMAS Web site.

Discretionary Issues

Minor. These are policy areas with an exceptionally narrow or insignificant impact on federal policy. Such bills mainly fell into four easily identifiable categories according to the coding in the Congressional Bills Project.

1. *Private bills*: Bills that provide relief or confer benefits on specific individuals or organizations. **Coding:** Bills falling within subtopic 9999.
2. *Commemorative bills*: Bills that propose commemorative actions such as the coining of a medal or the naming of a building. **Coding:** All bills that the Congressional Bills Project designates as "commemorative," as well as all bills falling within subtopics 2008, 2015, and 1699.
3. *Land conveyance bills*: Bills transferring control of federal lands. **Coding:** Bills falling within subtopic 2103.
4. *Tariff and duty bills*: Bills proposing or suspending tariffs or duties on particular commodities. **Coding:** Bills falling within subtopic 1807.

Ordinary. These are policy areas that are of greater significance than the "minor" category, but do not qualify as being important or compulsory.

Coding: This is the residual category – all noncompulsory bills that are not otherwise coded as minor.

Appendix C

Calculating Committee Roll Rates

A "roll" occurs when a majority of a subset of the legislature (e.g., a party caucus) unsuccessfully opposes a particular bill's passage. Rohde (2005b) tallies the yeas and nays for members of each party on roll call votes. Final passage roll rates are based on Rohde's Vote Types: 11, 12, 15, and 30. Amendment roll rates are based on the vote types: 21 through 29.

To calculate committee of jurisdiction roll rates, we obtained individual voting positions on each roll call from Poole's VOTEVIEW and then merged them with committee membership information (Stewart and Woon n.d.) so that we were able to calculate the proportion of voting committee members taking yea and nay positions on each roll call.

Next we use committee of jurisdiction information drawn from the Congressional Bills Project to identify which of these committees was the committee of jurisdiction for the bill that was the focus of each roll call. A committee was rolled if the majority position of the committee members was different than the majority position of the legislature.

The central limitation of this approach is that some of the bills considered on the floor (about 15%) are multiple referrals. We thus identify a committee roll for multiple referrals when most of the committees of jurisdiction are rolled in cases of multiple referrals. Restricting the focus of this analysis to singly referred bills only does not substantively alter its conclusions.

Bibliography

Aberbach, Joel. 2002. "What's Happened to the Watchful Eye?" *Congress & the Presidency: A Journal of Capital Studies* 29(1): 3.

Abramowitz, Alan. 2010. "Does Congressional Popularity Matter?" *Sabato's Crystal Ball*, February 11. http://www.centerforpolitics.org/crystalball /articles/aia2010021101/ (accessed April 20, 2012).

—— 1984. "National Issues, Strategic Politicians, and Voting Behavior in the 1980 and 1982 Congressional Elections." *American Journal of Political Science* 28(4): 710–21.

Abramowitz, Alan, Albert Cover, and Helmut Norpoth. 1986. "The President's Party in Midterm Elections: Going from Bad to Worse." *American Journal of Political Science* 30(3): 562–76.

Abrams, Jim. 2008. "House Votes $8B Relief for Highway Trust Fund." *ABC News*. http://abcnews.go.com/Travel/BusinessTravel/wireStory?id=5782199.

Adler, E. Scott. 2011. "Congressional Reforms." In *The Oxford Handbook of the American Congress*, ed. Eric Schickler and Frances E. Lee. New York: Oxford University Press, 473–97.

—— 2002. *Why Congressional Reforms Fail: Reelection and the House Committee System*. Chicago: University of Chicago Press.

—— 2000. "Constituency Characteristics and the 'Guardian' Model of Appropriations Subcommittees, 1959–1998." *American Journal of Political Science* 44(1): 104–14.

Adler, E. Scott, and John Lapinski. 2006. *The Macropolitics of Congress*. Princeton, NJ: Princeton University Press.

—— 1997. "Demand-side Theory and Congressional Committee Composition: A Constituency Characteristics Approach." *American Journal of Political Science* 41: 895–918.

Ainsworth, Scott, and Frances Akins. 1997. "The Informational Role of Caucuses in the U.S. Congress." *American Politics Research* 25(4): 407–30.

Ainsworth, Scott, and Thad Hall. 2010. *Abortion Politics in Congress: Strategic Incrementalism and Policy Change*. New York: Cambridge University Press.

Ainsworth, Scott, and Douglas Hanson. 1996. "Bill Sponsorship and Legislative Success among Freshmen Senators, 1954–1986." *The Social Science Journal* 33(2): 211.

Ainsworth, Scott, Brian Harward, and Kenneth Moffett. 2010. "Congressional Oversight and Presidential Signing Statements." Paper presented at the 2010 Southern Political Science Association Meetings, Atlanta, GA.

Alchian, Armen, and Harold Demsetz. 1972. "Production, Information Costs, and Economic Organization." *American Economic Review* 62: 777–95.

Aldrich, John, and David Rohde. 2005. "Congressional Committees in a Partisan Era." In *Congress Reconsidered*, ed. Lawrence C. Dodd and Bruce I. Oppenheimer. Washington, DC: Congressional Quarterly Press.

   2001. "The Logic of Conditional Party Government: Revisiting the Electoral Connection." In *Congress Reconsidered*. Washington, DC: Congressional Quarterly Press, 269–92.

   2000. "The Republican Revolution and the House Appropriations Committee." *Journal of Politics* 62(1): 1–33.

Alesina, Alberto, and Howard Rosenthal. 1995. *Partisan Politics, Divided Government, and the Economy.* New York: Cambridge University Press.

Anderson, William, Janet Box-Steffensmeier, and Valeria Sinclair-Chapman. 2003. "The Keys to Legislative Success in the U.S. House of Representatives." *Legislative Studies Quarterly* 28(3): 357–86.

Ansolabehere, Stephen, and Philip Edward Jones. 2010. "Constituents' Responses to Congressional Roll-Call Voting." *American Journal of Political Science* 54(3): 583–97.

Ansolabehere, Stephen, Jonathan Rodden, and James Snyder. 2008. "The Strength of Issues: Using Multiple Measures to Gauge Preference Stability, Ideological Constraint, and Issue Voting." *American Political Science Review* 102(2): 215–32.

Arnold, Peri. 1998. *Making the Managerial Presidency: Comprehensive Reorganization Planning, 1905–1996.* Lawrence: University Press of Kansas.

Arnold, R. Douglas. 1990. *The Logic of Congressional Action.* New Haven, CT: Yale University Press.

Asher, Herbert, and Herbert Weisberg. 1978. "Voting Change in Congress: Some Dynamic Perspectives on an Evolutionary Process." *American Journal of Political Science* 22 (May): 391–425.

Bach, Stanley, and Steven Smith. 1988. *Managing Uncertainty in the House of Representatives: Adaptation and Innovation in Special Rules.* Washington, DC: Brookings Institution.

Bailey, Elizabeth. 2002. "Aviation Policy: Past and Present." *Southern Economic Journal* 69(1): 12–20.

Baker, Ross. 2008. *House & Senate.* 4th ed. New York: W. W. Norton and Company.

Barnes, Jeb. 2004. *Overruled? Legislative Overrides, Pluralism, and Contemporary Court-Congress Relations.* Stanford, CA: Stanford University Press.

Bartels, Larry. 2000. "Partisanship and Voting Behavior, 1952–1996." *American Journal of Political Science* 44(1): 35–50.

Basinger, Scott, and Michael Ensley. 2007. "Candidates, Campaigns, or Partisan Conditions? Reevaluating Strategic-Politicians Theory." *Legislative Studies Quarterly* 32: 361–94.

Basinger, Scott, and Howard Lavine. 2005. "Ambivalence, Information, and Electoral Choice." *American Political Science Review* 99(2): 169–84.

Bauer, Raymond, Ithiel De Sola Pool, and Lewis Anthony Dexter. 1963. *American Business and Public Policy.* 3rd ed. New York: Atherton Press.

Baughman, John. 2006. *Common Ground: Committee Politics in the U.S. House of Representatives.* Stanford, CA: Stanford University Press.

　2003. "To the Sponsor the Spoils: Preferences, Partisanship, and Legislative Success." Paper presented at the Annual Meeting of the Midwest Political Science Association, Chicago, IL.

Baumgartner, Frank, and Bryan Jones. 1993. *Agendas and Instability in American Politics.* Chicago: University of Chicago Press.

　1991. "Agenda Dynamics and Policy Subsystems." *Journal of Politics* 53: 1044–74.

Baumgartner, Frank, Bryan Jones, and Michael MacLeod. 2000. "The Evolution of Legislative Jurisdictions." *Journal of Politics* 62: 321–49.

Baumgartner, Frank, Jeffrey M. Berry, Marie Hojnacki, David C. Kimball, and Beth L. Leech. 2009. *Lobbying and Policy Change: Who Wins, Who Loses, and Why.* Chicago: University of Chicago Press.

Beck, Nathaniel, and Jonathan Katz. 1995. "What To Do (and Not To Do) with Time-Series – Cross-Section Data in Comparative Politics." *American Political Science Review* 89: 634–47.

Becker, Lawrence. 2005. *Doing the Right Thing: Collective Action and Procedural Choice in the New Legislative Process.* Columbus: Ohio State University Press.

Behn, Robert. 1977. "The False Dawn of Sunset Laws." *The Public Interest* 49: 103–18.

Benda, Susan. 1997. "Committees in Legislatures: A Division of Labour." In *The Changing Roles of Parliamentary Committees,* ed. Lawrence Longley and Attila Agh. Appleton, WI: Research Committee of Legislative Specialists, International Political Science Association, 17–50.

Bentley, Arthur. 1908. *The Process of Government.* Chicago: University of Chicago Press.

Berinsky, Adam J. 2004. *Silent Voices. Public Opinion and Political Participation in America.* Princeton, NJ: Princeton University Press.

Berry, Christopher, Barry Burden, and William Howell. 2010. "After Enactment: The Lives and Deaths of Federal Programs." *American Journal of Political Science* 54(1): 1–17.

Bibby, John. 1966. "Committee Characteristics and Legislative Oversight of Administration." *Midwest Journal of Political Science* 10: 78–98.

Bickford, Charlene Bangs, Kenneth R. Bowling, and Helen Veit, eds. 1992. *Debates in the House of Representatives.* Baltimore, MD: Johns Hopkins University Press.

Bimber, Bruce. 1996. *The Politics of Expertise in Congress: The Rise and Fall of the Office of Technology Assessment.* Albany: State University of New York Press.

Binder, Sarah. 2006. "Elections, Parties, and Governance." In *Institutions of American Democracy: The Legislative Branch*, ed. Paul Quirk and Sarah Binder. New York: Oxford University Press.

2003. *Stalemate: Causes and Consequences of Legislative Gridlock.* Washington, DC: Brookings Institution Press.

1997. *Minority Rights, Majority Rule: Partisanship and the Development of Congress.* New York: Cambridge University Press.

Birkland, Thomas. 1997. *After Disaster: Agenda Setting, Public Policy, and Focusing Events.* Washington, DC: Georgetown University Press.

Black, Duncan. 1948. "On the Rationale of Group Decision-Making." *Journal of Political Economy* 56: 23–34.

Blickle, Mark. 1985. "The National Sunset Movement." *Seton Hall Legislative Journal* 9: 209–32.

Blinder, Alan. 2010. "Opinion: Government to the Economic Rescue." *wsj.com.* http://online.wsj.com/article/SB1000142405274870432430457530707118 8294124.html (accessed February 18, 2011).

Boehner, John. 2011. "Interview with Christiane Amanpour." *This Week.* http://abcnews.go.com/Politics/week-transcript-speaker-john-boehner /story?id=14892830&page=6#.Tv3aFEqQOzh (accessed December 30, 2011).

Bolling, Richard. 1974. "Committees in the House." *The Annals of the American Academy of Political and Social Sciences* 411: 1–14.

1965. *House Out of Order.* New York: Dutton.

Bolton, Alexander. 2010. "111th Congress Comes to a Close; New Session Begins Jan. 5." *The Hill*, December 12. http://thehill.com/homenews/house/134917- 111th-congress-comes-to-a-close (accessed April 20, 2012).

Bond, Jon, Cary Covington, and Richard Fleisher. 1985. "Explaining Challenger Quality in Congressional Elections." *The Journal of Politics* 47(2): 510–29.

Born, Richard. 1990a. "Surge and Decline, Negative Voting, and the Midterm Loss Phenomenon: A Simultaneous Choice Analysis." *American Journal of Political Science* 34(3): 615–45.

1990b. "The Shared Fortunes of Congress and Congressmen: Members May Run from Congress, But They Can't Hide." *Journal of Politics* 52: 1223–41.

1984. "Reassessing the Decline of Presidential Coattails: U.S. House Elections from 1952–80." *The Journal of Politics* 46(1): 60–79.

Box-Steffensmeier, Janet, and Bradford Jones. 2004. *Event History Modeling: A Guide for Social Scientists.* New York: Cambridge University Press.

1997. "Time Is of the Essence: Event History Models in Political Science." *American Journal of Political Science* 41: 1414–61.

Brady, David, and Barbara Sinclair. 1984. "Building Majorities for Policy Changes in the House of Representatives." *Journal of Politics* 46: 1033–60.

Brady, David. 1988. *Critical Elections and Congressional Policy Making.* Stanford, CA: Stanford University Press.

Brady, David, and Craig Volden. 1998. *Revolving Gridlock: Politics and Policy from Carter to Clinton.* Boulder, CO: Westview Press.

Brady, David, John Ferejohn, and Laurel Harbridge. 2008. "Polarization and Public Policy: A General Assessment." In *Red and Blue Nation? Consequences and Correction of America's Polarized Politics*, ed. Pietro Nivola and David Brady. Washington, DC: Brookings Institution Press, 185–234.

Brownstein, Ronald. 2007. *The Second Civil War: How Extreme Partisanship Has Paralyzed Washington and Polarized America*. New York: The Penguin Press.

Burden, Barry, and David Kimball. 2004. *Why Americans Split Their Tickets: Campaigns, Competition, and Divided Government*. Ann Arbor: University of Michigan Press.

Burden, Barry, and Amber Wichowsky. 2010. "Local and National Forces in Congressional Elections." In *The Oxford Handbook on American Elections and Political Behavior*. New York: Oxford University Press.

Burstein, Paul, Shawn Bauldry, and Paul Froese. 2005. "Bill Sponsorship and Congressional Support for Policy Proposals, from Introduction to Enactment or Disappearance." *Political Research Quarterly* 58(2): 295–302.

Bustamante, Jeanette. 2008. "Lawmaker Perceptions of Constituent Priorities and the Effects on Legislative Behavior." Senior Honors Thesis. University of Colorado, Boulder.

Cain, Bruce, John Ferejohn, and Morris Fiorina. 1987. *The Personal Vote: Constituency Service and Electoral Independence*. Cambridge, MA: Harvard University Press.

Calabresi, Guido. 1982. *A Common Law for the Age of Statutes*. Cambridge, MA: Harvard University Press.

Calvert, Randall, and John Ferejohn. 1983. "Coattail Voting in Recent Presidential Elections." *American Political Science Review* 77(2): 407–19.

Campbell, Angus, Philip Converse, Warren Miller, and Donald Stokes. 1960. *The American Voter*. New York: John Wiley.

Campbell, James. 1991. "The Presidential Surge and Its Midterm Decline in Congressional Elections, 1868–1988." *Journal of Politics* 53(2): 477–87.

Campbell, James, and Joe Sumners. 1990. "Presidential Coattails in Senate Elections." *American Political Science Review* 84(2): 513–24.

Canes-Wrone, Brandice. 2005. *Who Leads Whom? Presidents, Policy, and the Public*. Chicago: University of Chicago Press.

Canes-Wrone, Brandice, David Brady, and John Cogan. 2002. "Out of Step, Out of Office: Electoral Accountability and House Members' Voting." *American Political Science Review* 96(1): 127–40.

Capehart, Jonathan. 2010. "America Really Hates Congress." *Post Partisan: Quick Takes by The Post's Opinion Writers*, February 10. http://voices .washingtonpost.com/postpartisan/2010/02/bipartisanship_as_possible_inc .html?hpid=opinionsbox1 (accessed April 20, 2012).

Carey, Mary Agnes. 2000. "GOP's Prescription Drug Bill: A 'Political Imperative'?" *Congressional Quarterly Weekly Report* (June 17): 1436.

Carpenter, Daniel, and David Lewis. 2004. "Political Learning from Rare Events: Poisson Inference, Fiscal Constraints, and the Lifetime of Bureaus." *Political Analysis* 12(3): 201–32.

Carrubba, Clifford, Matthew Gabel, and Simon Hug. 2008. "Legislative Voting Behavior, Seen and Unseen: A Theory of Roll-Call Vote Selection." *Legislative Studies Quarterly* 33(4): 543–72.

Carson, Jamie, Charles Finocchiaro, and David Rohde. 2010. "Consensus, Conflict, and Partisanship in House Decision Making: A Bill-Level Examination of Committee and Floor Behavior." *Congress & the Presidency* 37(3): 231–53.

CBS News. 2011. "House Republicans Blink, Payroll Tax Standoff Ends." http://newyork.cbslocal.com/2011/12/22/house-republicans-blink-payroll-tax-standoff-ends/ (accessed January 11, 2012).

Chaffee, Steven, and Donna Wilson. 1977. "Media Rich, Media Poor: Two Studies of Diversity in Agenda-Holding." *Journalism Quarterly* 54: 466–76.

Chan, Sewell. 2010. "In Study, 2 Economists Say Intervention Helped Avert a 2nd Depression." *The New York Times*. http://www.nytimes.com/2010/07/28/business/economy/28bailout.html?_r=3&partner=rss&emc=rss (accessed February 18, 2011).

Cillizza, Chris, and Shailagh Murray. 2008. "GOP Strategists Whisper Fears of Greater Losses in November." *Washington Post*, A11.

Clinton, Joshua, and John Lapinski. 2006. "Measuring Legislative Accomplishment, 1877–1994." *American Journal of Political Science* 50: 232–49.

Coase, Ronald. 1937. "The Nature of the Firm." *Economica* 4: 386–405.

Cohen, Richard, Siobhan Gorman, and Sydney Freedberg. 2003. "The Ultimate Turf War." *National Journal* (January 3): 16–23.

Coleman, John. 1999. "Unified Government, Divided Government, and Party Responsiveness." *American Political Science Review* 93: 821–35.

    1997. "The Decline and Resurgence of Congressional Party Conflict." *Journal of Politics* 59: 165–84.

Congressional Budget Office. 2001. *Unauthorized Appropriations and Expiring Authorizations*. Washington, DC: Congressional Budget Office.

Cooper, Joseph. 1970. "The Origins of the Standing Committees and the Development of the Modern House." *Rice University Studies* 56: 1–167.

Corder, Kevin. 2004. "Are Federal Programs Immortal?" *American Politics Research* 32(1): 3–25.

Cover, Albert. 1977. "One Good Term Deserves Another: The Advantage of Incumbency in Congressional Elections." *American Journal of Political Science* 21(3): 523–41.

Cover, Albert, and Bruce Brumberg. 1982. "Baby Books and Ballots: The Impact of Congressional Mail on Constituent Opinion." *American Political Science Review* 76(2): 347–59.

Cox, Gary. 2006. "The Organization of Democratic Legislatures." In *The Oxford Handbook of Political Economy*, ed. Barry Weingast and Donald Wittman. New York: Oxford University Press.

Cox, Gary, and Mathew McCubbins. 2005. *Setting the Agenda: Responsible Party Government in the U.S. House of Representatives*. New York: Cambridge University Press.

    1993. *Legislative Leviathan: Party Government in the House*. Berkeley: University of California.

Cox, Gary, and William Terry. 2008. "Legislative Productivity in the 93rd–105th Congresses." *Legislative Studies Quarterly* 33: 603–18.

Cox, James. 2004. *Reviewing Delegation: An Analysis of the Congressional Reauthorization Process*. Westport, CT: Praeger.

Congressional Quarterly Almanac. 1989. "Natural Gas Decontrol Bill Speeds through Congress." In *Congressional Quarterly Almanac*. Washington, DC: Congressional Quarterly Press, 674–7.

1985. "Transportation Funding Set at $11.6 Billion." In *Congressional Quarterly Almanac, 1984*. Washington, DC: Congressional Quarterly Press, 410–14.

Davidson, Roger, and Walter Oleszek. 2004. *Congress and Its Members*. 9th ed. Washington, DC: Congressional Quarterly Press.

1977. *Congress against Itself*. Bloomington: Indiana University Press.

Davidson, Roger, David Kovenock, and Michael O'Leary. 1966. *Congress in Crisis: Politics and Congressional Reform*. Belmont, CA: Wadsworth Publishing.

Davidson, Roger, Walter Oleszek, and Thomas Kephart. 1988. "One Bill, Many Committees: Multiple Referrals in the U.S. House of Representatives." *Legislative Studies Quarterly* 13: 3–28.

Davis, Julie Hirschfeld. 2002. "'Temporary' Breaks Keep Tax Writers and Lobbyists in Perpetual Motion." *Congressional Quarterly Weekly Report*: 293–6.

De Boef, Suzanne, and Luke Keele. 2008. "Taking Time Seriously." *American Journal of Political Science* 52(1): 184–200.

Deering, Christopher, and Steven Smith. 1997. 3rd ed. *Committees in Congress*. Washington, DC: Congressional Quarterly Press.

DeGregorio, Christine. 1999. *Networks of Champions: Leadership, Access, and Advocacy in the U.S. House of Representatives*. Ann Arbor: University of Michigan Press.

Delli Carpini, Michael, and Scott Keeter. 1996. *What Americans Know about Politics and Why It Matters*. New Haven, CT: Yale University Press.

Desposato, Scott, and John Petrocik. 2003. "The Variable Incumbency Advantage: New Voters, Redistricting, and the Personal Vote." *American Journal of Political Science* 47: 18–32.

Dionne, E. J. 2010. "Can Democrats Step Up Their Game?" *Washington Post*. http://www.washingtonpost.com/wp-dyn/content/article/2010/12/05/AR2010120503302.html (accessed December 30, 2011).

Dodd, Lawrence, and Richard Schott. 1979. *Congress and the Administrative State*. New York: John Wiley and Sons.

Donovan, Mark. 2001. *Taking Aim: Target Populations and the Wars on AIDS and Drugs*. Illustrated ed. Washington, DC: Georgetown University Press.

Donovan, Robert. 1960. *Joe Martin: My First Fifty Years in Politics*. New York: McGraw-Hill.

Döring, Herbert, ed. 1995. "Time as a Scarce Resource: Government Control of the Agenda." In *Parliaments and Majority Rule in Western Europe*, ed. Herbert Döring. Frankfurt, Germany: Campus, 223–46.

Downs, Anthony. 1972. "Up and Down with Ecology – The 'Issue-Attention Cycle.'" *Public Interest* 28: 38–50.

Drucker, Peter F. 1985. *Innovation and Entrepreneurship*. New York: Harper and Row.

Durr, Robert, John Gilmour, and Christina Wolbrecht. 1997. "Explaining Congressional Approval." *American Journal of Political Science* 41: 175–207.

Dukakis, Andrea. 2011. "Colorado's Push for Civility in Government." *Colorado Matters*, January 19. http://www.cpr.org/article/Colorados_Push_for_Civility (accessed April 20, 2012).

Dye, Thomas R. 2010. *Understanding Public Policy*. 13th ed. New York: Longman.

Edwards, George. 2003. *On Deaf Ears: The Limits of the Bully Pulpit*. New Haven, CT: Yale University Press.

Edwards, George, Andrew Barrett, and Jeffrey Peake. 1997. "The Legislative Impact of Divided Government." *American Journal of Political Science* 41: 545–63.

Eilperin, Juliet. 2007. *Fight Club Politics: How Partisanship Is Poisoning the House of Representatives*. Lanham, MD: Rowman and Littlefield Publishers.

Ellwood, John, and Eric Patashnik. 1993. "In Praise of Pork." *The Public Interest* (Winter): 19–33.

Epstein, Lee, and Jeffrey Segal. 2000. "Measuring Issue Salience." *American Journal of Political Science* 44(1): 66–83.

Erikson, Robert, and Gerald Wright. 2009. "Voters, Candidates and Issues in Congressional Elections." In *Congress Reconsidered*, ed. Lawrence Dodd and Bruce Oppenheimer. Washington, DC: Congressional Quarterly Press, 71–96.

    1993. "Voters, Candidates and Issues in Congressional Elections." In *Congress Reconsidered*, ed. Lawrence Dodd and Bruce Oppenheimer. Washington, DC: Congressional Quarterly Press.

Erikson, Robert, Michael Mackuen, and James Stimson. 2002. *The Macro Polity*. New York: Cambridge University Press.

    2006. "Public Opinion and Congressional Policy: A Macro-Level Perspective." In *The Macropolitics of Congress*, ed. E. Scott Adler and John S. Lapinski. Princeton, NJ: Princeton University Press, 79–95.

Eskridge, William. 1991. "Overriding Supreme Court Statutory Interpretation." *Yale Law Journal* 101: 331–456.

Esterling, Kevin. 2004. *The Political Economy of Expertise: Information and Efficiency in American National Politics*. Ann Arbor: University of Michigan Press.

Evans, C. Lawrence. 1999. "Legislative Structure: Rules, Precedents, and Jurisdictions." *Legislative Studies Quarterly* 24: 605–42.

    1991. *Leadership in Committee: A Comparative Analysis of Leadership Behavior in the U.S. Senate*. Ann Arbor: University of Michigan Press.

Evans, C. Lawrence, and Walter Oleszek. 1997. *Congress under Fire: Reform Politics and the Republican Majority*. Boston: Houghton Mifflin Company.

Evans, Diana. 2004. *Greasing the Wheels: Using Pork Barrel Projects to Build Majority Coalitions in Congress*. New York: Cambridge University Press.

Evans, Gary. 1997. *Red Ink: The Budget, Deficit, and Debt of the U.S. Government*. San Diego, CA: Academic Press.

Fahrenthold, David, Philip Rucker, and Felicia Sonmez. 2010. "Stormy 111th Congress Was Still the Most Productive in Decades." *Washington Post*. http://www.washingtonpost.com/wp-dyn/content/article/2010/12/22/AR2010122 205620.html (accessed February 10, 2011).

Fasone, Cristina. 2011. "Systems of Parliamentary Committees and Forms of Government: Comparing the U.S. Congress, the British, the French, and the Italian, and the European Parliaments." Paper presented at the Parliamentary Legitimization and Democratic Government in France and in the European Union Conference, Sciences Po Bordeaux, December 1–2.

Fenno, Richard. 1978. *Home Style: House Members in Their Districts*. Glenview, IL: Scott Foresman and Company.

    1975. "If, as Ralph Nader Says, Congress Is 'The Broken Branch,' How Come We Love Our Congressmen So Much?" In *Congress in Change: Evolution and Reform*, ed. Norman Ornstein. New York: Praeger Publishers, 277–87.

    1973. *Congressmen in Committees*. Boston: Little, Brown and Co.

    1966. *The Power of the Purse: Appropriations Politics in Congress*. Boston: Little, Brown and Co.

Ferejohn, John. 1977. "On the Decline of Competition in Congressional Elections." *American Political Science Review* 71(1): 166–76.

    1974. *Pork Barrel Politics: Rivers and Harbors Legislation, 1947–1968*. Stanford, CA: Stanford University Press.

Ferejohn, John, and Randall Calvert. 1984. "Presidential Coattails in Historical Perspective." *American Journal of Political Science* 28(1): 127–46.

Fiorina, Morris. 2006. "Parties as Problem Solver." In *Promoting the General Welfare: New Perspectives on Government Performance*, ed. Alan Gerber and Eric Patashnik. Washington, DC: Brookings Institution Press, 237–55.

    1996. *Divided Government*. Boston: Allyn and Bacon.

    1989. *Congress: Keystone of the Washington Establishment*. 2nd ed. New Haven, CT: Yale University Press.

    1981. *Retrospective Voting in American National Elections*. New Haven, CT: Yale University Press.

    1980. "The Decline of Collective Responsibility in American Politics." *Daedalus* 109(3): 25–45.

    1977. "The Case of the Vanishing Marginals: The Bureaucracy Did It." *The American Political Science Review* 71(1). 177–81.

Fiorina, Morris, Samuel Abrams, and Jeremy Pope. 2005. *Culture Wars? The Myth of a Polarized America*. New York: Longman.

Fisher, Louis. 1983. "Annual Authorizations: Durable Roadblocks to Biennial Budgeting." *Public Budgeting & Finance* 3(1): 23–40.

Frantzich, Stephen. 1979. "Who Makes Our Laws? The Legislative Effectiveness of Members of the U.S. Congress." *Legislative Studies Quarterly* 4(3): 409–28.

Gale, William, and Peter Orszag. 2003. *Sunsets in the Tax Code*. Falls Church, VA: Tax Analysts.

Galloway, George. 1946. *Congress at the Crossroads*. New York: Thomas Y. Crowell.

Gamm, Gerald, and Kenneth Shepsle. 1989. "Emergence of Legislative Institutions: Standing Committees in the House and Senate, 1810–1825." *Legislative Studies Quarterly* 14: 39–66.

Gerber, Alan, and Eric Patashnik. 2006. "Government Performance: Missing Opportunities to Solve Problems." In *Promoting the General Welfare: New*

Perspectives on Government Performance, ed. Alan Gerber and Eric Patashnik. Washington, DC: Brookings Institution Press, 3–18.

Gersen, Jacob E. 2007. "Temporary Legislation." *University of Chicago Law Review* 74: 247–98.

Gilligan, Thomas, and Keith Krehbiel. 1990. "Organization of Informative Committees by a Rational Legislature." *American Journal of Political Science* 34: 531–64.

1989. "Asymmetric Information and Legislative Rules with a Heterogeneous Committee." *American Journal of Political Science* 33: 459–90.

Granato, Jim, and Motoshi Suzuki. 1996. "The Use of the Encompassing Principle to Resolve Empirical Controversies in Voting Behavior: An Application to Voter Sophistication in Congressional Elections." *Electoral Studies* 15(3): 383–98.

Grant, J. Tobin, and Nathan Kelly. 2008. "Legislative Productivity of the U.S. Congress, 1789–2004." *Political Analysis* 16(3): 303–23.

Greene, William. 2007. *Econometric Analysis.* 6th ed. Englewood Cliffs, NJ: Prentice Hall.

Groseclose, Timothy. 1994. "The Committee Outlier Debate: A Review and a Reexamination of Some of the Evidence." *Public Choice* 80: 265–73.

Groseclose, Timothy, and Keith Krehbiel. 1994. "Golden Parachutes, Rubber Checks, and Strategic Retirements from the 102d House." *American Journal of Political Science* 38(1): 75–99.

Hall, Richard. 1996. *Participation in Congress.* New Haven, CT: Yale University Press.

1995. "Empiricism and Progress in Positive Theories of Legislative Institutions." In *Positive Theories of Congressional Institutions.* Ann Arbor: University of Michigan Press, 273–302.

Hall, Thad. 2004. *Authorizing Policy.* Columbus: Ohio State University Press.

Hamilton, Lee. 2009. *Strengthening Congress.* Bloomington: Indiana University Press.

Hamm, Keith, and Roby Robertson. 1981. "Factors Influencing the Adoption of New Methods of Legislative Oversight in the U.S. States." *Legislative Studies Quarterly* 6(1): 133–50.

Harbridge, Laurel. 2011. "Congressional Agenda Control and the Decline of Bipartisan Cooperation." Paper presented at Annual Meetings of the American Political Science Association, Seattle, WA.

Harbridge, Laurel, and Neil Malhotra. 2011. "Electoral Incentives and Partisan Conflict in Congress: Evidence from Survey Experiments." *American Journal of Political Science* 55(3): 494–510.

Hardin, John. 1998. "Advocacy versus Certainty: The Dynamics of Committee Jurisdiction Concentration." *Journal of Politics* 60: 374–97.

Hasecke, Edward, and Jason Mycoff. 2007. "Party Loyalty and Legislative Success: Are Loyal Majority Party Members More Successful in the U.S. House of Representatives?" *Political Research Quarterly* 60(4): 607–17.

Haynes, George. 1938. *The Senate of the United States.* Boston: Houghton Mifflin.

Heitshusen, Valerie, and Garry Young. 2006. "Macropolitics and Changes in the U.S. Code: Testing Competing Theories of Policy Production, 1874–1946." In *The Macropolitics of Congress*, ed. E. Scott Adler and John S. Lapinski. Princeton, NJ: Princeton University Press, 129–50.

Herszenhorn, David. 2008. "Rematch in Senate Race Finds a New Climate." *The New York Times*.

Hibbing, John. 2005. "Images of Congress." In *The Legislative Branch*, ed. Paul Quirk and Sarah Binder. New York: Oxford University Press, 461–89.

  1991. *Congressional Careers: Contours of Life in the U.S. House of Representatives*. Chapel Hill: University of North Carolina Press.

Hibbing, John, and John Alford. 1981. "The Electoral Impact of Economic Conditions: Who Is Held Responsible?" *American Journal of Political Science* 25(3): 423–39.

Hibbing, John, and Christopher Larimer. 2008. "The American Public's View of Congress." *The Forum* 6(3). http://www.bepress.com/forum/vol6/iss3/art6 (accessed January 4, 2012).

Hibbing, John, and Elizabeth Theiss-Morse. 2002. *Stealth Democracy: Americans' Beliefs about How Government Should Work*. New York: Cambridge University Press.

Holmström, Bengt, and John Roberts. 1998. "The Boundaries of the Firm Revisited." *Journal of Economic Perspectives* 12(4): 73–94.

House Select Committee on Committees. 1974. *Monographs on the Committees of the House of Representatives*. Washington, DC: Government Printing Office.

Howell, William. 2003. *Power without Persuasion: The Politics of Direct Presidential Action*. Princeton, NJ: Princeton University Press.

Howell, William, Scott Adler, Charles Cameron, and Charles Riemann. 2000. "Divided Government and the Legislative Productivity of Congress, 1945–94." *Legislative Studies Quarterly* 25: 285–312.

Hughes, John. 2011. *Slade Gorton: A Half Century in Politics*. Tumwater: Washington State Heritage Center Legacy Project.

Hulse, Carl. 2008. "Behind a G.O.P. Revolt, Ideology, and Politics." *The New York Times*, A13.

Hulse, Carl, and David Herszenhorn. 2010. "111th Congress, One for History Books – Congressional Memo." *The New York Times*. http://www.nytimes.com/2010/12/23/us/politics/23cong.html (accessed February 10, 2011).

Hulse, Carl, and Adam Nagourney. 2010. "McConnell Strategy Shuns Bipartisanship." *The New York Times*. http://www.nytimes.com/2010/03/17/us/politics/17mcconnell.html (accessed January 11, 2012).

Hurley, Patricia, David Brady, and Joseph Cooper. 1977. "Measuring Legislative Potential for Policy Change." *Legislative Studies Quarterly* 2: 385–98.

Iyengar, Shanto, and Donald Kinder. 2010. *News That Matters: Television and American Opinion*. Chicago: University of Chicago Press.

Jacobs, Lawrence, and Robert Shapiro. 1994. "Questioning the Conventional Wisdom on Public Opinion toward Health Reform." *PS: Political Science and Politics* 27(2): 208–14.

Jacobson, Gary. 2009. *The Politics of Congressional Elections.* 7th ed. New York: Pearson Longman.

1989. "Strategic Politicians and the Dynamics of U.S. House Elections, 1946–86." *American Political Science Review* 83(3): 773–93.

Jacobson, Gary, and Michael A. Dimock. 1994. "Checking Out: The Effects of Bank Overdrafts on the 1992 House Elections." *American Journal of Political Science* 38(3): 601–24.

Jacobson, Gary, and Samuel Kernell. 1983. *Strategy and Choice in Congressional Elections.* 2nd ed. New Haven, CT: Yale University Press.

Jameson, J. Franklin. 1894. "The Origin of the Standing-Committee System in American Legislative Bodies." *Political Science Quarterly* 9(2): 246–67.

Jeydel, Alana, and Andrew Taylor. 2003. "Are Women Legislators Less Effective? Evidence from the U.S. House in the 103rd–105th Congress." *Political Research Quarterly* 56(1): 19–27.

Johannes, John, and John McAdams. 1981. "The Congressional Incumbency Effect: Is It Casework, Policy Compatibility, or Something Else?" *American Journal of Political Science* 41: 512–42.

Jones, Bryan, and Frank Baumgartner. 2005. *The Politics of Attention: How Government Prioritizes Problems.* Chicago: University of Chicago Press.

Jones, Bryan, Frank Baumgartner, and Jeffery Talbert. 1993. "The Destruction of Issue Monopolies in Congress." *American Political Science Review* 87: 657–71.

Jones, Bryan, Heather Larsen-Price, and John Wilkerson. 2009. "Representation and American Governing Institutions." *Journal of Politics* 71(1): 277–90.

Jones, Charles. 1994. *The Presidency in a Separated System.* Washington, DC: Brookings Institution.

Jones, David. 2010. "Partisan Polarization and Congressional Accountability in House Elections." *American Journal of Political Science* 54(2): 323–37.

2001. "Party Polarization and Legislative Gridlock." *Political Research Quarterly* 54(1): 125–41.

Jones, David, and Monika McDermott. 2009. *Americans, Congress, and Democratic Responsiveness: Public Evaluations of Congress and Electoral Consequences.* Ann Arbor: University of Michigan Press.

2004. "The Responsible Party Government Model in House and Senate Elections." *American Journal of Political Science* 48: 1–12.

Kearney, Richard. 1990. "Sunset: A Survey and Analysis of the State Experience." *Public Administration Review* 50(1): 49–57.

Kearney, Richard, and Deena Bayoumi. 2010. "Sunset Review in the State: A Reassessment." Unpublished manuscript. Raleigh: North Carolina State University.

Keele, Luke, and Nathan J. Kelly. 2006. "Dynamic Models for Dynamic Theories: The Ins and Outs of Lagged Dependent Variables." *Political Analysis* 14(2): 186–205.

Kelly, Sean. 1993. "Divided We Govern: A Reassessment." *Polity* 25: 475–84.

Kernell, Samuel. 2006. *Going Public: New Strategies of Presidential Leadership.* 4th ed. Washington, DC: Congressional Quarterly Press.

1977. "Presidential Popularity and Negative Voting: An Alternative Explanation of the Midterm Congressional Decline of the President's Party." *American Political Science Review* 71(1): 44–66.

Kessler, Daniel, and Keith Krehbiel. 1996. "Dynamics of Cosponsorship." *American Political Science Review* 90: 555–66.

Kiewiet, D. Roderick. 1983. *Macroeconomics and Micropolitics: Electoral Effects of Economic Issues.* Chicago: University of Chicago Press.

Kiewiet, D. Roderick, and Mathew McCubbins. 1991. *The Logic of Delegation: Congressional Parties and the Appropriations Process.* Chicago: University of Chicago Press.

Kinder, Donald, and D. Roderick Kiewiet. 1979. "Economic Discontent and Political Behavior: The Role of Personal Grievances and Collective Economic Judgments in Congressional Voting." *American Journal of Political Science* 23(3): 495–527.

King, David. 1997. *Turf Wars: How Congressional Committees Claim Jurisdictions.* Chicago: University of Chicago Press.

1994. "The Nature of Congressional Committee Jurisdictions." *American Political Science Review* 88: 48–62.

Kingdon, John. 1995. *Agendas, Alternative, and Public Policies.* 2nd ed. New York: HarperCollins.

1989. *Congressman's Voting Decisions.* 3rd ed. Ann Arbor: University of Michigan Press.

Koger, Gregory, and James Fowler. 2006. "Parties and Agenda-Setting in the Senate, 1973–1998." University of California, San Diego. Manuscript.

Koper, Christopher, Daniel Woods, and Jeffrey Roth. 2004. *An Updated Assessment of the Federal Assault Weapons Ban: Impacts on Gun Markets and Gun Violence, 1994–2003.* Philadelphia: Jerry Lee Center of Criminology, University of Pennsylvania. Report to the National Institute of Justice, U.S. Department of Justice.

Kramer, Gerald. 1971. "Short-Term Fluctuations in U.S. Voting Behavior, 1896–1964." *American Political Science Review* 65(1): 131–43.

Krehbiel, Keith. 2007. "Partisan Roll Rates in a Nonpartisan Legislature." *Journal of Law, Economics, and Organization* 23(1): 1–23.

1998. *Pivotal Politics: A Theory of U.S. Lawmaking.* Chicago: University of Chicago Press.

1991. *Information and Legislative Organization.* Ann Arbor: University of Michigan.

Krehbiel, Keith, and Jonathan Woon. 2005. "Selection Criteria for Roll Call Votes." *SSRN eLibrary.* http://papers.ssrn.com/sol3/papers.cfm?abstract _id=937937 (accessed November 4, 2011).

Krutz, Glen. 2005. "Issues and Institutions: 'Winnowing' in the U.S. Congress." *American Journal of Political Science* 49: 313–26.

2001. *Hitching a Ride: Omnibus Legislating in the U.S. Congress.* Columbus: Ohio State University Press.

Kysar, Rebecca. 2006. "The Sun Also Rises: The Political Economy of Sunset Provisions in the Tax Code." *Georgia Law Review* 40: 335–405.

Lapinski, John. Forthcoming. *The Substance of Representation: Congress, American Political Development and Policy Making, 1877–1994.* Princeton, NJ: Princeton University Press.

——— 2008. "Policy Substance and Performance in American Lawmaking, 1877–1994." *American Journal of Political Science* 52: 235–51.

Leamer, Edward. 1983. "Let's Take the Con Out of Econometrics." *The American Economic Review* 73(1): 31–43.

Lee, Frances. 2009. *Beyond Ideology: Politics, Principles, and Partisanship in the U.S. Senate.* Chicago: University of Chicago Press.

——— 2005. "Interests, Constituencies, and Policy Making." In *The Legislative Branch*, ed. Paul Quirk and Sarah Binder. New York: Oxford University Press, 281–313.

——— 2003. "Geographic Politics in the U.S. House of Representatives: Coalition Building and Distribution of Benefits." *American Journal of Political Science* 47(4): 714–28.

Lenz, Gabriel. 2012. *Policy, Performance, and Democracy: Do Citizens Lead or Follow Politicians.* Chicago: University of Chicago Press.

——— 2009. "Learning and Opinion Change, Not Priming: Reconsidering the Priming Hypothesis." *American Journal of Political Science* 53(4): 821–37.

Levine, Ross, and David Renelt. 1992. "A Sensitivity Analysis of Cross-Country Growth Regressions." *American Economic Review* 82(4): 942–63.

Levitt, Steven, and James Snyder. 1997. "The Impact of Federal Spending on House Election Outcomes." *Journal of Political Economy* 105(1): 30–53.

Lewis, David. 2002. "The Politics of Agency Termination: Confronting the Myth of Agency Immortality." *Journal of Politics* 64(1): 89–107.

Life Magazine. 1947. "That 'Streamlined' Congress: One Reform of Our Legislative Machinery Wasn't Enough. So Let's Try Again." *Life Magazine.*

Lindblom, Charles. 1959. "The Science of 'Muddling Through.'" *Public Administration Review* 19(2): 79–88.

Lipinski, Daniel. 2004. *Congressional Communication: Content and Consequences.* Ann Arbor: University of Michigan Press.

Lippmann, Walter. 1922. *Public Opinion.* New York: Macmillan.

Longley, Lawrence, and Roger Davidson. 1998. *The New Role of Parliamentary Committees.* London: Frank Cass and Company.

Lowi, Theodore. 1964. "American Business, Public Policy, Case-Studies, and Political Theory." *World Politics* 16: 677–715.

Lynch, Michael, and Anthony Madonna. 2008. "Viva Voce: Implications from the Disappearing Voice Vote, 1807–1990." Paper presented at the Annual Meeting of the Midwest Political Science Association, Chicago, IL.

Maass, Arthur. 1983. *Congress and the Common Good.* New York: Basic Books.

MacDonald, Jason. 2007. "Legislative Productivity and Policy Conflict: Reauthorizing Laws in the U.S. Congress, 1987–2007."

Maltzman, Forrest. 1997. *Competing Principals: Committees, Parties, and the Organization of Congress.* Ann Arbor: University of Michigan Press.

Maltzman, Forrest, and Charles Shipan. 2008. "Continuity and Change: The Evolution of the Law." *American Journal of Political Science* 52: 252–67.

Mann, Thomas, and Norman Ornstein. 2006. *The Broken Branch: How Congress Is Failing America and How to Get It Back on Track*. New York: Oxford University Press.

Mann, Thomas, and Raymond Wolfinger. 1980. "Candidates and Parties in Congressional Elections." *American Political Science Review* 74(3): 617–32.

March, James, and Herbert Simon. 1993. *Organizations*. 2nd ed. Cambridge, MA: Blackwell Publishers.

Matthews, Donald. 1960. *U.S. Senators and Their World*. New York: Vintage Books.

Matthews, Dylan. 2011. "Everything You Need to Know about the FAA Shutdown in One Post." *Washington Post*. http://www.washingtonpost.com/blogs/ezra-klein/post/everything-you-need-to-know-about-the-faa-shutdown-in-one-post/2011/07/11/gIQAfatTsI_blog.html (accessed January 11, 2012).

Mayer, Kenneth, and David Canon. 1999. *The Dysfunctional Congress: The Individual Roots of an Institutional Dilemma*, Boulder, CO: Westview Press.

Mayhew, David. 2006. "Congress as Problem Solver." In *Promoting the General Welfare: New Perspectives on Government Performance*, ed. Alan Gerber and Eric Patashnik. Washington, DC: Brookings Institution Press, 219–36.

   1991. *Divided We Govern: Party Control, Lawmaking, and Investigations, 1946–1990*. New Haven, CT: Yale University Press.

   1974. *Congress: The Electoral Connection*. New Haven, CT: Yale University Press.

McCarty, Nolan. 2007. "The Policy Consequences of Political Polarization." In *The Transformation of American Politics: Activist Government and the Rise of Conservatism*, ed. Paul Pierson and Theda Skocpol. Princeton, NJ: Princeton University Press, 223–55.

McCarty, Nolan, Keith Poole, and Howard Rosenthal. 2006. *Polarized America: The Dance of Ideology and Unequal Riches*. Cambridge, MA: MIT Press.

McCombs, Maxwell, and Donald Shaw. 1972. "The Agenda setting Function of Mass Media." *Public Opinion Quarterly* 36(2): 176–87.

McCombs, Maxwell, and Jian-Hua Zhu. 1995. "Capacity, Diversity, and Volatility of the Public Agenda: Trends from 1954 to 1994." *Public Opinion Quarterly* 59(4): 495–525.

McConachie, Lauros. 1898. *Congressional Committees: A Study of the Origins and Development of Our National and Local Legislative Methods*. New York: Crowell.

McCubbins, Mathew, and Thomas Schwartz. 1984. "Congressional Oversight Overlooked: Police Patrols versus Fire Alarms." *American Journal of Political Science* 28(1): 165–79.

McCurley, Carl, and Jeffery Mondak. 1995. "Inspected by #1184063113: The Influence of Incumbents' Competence and Integrity in U.S. House Elections." *American Journal of Political Science* 39(4): 864–85.

McDermott, Monika, and David Jones. 2003. "Do Public Evaluations of Congress Matter? Retrospective Voting in Congressional Elections." *American Politics Research* 31: 155–77.

McGowan, Elizabeth. 2011. "Most Americans Oppose Restrictions on EPA, Poll Finds." *Reuters News Service*, February 7. http://www.reuters.com/article/2011/02/07/idUS140003086120110207?pageNumber=2 (accessed April 20, 2012).

Miller, Warren, and Donald Stokes. 1963. "Constituency Influence in Congress." *American Political Science Review* 57: 45–56.

Mitchell, Dona-Gene, and Jeffery Mondak. 2009. "The Context of Defeat." In *Fault Lines: Why The Republicans Lost Congress*. New York: Routledge, 1–21.

Moe, Terry. 1984. "The New Economics of Organization." *American Journal of Political Science* 28: 739–77.

Monroe, Nathan, and Thomas Hammond. 2006. "A Multi-institutional Explanation for the Emergence of Standing Committees in the U.S. House, 1789–1829." Paper presented at the Annual Meetings of the American Political Science Association, Washington, DC.

Moore, Michael, and Sue Thomas. 1991. "Explaining Legislative Success in the U.S. Senate: The Role of the Majority and Minority Parties." *Western Political Quarterly* 44(4): 959–70.

Muir, William. 1982. *Legislature: California's School for Politics*. Chicago: University of Chicago Press.

Mutz, Diana, and Gregory Flemming. 1999. "How Good People Make Bad Collectives: A Social-psychological Perspective on Public Attitudes toward Congress." In *Congress and the Decline of Public Trust*, ed. Joseph Cooper. Boulder, CO: Westview Press, 79–100.

Nather, David, and Karen Foerstel. 2002. "Proposal Presages Turf Wars." *Congressional Quarterly Weekly Report*: 1505.

National Commission on Terrorist Attacks upon the United States. 2004. *The 9/11 Commission Report: Final Report of the National Commission on Terrorist Attacks upon the United States*. Washington, DC: Government Printing Office.

Nelson, Caleb. 2003. "Originalism and Interpretive Conventions." *University of Chicago Law Review* 70(2): 519–98.

Nelson, Candice. 1978. "The Effect of Incumbency on Voting in Congressional Elections, 1964–1974." *Political Science Quarterly* 93(4): 665–78.

Newport, Frank. 2011a. *Americans Again Call for Compromise in Washington*. Princeton, NJ: Gallup. Online Report, September 26. http://www.gallup.com/poll/149699/Americans-Again-Call-for-Compromise-Washington.aspx (accessed April 20, 2012).

  2011b. *Americans, Including Republicans, Want Debt Compromise*. Princeton, NJ: Gallup. Online Report, July 18. http://www.gallup.com/poll/148562/Americans-Including-Republicans-Debt-Compromise.aspx (accessed April 20, 2012).

Nicholson, Stephen, and Gary Segura. 1999. "Midterm Elections and Divided Government: An Information-Driven Theory of Electoral Volatility." *Political Research Quarterly* 52(3): 608–29.

O'Donnell, Thomas. 1981. "Controlling Legislative Time." In *The House at Work*, ed. Joseph Cooper and Mackenzie. Austin: University of Texas Press, 127–50.

Ogul, Morris. 1976. *Congress Oversees the Bureaucracy*. Pittsburgh, PA: University of Pittsburgh Press.

Oleszek, Walter. 2007. *Congressional Procedures and the Policy Process*. 7th ed. Washington, DC: Congressional Quarterly Press.

Oliver, Thomas, Philip Lee, and Helene Lipton. 2004. "A Political History of Medicare and Prescription Drug Coverage." *Milbank Quarterly* 82(2): 283–354.

Olson, David, and Cynthia Nonidez. 1972. "Measures of Legislative Performance in the U.S. House of Representatives." *Midwest Journal of Political Science* 16(2): 269–77.

Oppel, Richard, Jr., and Diana Jean Schemo. 2000. "The 43rd President: The President-Elect; Bush Is Warned Vouchers Might Hurt School Plans." *The New York Times*. http://www.nytimes.com/2000/12/22/us/43rd-president-president-elect-bush-warned-vouchers-might-hurt-school-plans.html?scp=6&sq=george+bush+%22head+start%22&st=nyt (accessed December 18, 2011).

Page, Benjamin, and Robert Shapiro. 1992. *The Rational Public: Fifty Years of Trends in Americans' Policy Preferences*. Chicago: University of Chicago Press.

Patashnik, Eric. 2008. *Reforms at Risk: What Happens After Major Policy Changes Are Enacted*. Princeton, NJ: Princeton University Press.

Pear, Robert. 2012. "After Three Decades, Federal Tax Credit for Ethanol Expires." *The New York Times*. http://www.nytimes.com/2012/01/02/business/energy-environment/after-three-decades-federal-tax-credit-for-ethanol-expires.html (accessed January 10, 2012).

Penner, Rudolph, and Alan Abramson. 1988. *Broken Purse Strings: Congressional Budgeting, 1974–88*. Lanham, MD: University Press of America.

Perry, Brittany. 2007. "Finding a Focus: Immigration Policy Specialization in the United States Congress." Senior Honors Thesis. University of Colorado, Boulder.

Petrocik, John. 1989. "Issue Ownership in Presidential Elections, with a 1980 Case Study." *American Journal of Political Science* 40: 825–50.

Pew Research Center. 2011. *Beyond Red vs. Blue: The Political Typology*. Washington, DC: Pew Research Center for the People and the Press.

Poole, Keith, and Howard Rosenthal. 2007. *Ideology and Congress*. 2nd ed. New Brunswick, NJ: Transaction Publishers.

Pope, Jeremy, and Jonathan Woon. 2008. "Measuring Changes in American Party Reputations, 1939–2004." *Political Research Quarterly* 61: 653–61.

Potoski, Matthew, and Jeffery Talbert. 2000. "The Dimensional Structure of Policy Outputs: Distributive Policy and Roll Call Voting." *Political Research Quarterly* 53(4): 695–710.

Pressman, Jeffrey, and Aaron Wildavsky. 1984. *Implementation: How Great Expectations in Washington Are Dashed in Oakland: Or, Why It's Amazing That Federal Programs Work At All, This Being a Saga of the Economic Development Administration as Told by Two Sympathetic Observers Who Seek to Build Morals on a Foundation of Ruined Hopes*. Berkeley: University of California Press.

Price, David. 1978. "Policy Making in Congressional Committees: The Impact of 'Environmental Factors.'" *American Political Science Review* 72: 548–74.

Quirk, Paul. 2006. "Deliberation and Decision Making." In *Institutions of American Democracy: The Legislative Branch*, ed. Paul Quirk and Sarah Binder. New York: Oxford University Press, 314–48.

Ragsdale, Lyn. 1994. "Old Approaches and New Challenges in Legislative Election Research." *Legislative Studies Quarterly* 19(4): 537–82.

Ragusa, Jordan Michael. 2010. "The Lifecycle of Public Policy: An Event History Analysis of Repeals to Landmark Legislative Enactments, 1951–2006." *American Politics Research* 38(6): 1015–51.

Ramirez, Mark. 2009. "The Dynamics of Partisan Conflict on Congressional Approval." *American Journal of Political Science* 53(3): 681–94.

Restuccia, Andrew. 2011. "Gingrich Calls for Replacing the EPA." *The Hill*, January 25. http://thehill.com/blogs/e2-wire/e2-wire/140173-gingrich-calls -for-eliminating-epa-creating-new-agency (accessed April 20, 2012).

Rieselbach, Leroy. 1994. *Congressional Reform: The Changing Modern Congress*. Washington, DC: Congressional Quarterly Press.

Ripley, Randall, and Grace Franklin. 1990. *Congress, the Bureaucracy, and Public Policy*. 5th ed. Boston: Houghton Mifflin Harcourt Press.

Roberts, Jason, and Steven Smith. 2003. "Procedural Contexts, Party Strategy, and Conditional Party Voting in the U.S. House of Representatives, 1971–2000." *American Journal of Political Science* 47(2): 305–17.

Robinson, Peter. 1995. *Can Congress Be Fixed? And Is It Broken? Five Essays on Congressional Reform*. Stanford, CA: Hoover Institution Press.

Rochester Business Journal. 2010. "Large Majority Disapproves of Congress' Performance." *Rochester Business Journal*, September 10. http://www.rbj .net/article.asp?aID=185061 (accessed April 20, 2012).

Rohde, David. 2005a. "Committees and Policy Formulation." In *Institutions of American Democracy: The Legislative Branch*, ed. Paul Quirk and Sarah Binder. New York: Oxford University Press, 201–23.

   2005b. *Roll Call Voting Data for the United States House of Representatives, 1953–2004*. Compiled by the Political Institutions and Public Choice Program, East Lansing: Michigan State University.

   1991. *Parties and Leaders in the Postreform House*. Chicago: University of Chicago.

Rudalevige, Andrew. 2002. *Managing the President's Program: Presidential Leadership and Legislative Policy Formulation*. Princeton, NJ: Princeton University Press.

Sack, Kevin. 2010. "Experts Split on State Lawsuits over Health Care Law." *The New York Times*. http://www.nytimes.com/2010/05/11/health/policy/11lawsuit .html (accessed January 11, 2012).

Schattschneider, E. E. 1960. *The Semi-sovereign People: A Realist's View of Democracy in America*. New York: Holt, Reinhart and Winston.

Schick, Allen. 2007. *The Federal Budget: Politics, Policy, Process*. 3rd ed. Washington, DC: The Brookings Institution.

   1987. *Making Economic Policy in Congress*. Washington, DC: AEI Press.

1980. *Congress and Money: Budgeting, Spending and Taxing.* Washington, DC: The Urban Institute.

Schickler, Eric. 2001. *Disjointed Pluralism: Institutional Innovation and the Development of the U.S. Congress.* Princeton, NJ: Princeton University Press.

Schickler, Eric, and Andrew Rich. 1997. "Controlling the Floor: Parties as Procedural Coalitions in the House." *American Journal of Political Science* 41: 1340–75.

Schickler, Eric. 2011. "The Development of the Congressional Committee System." In *The Oxford Handbook of the American Congress*, eds. Eric Schickler and Frances Lee. New York: Oxford University Press, 712–37.

Schiller, Wendy. 1995. "Senators as Political Entrepreneurs: Using Bill Sponsorship to Shape Legislative Agendas." *American Journal of Political Science* 39: 186–203.

Sellers, Patrick. 1998. "Strategy and Background in Congressional Campaigns." *American Political Science Review* 92: 159–72.

Serra, George, and David Moon. 1994. "Casework, Issue Positions and Voting in Congressional Elections." *Journal of Politics* 56: 200–13.

Shannon, Claude, and Warren Weaver. 1998. *The Mathematical Theory of Communication.* 1st ed. Champaign: University of Illinois Press.

Sheingate, Adam. 2006. "Structure and Opportunity: Committee Jurisdiction and Issue Attention in Congress." *American Journal of Political Science* 50(4): 844–59.

Sheppard, Burton. 1985. *Rethinking Congressional Reform: The Reform Roots of the Special Interest Congress.* Cambridge, MA: Schenkman Books.

Shepsle, Kenneth. 1978. *The Giant Jigsaw Puzzle.* Chicago: University of Chicago Press.

Shepsle, Kenneth, and Barry Weingast. 1987. "The Institutional Foundations of Committee Power." *American Political Science Review* 81: 85–104.

Shipan, Charles. 2006. "Does Divided Government Increase the Size of the Legislative Agenda?" In *The Macropolitics of Congress*, ed. E. Scott Adler and John S. Lapinski. Princeton, NJ: Princeton University Press, 151–70.

Shoemaker, Pamela, and Stephen Reese. 1996. *Mediating the Message: Theories of Influence on Mass Media Content.* 2nd ed. White Plains, NY: Longman.

Shuman, Howard. 1988. *Politics and the Budget: The Struggle between the President and the Congress.* 2nd ed. Englewood Cliffs, NJ: Prentice Hall.

Sinclair, Barbara. 2007. *Unorthodox Lawmaking: New Legislative Processes in the U.S. Congress.* 3rd ed. Washington, DC: Congressional Quarterly Press.

2006. *Party Wars: Polarization and the Politics of National Policy Making.* Norman: University of Oklahoma Press.

2001. "Structure, Preferences and Outcomes: Explaining When Bills Do – and Don't – Become Law." Paper presented at the Annual Meetings of the American Political Science Association, Los Angeles, CA.

1986. "The Role of Committees in Agenda Setting in the U.S. Congress." *Legislative Studies Quarterly* 11: 35–45.

Sontag, Deborah. 2005. "Assault Weapons Ban Comes to End: A Dud?" *The New York Times.*

Stanfield, Rochelle. 1988. "Plotting Every Move." *National Journal* (March 26): 792–97.

Stein, Robert, and Kenneth Bickers. 1995. *Perpetuating the Pork Barrel: Policy Subsystems and American Democracy.* New York: Cambridge University Press.

  1994. "Congressional Elections and the Pork Barrel." *Journal of Politics* 56: 377–99.

Steinberg, Jacques. 2001. "Bush's Plan to Push Reading in 'Head Start' Stirs Debate." *The New York Times.*

Stewart, Charles. 2001. *Analyzing Congress.* New York: W. W. Norton and Company.

  1989. *Budget Reform Politics: The Design of Appropriations Process in the House of Representatives, 1865–1921.* New York: Cambridge University Press.

Stewart, Charles, and Jonathan Woon. n.d. *Congressional Committee Assignments, 103rd to 105th Congresses, 1993–1998.* Cambridge, MA: MIT. http://web.mit.edu/17.251/www/data_page.html (accessed July 14, 2007).

Stimson, James. 2004. *Tides of Consent: How Public Opinion Shapes American Politics.* New York: Cambridge University Press.

  1999. *Public Opinion in America: Moods, Cycles, and Swings.* 2nd ed. Boulder, CO: Westview Press.

Stimson, James, Michael Mackuen, and Robert Erikson. 1995. "Dynamic Representation." *American Political Science Review* 89(3): 543–65.

Stokes, Donald, and Warren Miller. 1962. "Party Government and the Saliency of Congress." *Public Opinion Quarterly* 26: 531–46.

Stone, Walter, and Elizabeth Simas. 2010. "Candidate Valence and Ideological Positions in U.S. House Elections." *American Journal of Political Science* 54(2): 371–88.

Stone, Walter, L. Sandy Maisel, and Cherie Maestas. 2010. "Incumbency Reconsidered: Prospects, Strategic Retirement, and Incumbent Quality in U.S. House Elections." *Journal of Politics* 72(1): 178–90.

Sulkin, Tracy. 2011. *The Legislative Legacy of Congressional Campaigns.* 1st ed. New York: Cambridge University Press.

  2005. *Issue Politics in Congress.* New York: Cambridge University Press.

Talbert, Jeffery, and Matthew Potoski. 2002. "Setting the Legislative Agenda: The Dimensional Structure of Bill Cosponsoring and Floor Voting." *Journal of Politics* 64(3): 864–91.

Theriault, Sean. 2008. *Party Polarization in Congress.* New York: Cambridge University Press.

Thurber, James, and Roger Davidson, eds. 1995. *Remaking Congress: Change and Stability in the 1990s.* Washington, DC: Congressional Quarterly Press.

Tiefer, Charles. 1989. *Congressional Practice and Procedure: A Reference, Research and Legislative Guide.* Westport, CT: Greenwood Press.

Trubowitz, Peter, and Nicole Mellow. 2005 "Going Bipartisan: Politics by Other Means." *Political Science Quarterly* 120(3): 433–53.

Tufte, Edward. 1978. *Political Control of the Economy*. Princeton, NJ: Princeton University Press.

1975. "Determinants of the Outcomes of Midterm Congressional Elections." *American Political Science Review* 69(3): 812–26.

Vietor, Richard. 1990. "Contrived Competition: Airline Regulation and Deregulation, 1925–1988." *Business History Review* 64(1): 61–108.

Viswanathan, Manoj. 2007. "Sunset Provisions in the Tax Code: A Critical Evaluation and Prescriptions for the Future." *New York University Law Review* 82: 656–88.

Volden, Craig, and Alan Wiseman. 2009. "Legislative Effectiveness in Congress." Paper presented at the Annual Meetings of Midwest Political Science Association, Chicago, IL.

Walker, Jack. 1977. "Setting the Agenda in the US Senate: A Theory of Problem Selection." *British Journal of Political Science* 7: 423–45.

Ward, Jon. 2010. "Paul Ryan Explains His Votes for TARP, Bailouts and Tax on AIG Bonuses." *The Daily Caller*. http://dailycaller.com/2010/02/14/paul-ryan-explains-his-votes-for-tarp-auto-bailouts-and-tax-on-aig-bonuses/ (accessed January 11, 2012).

Waterman, Shaun. 2005. "New Homeland Security Committee off to Shaky Start." *United Press International*, January 4. http://www.upi.com/Business_News/Security-Industry/2005/01/04/New-Homeland-Security-Committee-off-to-shaky-start/UPI-86311104884999/ (accessed April 20, 2012).

Wawro, Gregory. 2000. *Legislative Entrepreneurship in the U.S. House of Representatives*. Ann Arbor: University of Michigan.

2002. "Estimating Dynamic Panel Data Models in Political Science." *Political Analysis* 10(1): 25–48.

Waxman, Henry. 2010. *The Waxman Report: How Congress Really Works*. New York: Twelve.

Wayne, Alex, and Bill Swindell. 2004. "2004 Legislative Summary: Capitol Hill Gridlock Leaves Programs in Limbo." *Congressional Quarterly Weekly Report*: 2834–37.

Weaver, R. Kent. 1988. *Automatic Government: The Politics of Indexation*. Washington, DC: Brookings Institution Press.

Weingast, Barry, and William Marshall. 1988. "The Industrial Organization of Congress; or, Why Legislatures, Like Firms, Are Not Organized as Markets." *Journal of Political Economy* 96: 132–63.

Welna, David. 2011. "Even Lawmakers Ask: Does Anyone Like Congress?" *National Public Radio: All Things Considered*, November 25. http://www.npr.org/2011/11/25/142705292/even-lawmakers-ask-does-anyone-like-congress (accessed April 20, 2012).

Wildavsky, Aaron. 1984. *Politics of the Budgetary Process*. 4th ed. Glenview, IL: Scott Foresman and Company.

Wilkerson, John, T. Jens Feeley, Nicole S. Schiereck, and Christina Sue. 2002. "Using Bills to Trace Attention in Congress: Policy Windows in Health Care Legislating." In *Policy Dynamics*, ed. Frank Baumgartner and Bryan Jones. Chicago: University of Chicago Press, 250–69.

Williamson, Oliver. 1975. *Markets and Hierarchies: Analysis and Antitrust Implications*. New York: Free Press.

Wilson, Rick, and Cheryl Young. 1997. "Cosponsorship in the U.S. Congress." *Legislative Studies Quarterly* 22: 25–44.

Wilson, Woodrow. 1981. *Congressional Government: A Study in American Politics*. Baltimore, MD: Johns Hopkins University Press [1885].

Wlezien, Christopher. 2005. "On Salience of Political Issues: The Problem with 'Most Important Problem.'" *Electoral Studies* 24: 555–79.

　　1995. "The Public as Thermostat: Dynamics of Preferences for Spending." *American Journal of Political Science* 39(4): 981–1000.

Wolak, Jennifer. 2007. "Strategic Retirements: The Influence of Public Preferences on Voluntary Departures from Congress." *Legislative Studies Quarterly* 32: 285–308.

Wolfensberger, Donald. 2004. "Reorganizing Congress and the Executive in Response to Focusing Events: Lessons of the Past, Portents of the Future." Paper presented at the Annual Meetings of the Southern Political Science Association, New Orleans, LA.

Woll, Peter. 1977. *American Bureaucracy*. 2nd ed. New York: W. W. Norton and Company.

Woon, Jonathan. 2009. "Issue Attention and Legislative Proposals in the U.S. Senate." *Legislative Studies Quarterly* 34: 29–54.

Woon, Jonathan, and Jeremy Pope. 2007. "Made in Congress? Testing the Electoral Implications of Party Ideological Brand Names." *Journal of Politics* 70: 823–36.

Workman, Samuel, Bryan Jones, and Ashley Jochim. 2009. "Information Processing and Policy Dynamics." *Policy Studies Journal* 37(1): 75–92.

Wright, Gerald. 1978. "Candidates' Policy Positions and Voting in U.S. Congressional Elections." *Legislative Studies Quarterly* 3(3): 445–64.

Wright, John. 1996. *Interest Groups and Congress: Lobbying, Contributions, and Influence*. Boston: Allyn and Bacon.

Yamamoto, Hironori. 2007. *Tools for Parliamentary Oversight: A Comparative Study of 88 National Parliaments*. Geneva, Switzerland: Inter-Parliamentary Union.

Yiannakis, Diana Evans. 1982. "House Members' Communication Styles: Newsletters and Press Releases." *Journal of Politics* 44: 1049–71.

　　1981. "The Grateful Electorate: Casework and Congressional Elections." *American Journal of Political Science* 25(3): 568–80.

Yin, George. 2009. "Temporary-Effect Legislation, Political Accountability, and Fiscal Restraint." *New York University Law Review* 84: 174–257.

Young, Garry, and Joseph Cooper. 1993. "Multiple Referral and the Transformation of House Decision Making." In *Congress Reconsidered*, ed. Lawrence Dodd and Bruce Oppenheimer. Washington, DC: Congressional Quarterly Press, 211–34.

Young, McGee. 2009. "The Free Trade Movement and the New Deal: Reassessing the Role of Interest Groups in Securing Policy Change." Charlottesville, VA. Paper presented at the 8th Annual Congress and History Conference.

Index